AMERICA THE VANISHING

Mount Washington and the White Mountains, New Hampshire, 1852

AMERICA THE VANISHING

Rural Life and the Price of Progress

Edited by
SAMUEL R. OGDEN

Illustrated with nineteenth-century engravings and twentieth-century
photographs by David Plowden

HAYDEN BOOK COMPANY, INC., NEW YORK

The author and publisher are grateful to the following individuals and publishers for their permission to use material in this book:

"Talking Myself to Sleep in One More Hilton" from *This Strangest Everything* by John Ciardi. Copyright 1966 by Rutgers, The State University. Reprinted by permission of the author. "The Garden of Ashes" from *The Machine in the Garden: Technology and the Pastoral Ideal in America* by Leo Marx. Copyright © 1964 by Oxford University Press, Inc. Reprinted by permission. THE UNSPOILED LAND. "The General Survey of the Country" from "New English Canaan" from *Early American Writers*, edited by William B. Cairns. Copyright 1915 by The MacMillan Company. "De Soto," "The Wild Middle West" and "Father of Waters" from *The Eyes of Discovery* by John Bakeless. Copyright © 1950 by John Bakeless. Copyright © 1961 by Dover Publications, Inc. Reprinted by permission of Curtis Brown, Ltd. "On the St. John River in Florida" from *The Travels of William Bartram* by William Bartram, published by Dover Publications, Inc. "The Ohio," "Hospitality in the Woods" and "Great Egg Harbor" by John Audubon from *Audubon and His Journals* edited by Maria Audubon, published by Dover Publications in 1960. "Breaking the Ice" and "Jumping Off" from *The Oregon Trail* by Francis Parkman, published by Ginn & Co. in 1910. "The Passes" from *The Mountains of California* by John Muir, published by Doubleday & Co. in 1961. YEARS OF SPACIOUS LIVING. "The Profits of Idleness" from *American Note-Books* by Nathaniel Hawthorne, published by Riverside Press in 1883. "Sounds" from *Walden* by Henry David Thoreau, published by Houghton Mifflin in 1881. "Quincy" from *A Henry Adams Reader* edited by Elizabeth Stevenson, published by Doubleday & Co. in 1958. Permission of the editor. "My First Visit to New England" from *Literary Friends and Acquaintance* by William Dean Howells, published by W. W. Norton in 1956. "Prairie Farm" from Chapter IV *The Autobiography of Mark Twain*, edited by Charles Neider. Copyright © 1917, 1940, 1958, 1959, by The Mark Twain Company; Copyright 1924, 1945, 1952, by Clara Clemens Samossoud; Copyright © 1959 by Charles Neider. Reprinted by permission of Harper & Row, Publishers. "The Most Difficult Step" from *This Country Life* by Samuel Ogden, published by A. S. Barnes & Co., in 1946. "Farthest Field to the North" from *Cold Friday* by Whittaker Chambers. © Copyright 1964 by Whittaker Chambers. Reprinted by permission of Random House, Inc. "A Time for Summary" from *Countryman: A Summary of Belief* by Hal Borland. Copyright © 1957, 1958, 1961, 1962, 1963,1964 and 1965 by Hal Borland. Published by J. B. Lippincott Company. "A Judicial Wedding" from *A Daughter of the Middle Border* by Hamlin Garland; copyright 1915 by Hamlin Garland. Reprinted by permission of The MacMillan Company. "The Frontier of Indiana" from *A Hoosier Holiday* by Theodore Dreiser, published by John Lane Co., N. Y., in 1916. "Growing Up Along the Brandywine" from *The Brandywine* by Henry Seidel Canby, published by Farrar & Rinehart, Inc. in 1941. "Summer on the Old Farm" and "Mill and Village" from *Over Cram Hill* by Russell W. Farnsworth. "Miss Lock's" from *I Was a Summer Boarder* by Ruth Crosby, published by The Christopher Publishing House in 1966. "Cedar River, Maine" from *Maine Is in My Heart* by William M. Clark, published by David McKay Company, Inc., New York, in 1964. Reprinted by permission of David McKay Company, Inc. "Solo in Wyoming" from *It Has Its Charms* by Charles W. Morton. Copyright © 1960, 1961, 1963, 1965, 1966 by Charles W. Morton. Published by J. B. Lippincott Company. GOING BACK TO THE SOIL. "July" from *The Countryman's Year* by David Grayson. Permission of the heirs of Ray Stannard Baker. "The Pleasures of Lake Champlain" from *Green Mountain Farm* by Elliott Merrick; copyright 1948 by Elliott Merrick. Reprinted by permission of The MacMillan Company. THE PRICE OF PROGRESS. "The Poisoned Hills" from *North with the Spring* by Edwin Way Teale. Copyright 1951 by Edwin Way Teale. Reprinted by permission of Dodd, Mead & Company, Inc. "Fro-Joy—January 1940," Copyright 1940, 1968, by E. B. White. "Walden—June 1939" Copyright 1939, 1967 by E. B. White, from *One Man's Meat* (1944) by E. B. White. Reprinted by permission of Harper & Row, Publishers. "Earthly Paradise: El Centro, California" from *Tomorrow is Already Here* by Robert Jungk. Reprinted by permission of Antrium Verlag, A. G. Zuerich, and Rupert Hart-Davis Limited, London publishers. "The Greatest Threat to Life on Earth" from *The Balance of Nature* by Lorus J. and Margery Milne. © Copyright 1960 by Lorus J. and Margery Milne. Reprinted by permission of Alfred A. Knopf, Inc. "To Survive on Earth" from *Science and Survival* by Barry Commoner. Copyright © 1963, 1964, 1966 by Barry Commoner. All rights reserved. Reprinted by permission of The Viking Press, Inc. "A Fable for Tomorrow" from *Silent Spring* by Rachel Carson, published by Houghton Mifflin Company in 1962. LOOKING FOR A SILVER LINING. "The Twentieth Century: Dawn or Twlight?" from *Human Nature and the Human Condition* by Joseph Wood Krutch. © Copyright 1959 by Joseph Wood Krutch. Reprinted by permission of Random House, Inc. "Patterns of the Future" from *The Challenge of Man's Future* by Harrison Brown. Copyright 1954 by Harrison Brown. Reprinted by permission of The Viking Press, Inc. "The Human Implications" from *Mechanization Takes Command* by Siegfried Giedion. Copyright 1948 by Oxford University Press, Inc. Reprinted by permission.

The halftone illustrations on pages 168, 172-173, 183, 200-201, 210-211, 223-224, 232-233, 238-239, and 241 are reprinted with the permission of David Plowden.

HAYDEN BOOK COMPANY, INC.
116 W. 14th Street, New York, N.Y. 10011

Library of Congress Catalog Number 77-76524
ISBN 0-8104-6105-6

Reprinted by arrangement with The Stephen Greene Press, Brattleboro, Vermont.

1   2   3   4   5   6   7   8   9   PRINTING

72 73 74 75 76 77 78   YEAR

CONTENTS

Prologue

Till swoln with cunning, of a self conceit,
His (Faustus) waxen wings did mount above his reach,
And, melting, heavens conspir'd his over-throw;
For, falling to a devilish exercise,
And glutted now with learning's golden gifts,
He surfeits upon cursed necromancy;
Nothing so sweet as magic (science) is to him,
Which he prefers before his chiefest bliss:
And this the man that in his study sits.

Christopher Marlowe
Prologue to the Tragical
History of Doctor Faustus

To the Reader

THE ORIGINAL IDEA for this anthology came from Stephen Greene. There were a number of bucolic collections already in existence, diverse in geography and in selectiveness, but none that we knew of had its scope confined entirely to the United States. Nor could we recall any that was not principally preoccupied with animal husbandry and the tillage of the soil or with the passage of the seasons. My selections, then, were to be strictly limited to the territory within our national boundaries, including all aspects of living in the country. The anthology as originally conceived was to be suitable, I presume, for use on the bedside table—to entertain, to soothe, to lead one quietly down the slopes of consciousness to the valley of pleasant dreams.

It has not worked out quite that way. Once caught up in the project which I must say has been a delight to me, I soon discovered that my subconscious was weaving a polemical cast into the pattern of my selections. Without intending to adduce proof that the old days of living in the country in America were the best ones, I found that the authors of the excerpts, which I chose from books in my library, were unmistakably making just that point. You may not agree with it, but the signs of what E. B. White calls "a dim degeneracy of progress" seem to me to be impossible to ignore. The way Ogden Nash put it was, "Progress may have been all right once, but it went on too long." Thus this anthology may be construed as both a nostalgic memorial to what was, and a disapproving commentary on what is.

The choices which with frightening acceleration are available to us now, each new one, whether it be to embark on travel to the moon or to turn atomic energy into electricity, represents a further victory in man's conquest of nature, and these things we accept as progress. They are toward a materialistic utopia wherein all of mankind will eventually possess complete freedom from fear, from competition, from hunger; every whim or wish in the direction of self-gratification will immediately be granted; there will be no pain, and eventually death will be conquered. But that these are worthy goals, many have doubted, and this collection will serve, I hope, to give these doubts significance. Though to what end, I cannot be certain.

At any rate the trend I am talking about is beautifully expressed in the poem I have chosen to stand at the head of the whole troop. But do not let this conviction of mine put you off. There is a lot of good stuff between these covers in spite of whatever doubts Mr. Ciardi or I may entertain concerning what is taking place in these times.

In further and more explicit introduction I have chosen to use the essay by Leo Marx called "The Garden of Ashes." I find that its inclusion at the start is justifiable in view of the direction this work has taken, even though I do not agree with Professor Marx's conclusion that the solution of our dilemma rests with politics, not with art. In my mind, the machine and politics contain exactly the same technological ingredients, and if, as Henry Adams put it, the dynamo is about to destroy the Virgin (or art), then, in my view, we of this civilization have had it: politics cannot save us.

I have chosen to present the following selections in five groups, with self-explanatory captions.

At this point I would like to acknowledge with deep gratitude the help Wesley Griswold has given me in the preparation of this manuscript.

SAMUEL R. OGDEN

Landgrove, Vermont
February, 1969

Talking Myself to Sleep at One More Hilton

by JOHN CIARDI

I have a country but no town.
Home ran away from me. My trees
ripped up their white roots and lay down.
Bulldozers cut my lawn. All these
are data toward some sentiment
like money: God knows where it went.

There was a house as sure as time,
sure as my father's name and grave,
sure as trees for me to climb,
sure as behave and misbehave,
sure as lamb stew, sure as sin,
as warts, as games, as a scraped shin.

There was a house, a chicken run,
a garden, guilt, a rocking chair.
I had six dogs and every one
was killed in traffic. I knew where
their graves were once. Now I'm not sure.
Roses used them for manure.

There was a house early and late.
One day there came an overpass.
It snatched the stew right off my plate.
It snatched the plate. A whiff of gas
blew up the house like a freak wind.
I wonder if I really mind.

My father died. My father's house
fell out of any real estate.
My dogs lie buried where time was
when time still flowed, where now a slate
stiff river flows, called Exit Nine.
Why should I mind? It isn't mine.

I have the way I think I live.
The doors of my expense account
open like arms when I arrive.
There is no cloud I cannot mount
and sip good bourbon as I ride.
My father's house is Hilton-wide.

What are old dog bones? Were my trees
still standing, would I really care?
What's the right name for this disease
of wishing they might still be there
if I went back, though I will not
and never meant to?—Smash the pot,

knock in the windows, blow the doors.
I am not and mean not to be
what I was once. I have two shores
five hours apart, soon to be three.
And home is anywhere between.
Such as the airport limousine,

Sure as credit, sure as a drink,
as the best steak you ever had,
as thinking—when there's time to think—
it's good enough. At least not bad.
Better than dog bones and lamb stew.
It does. Or it will have to do.

The Garden of Ashes

OURS IS AN intricately organized, urban, industrial, nuclear-armed society. For more than a century our most gifted writers have dwelt upon the contradiction between rural myth and technological fact. In the machinery of our collective existence, Thoreau says, we have "constructed a fate, an *Atropos*" that never will turn aside. And until we confront the unalterable, he would add, there can be no redemption from a system that makes men the tools of their tools. A similar insight informs *Moby-Dick*. But in the penchant for illusion Melville saw more dire implications. It is suicidal, Ishmael learns, to live "as in a musky meadow" when in truth one is aboard a vessel plunging into darkness. What was a grim possibility for Melville became a certainty for Mark Twain and Henry Adams; neither was able to imagine a satisfactory resolution of the conflict figured by the machine's incursion into the garden. By the turn of the century they both envisaged the outcome as a vast explosion of new power. Power, Adams said, now leaped from every atom. The closing chapters of *The Education of Henry Adams* are filled with images of mankind in the grip of uncontrollable forces. He pictured the forces grasping the wrists of man and flinging him about "as though he had hold of . . . a runaway automobile. . . ." Adams was haunted by the notion that bombs were about to explode. "So long as the rates of progress held good," he observed, "these bombs would double in force and number every ten years."

* * *

The ending of *The Great Gatsby* reminds us that American writers seldom, if ever, have designed satisfactory resolutions for their pastoral fables. The power of these fables to move us derives from the magnitude of the protean conflict figured by the machine's increasing domination of the visible world. This recurrent metaphor of contradiction makes vivid, as no other figure does, the bearing of public events upon private lives. It discloses that our inherited symbols of order and beauty have been divested of meaning. It compels us to recognize that the aspirations once represented by the symbol of an ideal landscape have not, and probably cannot, be embodied in our traditional institutions. It means that an inspiriting vision of a humane community has been reduced to a token of individual survival. The outcome of *Walden*, *Moby-Dick*, and *Huckleberry Finn* is repeated in the typical modern version of the fable; in the end the American hero is either dead or totally alienated from society, alone and powerless, like the evicted shepherd of Virgil's eclogue. And if, at the same time, he pays a tribute to the image of a green landscape, it is likely to be ironic and bitter. The resolutions of our pastoral fables are unsatisfactory because the old symbol of reconciliation is obsolete. But the inability of our writers to create a surrogate for the ideal of the middle landscape can hardly be accounted artistic failure. By incorporating in their work the root conflict of our culture, they have clarified our situation. They have served us well. To change the situation we require new symbols of possibility, and although the creation of those symbols is in some measure the responsibility of artists, it is in greater measure the responsibility of society. The machine's sudden entrance into the garden presents a problem that ultimately belongs not to art but to politics.

Leo Marx

Mount Tom, and the Connecticut River, Massachusetts, U. S.

I

The Unspoiled Land

MY PURPOSE HERE is to evoke, at the time of its exploration and early settlement, a vision of the pristine and unspoiled land that was to become the United States of America, and later, of the nation itself as it was in its robustious youth. Here is an amazing and beautiful country to wander in with its strange beasts and lush vegetation which included all sorts of new fruits and grains and vegetables.

These writings will introduce the reader to at least three lodes of great richness, the writings of Marquette, Bartram and Audubon, and will, I hope, excite in him a desire for further investigation. It is significant to note that Audubon, in his American paradise of a century and a half ago, was even then discovering with alarm that the machine was already making inroads in the garden.

View from Mount Washington, New Hampshire, 1853.

The Generall Survey of the Country

IN THE MONETH OF June, Anno Salutis 1622, it was my chaunce to arrive in the parts of New England with 30 Servants, and provision of all sorts fit for a plantation: and whiles our howses were building, I did indeavour to take a survey of the Country: The more I looked, the more I liked it. And when I had more seriously considered of the bewty of the place, with all her faire indowments, I did not thinke that in all the knowne world it could be paralel'd, for so many goodly groves of trees, dainty fine round rising hillucks, delicate faire large plaines, sweete cristall fountaines, and cleare running streames that twine in fine meanders through the meads, making so sweete a murmering noise to heare as would even lull the sences with delight a sleepe, so pleasantly doe they glide upon the pebble stones, jetting most jocundly where they doe meete and hand in hand runne downe to Neptunes Court, to pay the yearely tribute which they owe to him as soveraigne Lord of all the springs. Contained within the volume of the Land, Fowles in abundance, Fish in multitude; and discovered, besides, Millions of Turtledoves one the greene boughes, which sate pecking of the full ripe pleasant grapes that were supported by the lusty trees, whose fruitfull loade did cause the armes to bend: which here and there dispersed, you might see Lillies and of the Daphnean-tree: which made the Land to mee seeme paradice: for in mine eie 'twas Natures Masterpeece; Her cheifest Magazine of all where lives her store: if this Land be not rich, then is the whole world poore.

JOHN BAKELESS

The Eyes of Discovery

De Soto Tours the New World

Marching through Georgia, the Spaniards found the country "abundant, picturesque, and luxuriant, well watered, and having good river margins." Most of the route, from the moment they landed in Florida and far on into Georgia and the Carolinas, was covered with longleaf pine. They had already begun to admire the pines in Florida—"well proportioned and as tall as the tallest in Spain." Some of the country, especially Florida and southern Georgia, was "low, having many ponds." Elsewhere there were "high and dense forests, into which the Indians that were hostile betook themselves, where they could not be found; nor could horses enter there." This was unlike most northern forests where, from Virginia north, horses could move easily in spite of the heavy growth of trees. Northern Georgia and South Carolina country was "delightful and fertile, having good interval lands upon the streams; the forest was open, with abundance of walnut (probably hickory or pecan) and mulberry trees." The mulberries, De Soto's secretary noted, were "quite like those of Spain, just as tall and larger, but the leaf is softer and better for silk, and the mulberries are better eating and larger than those of Spain, and they were frequently of great advantage to the Spaniards for food." Sometimes the column passed large empty spaces, overgrown with grass, where towns had once stood—abandoned now, the Indians explained, because of pestilence two years before. . . .

These birds (turkeys) flourished in the prehistoric South and were remarkably good eating. American pioneers used slices of the white meat of the breast instead of the bread they could not get in the wilderness. Wild turkeys then were about as large as the biggest modern domesticated fowl. A really big gobbler might stand three feet high and weigh twenty to forty pounds. There are even tales of fifty-pound birds in the North. From March to April, they made the early morning ring with their gobbling from the magnolia trees in which they roosted. It is hard to see why the Spaniards fail to mention the dawn-gobbling of the turkeys. Certainly they heard it regularly, and it was a sound that ought to have impressed any traveler. The calls started at the first hint of dawn and continued till the sun was over the horizon. . . .

The southern tribes had an advanced agriculture, cultivating "many fine fields," in which they raised the usual Indian crops, including two kinds of corn—yellow for ordinary eating, white for flour. Near each Indian dwelling was a small field, fenced with saplings fastened to stakes in the ground. More distant fields, too big to fence, were not planted until the wild fruit began to ripen, drawing the birds away from the new seed. The planting date for these big communal fields was set by an old warrior, bearing the usual ceremonial title of "old beloved man," who gave warning to his village the day before the planting was to begin. Everyone, including the most distinguished chiefs and warriors, turned out to help with the planting. Everyone worked from one field to another till the seed was all in, their labors cheered by story-tellers, singers, and musicians performing on deer-skin drums.

The planting was not very skillful, the cornstalks being only two inches apart (one foot is an absolute minimum in modern agriculture); and the squaws, like many modern gardeners, were often rather careless about weeding and cultivating; but the richness of their soil made up for everything. . . .

Passing through the country in the spring, the Spaniards saw the pre-historic South at its very best. "They found there along the trails countless roses growing wild like those of Spain; and although they have not so many leaves since they are in the woods they are none the less fragrant and finer and sweeter." They admired the great forests of southern longleaf pine, "walnuts" (which may have been hickory nuts), oak, live oak, cedar, liquidambar, the fertile fields, the rich dress of the natives.

The newcomers were particularly impressed, as were all later Europeans, by the wild strawberries, "very savoury, palatable, and fragrant," rather better than those in Europe, "a finer delicate fruit." The plants grew in a thickness inconceivable today. One traveler notes that strawberries of large size "covered the ground as with a red cloth." Wild potatoes and the "nuts," i.e., roots, of wild flag added to the varied diet, which could at need be supplemented by green salad herbs or potherbs, of which the American woodlands and meadows, even today, produce an abundance—poke, lamb's-quarters, milk weed, purslane, nettle, wild spinach, wild onion—which for the most part goes to waste. . . .

The column must have presented a remarkable appearance, as it wound in single file along the narrow wilderness trails: caballeros with swords, lances, and armor, rather dingy and a bit rusty by this time; infantry cursing the weight of their packs and armor; arquebusiers, crossbowmen; squealing, rebellious hogs; Indian prisoners in chains; other Indian tamenes, or bearers; and the copper-colored ladies, who must have been fairly attractive (as Creek girls often were), or they wouldn't have been asked to go along.

By this time, careful breeding en route had increased the herd of swine to several hundred. Anyone who has ever tried to persuade an unwilling pig to go in any given direction will appreciate the labors of De Soto's swineherds. They coaxed hundreds of hogs through forests filled with edible nuts, succulent roots, and other porcine tidbits, over wilderness trails, with chances of escape into the bushes on every hand, with wild animals hungry for a little pork each night, for a distance of several thousand miles, from Florida to Texas, to Oklahoma, and half way back! There has been nothing like it since the *Odyssey;* and even in the *Odyssey,* the pigs stayed at home.

The Wild Middle West

As early as 1692 or 1693, Cornelissen Arnout Viele, an Albany Dutchman skilled in Indian languages, took a party down the Ohio, greatly to the distress of French officials who soon learned of his exploit, though they never intercepted him. By 1735, one Abraham Wendall was trading along the Allegheny. Other traders quickly followed. It is said that by the middle of the eighteenth century there were three hundred traders in the Ohio country, but these men kept their business secrets as close as possible. They did not want to interest possible rivals in the Indian trade and hence left practically no record of what they found. Enough information drifted East, however, to interest capitalists. The Ohio Company was formed and in 1750 sent the famous and resourceful frontiersman, Christopher Gist, to explore both Ohio and Kentucky.

Gist was no ordinary backwoodsman. Bold, resourceful, fearless and skillful in the big woods as any redskin, he was much better educated than the average Virginia gentleman. In a day when the formal business and official letters of Virginia leaders were marvels of illiteracy, even Gist's rough wilderness diaries were prose models, clear, simple, direct—and properly spelled! Yet he could be ruthless as the roughest backwoodsman upon occasion. It took definite orders from George Washington to keep him from dispatching out-of-hand an Indian who had, he thought, tried to shoot "the Major," while Gist and Major Washington were returning from their trip to warn the French off the Ohio. Acquaintance either with Gist himself or with his son, Nathaniel, probably helped arouse Daniel Boone's interest in Kentucky.

Gist made three western trips, the journals of which have been preserved, between 1750 and 1754, the last recording his famous journey with Washington, to warn off French troops at Fort Duquesne (Pittsburgh). His first and most ambitious journey in 1750 took him through Pennsylvania, down the river, through Ohio as far west as Piqua and Dayton, then still farther west in Kentucky almost to Louisville, then homeward southwest (sic) across Kentucky to westernmost Virginia and south to his home in North Carolina.

Most travelers floated down the Ohio in a canoe, or, in later years, in a flatboat or a keelboat. Gist, however, was traveling to "find a large Quantity of good, level Land" for the Ohio Company. There was plenty of good, rich bottom land along the Ohio itself—the early travelers are always talking about it—but Gist wanted to make a thorough survey of the country.

Ohio in those days was wooded, but as Gist moved west toward the prairies beyond the Mississippi, he found the woods becoming less dense. Much of the landscape, even in forested Ohio, was "fine rich level Land, with large Meadows, fine Clover Bottoms & spacious Plains covered with wild Rye: the wood chiefly large Walnuts and Hickories, here and there mixed with Poplars Cherry Trees and Sugar Trees." Like the eastern forests, these were open underfoot. There was practically no underbrush and the trunks were long and straight, their lower branches having died from lack of sunlight and dropped off. Early Ohio settlers found that they could drive about through the forests with sleds and horses.

Eventually these huge forests were cleared by an odd labor-saving device. Settlers would cut each tree half way through over a space of several acres, thereby saving themselves half the work. Then, when the wind was right, they felled a few of the big trees to windward which, as they crashed down, carried the rest with them, sending thousands of tall trees toppling to the ground like so many dominoes. Most of this magnificent timber was simply burned on the spot. The ashes were good for the soil, no one needed lumber, and no one worried over the lost beauty of the forest.

The soil was, in fact, already fertile enough without the ashes. One enterprising traveler proposed gathering them up and starting a potash industry, since the land did not need them. The rapid growth of new trees and plants in prairie soil astonished the first white men who cultivated it. If we can believe an early visitor to the settlements, apples would bear fruit four years from seed (he may have meant "seedlings"), peaches three years from seed were loaded with fruit, locusts two years from seed reached heights of twelve to fifteen feet. This enthusiast even insisted that "in six years a farmer may raise from the seed a forest which will meet every want."

Wild rye grew everywhere in Ohio, westward to the Mississippi, and even beyond. It was almost like the cultivated variety except for a longer beard. Thomas Pownall observes that it "shoots in its spontaneous Vegetations about the Middle of November as the cultivated rye doth." Pines seem to have stopped at the western boundary of Pennsylvania, though there were immense pine forests to the northwest and in the South. The sulphur springs of Pennsylvania gave way to numerous salt licks and springs. Even the bushes around them were sometimes encrusted with salt crystals. Occasionally the streams themselves were salt. The water, when boiled in enormous flat kettles made for the purpose, yielded a fairly good table salt. When first boiled out, the salt had a blue color, giving a bluish sediment to salt creeks and springs. In some streams and ponds even the water was blue—hence the name of the famous Blue Licks in Kentucky, or the Blue River in Indiana, which kept its clear blue color until it emptied into the Ohio.

If, however, the blue crystals were dissolved in pure water and boiled a second time they became "tolerable pure Salt." Earth near the springs was impregnated, creating "licks"—so called because deer and buffalo which craved salt as much as barnyard cattle, came from all the country around to lick eagerly at the saline earth. It was always easy to kill game by lying in wait at any of the licks. In the few wilderness areas now remaining, moose and deer are so eager for salt that it is easy to attract them by spreading it about on the ground—a practice usually forbidden by the game laws because of the slaughter it makes possible.

In some places the buffalo actually ate the salt earth. At the famous Blue Licks the earth had been eaten away to such a depth that the huge bodies of the buffalo were completely concealed. Sometimes the great trenches ran side by side with only a thin wall of earth dividing them. Michael Stoner, the famous Pennsylvania Dutch frontiersman of Kentucky, was nearly killed by attempting a prank in one of these excavations. Traveling past the Blue Licks with Daniel Boone, he saw a buffalo eagerly licking the earth of one such trench. The two woodsmen were in no need of meat but Stoner thought it would be amusing to scare the animal. He crept down the parallel trench, which earlier buffalo had dug in their search for salt, until he was opposite his own buffalo, whose attention was wholly taken up with the salt. Then rising suddenly, he thrust his cap across the thin dividing wall almost into the animal's face. Instead of running, the great brute charged straight into the thin earth wall. As the huge horns, head, and shoulders burst through the earth, almost on top of him, Stoner ran for his life, wildly yelling to Boone in Pennsylvania Dutch-English. "Schoot her, Gaptain! Schoot her, Gaptain!" Stoner was still running when the buffalo gave up the chase, while Boone, seeing that his companion was in no real danger, rolled upon the ground with laughter.

There were relatively few buffalo in the heavily wooded country north of the Ohio, for the salt licks and the heavy growth of cane, rushes, and "wild peas" attracted the animals to Kentucky. A herd of twenty is mentioned as remarkable, and an English visitor was very much excited at seeing "more than a hundred together"—which would have amused a Sioux or Comanche. There were rather larger herds on the lower Ohio, and buffalo roamed Kentucky in herds of several hundred at a time, though never in the huge masses of the western plains where far into the nineteenth century one might see a hundred thousand or more at a time.

Except when an individual animal was wounded or a whole herd was frightened and stampeded, these small herds were seldom dangerous. Daniel Boone and his friends on one occasion amused themselves by chasing a Kentucky herd across a river, simply for the fun of counting them. This kind of thing was all very well if you knew which way the herd was going to head, but it was almost certain death to get in the way of a stampede. The quick-witted Boone once saved himself in such a predicament by shooting one animal and crouching behind the huge carcass while the others thundered past it.

White hunters soon exterminated buffalo and elk. They were all gone east of the Mississippi by the second quarter of the nineteenth century, or earlier; but the deer, as usual, increased as hunters kept down beasts of prey, and as settlers opened up the forests to provide more grazing lands. Just before 1840, there was a brisk trade in deer hides and venison hams, the latter worth seventy-five cents to $1.50 a pair. Wolves remained a pest for a long time and often frightened farm wives by prowling about in broad daylight, always seeming to choose the hour when the farmer was in the fields, and there was no danger from his rifle. "Partridges," which seem to have been Bob-White quail, could be netted in winter by the hundreds, long after settlement began. The clearing of the forests probably benefited them as much as it did the deer.

Father of Waters

THE (FRENCH) GOVERNMENT, about 1672, proposed to send Louis Jolliet "to discover the south sea," and to explore "the great river Mississippi, which is believed to empty in the California sea."

In Jolliet, they had found an almost ideal man for their purpose. Born at Beauport, near Quebec, in 1645, he had been educated in the Jesuit College at Quebec, had received minor orders, and had at one time intended to become a member of the Society of Jesus. Giving up his studies for the priesthood, he had visited France, returned to Canada, and plunged into the wilderness.

Father Dablon, Jesuit Superior in Canada, under whom Jolliet had studied, wrote that he was "endowed with every quality that could be desired in such an enterprise. He possessed experience and a knowledge of the languages of the Ottawa country, where he had spent several years; he had the tact and prudence so necessary for the success of a voyage equally dangerous and difficult; and, lastly, he had courage to fear nothing where all is to be feared."

As usual in expeditions of this sort, both French and Spanish, a priest was sent along to do missionary work—in this case, the famous Father Jacques Marquette.

The daring little band was under Jolliet's command, while Father Marquette was attached to the expedition for religious purposes only. Because Jolliet's map and papers were destroyed while those of Père Marquette were preserved, the story of the two men's exploration is usually told from Marquette's point of view rather than Jolliet's. Nothing, one may be sure, would have distressed the devout and unworldly priest more than this.

A better companion for the dangerous task, it would have been hard to find. Père Marquette had, of course, passed through the usual rigorous intellectual training which the Society of Jesus has always required of its priests. He spoke six Indian languages fluently and had already had long experience in the wilderness. Moreover, he was a man of singular sweetness and gentleness, utterly indifferent to worldly matters, equally incapable of fear, jealousy, or personal ambition, with a temper by nature so placid that the worst hardships of the wilderness left it wholly undisturbed.

With five companions in two birchbark canoes, Jolliet and Marquette started from Mackinac Island, May 17, 1673. Determined that "if our enterprise was hazardous, it should not be foolhardy," they had been at pains to learn in advance everything that the Indians of the Great Lakes could tell them about the route overland to the Mississippi, the course of the river itself, and the tribes living on its banks. Like Nicolet and Allouez, they followed the usual Indian route, from Green Bay on Lake Michigan, up the Fox River, over the low watershed at its source, and down the Wisconsin into the Mississippi itself.

At Green Bay, they turned into the Fox River with a gentle current—a matter of no small importance to canoemen pushing upstream —and full of migrating waterfowl, attracted by the abundant wild rice. They were traveling in wild rice country. In modern times the growth of this staple grocery of the wilderness is so restricted and the demand for it so great that it is all gathered long before winter sets in. But in these early days there was so much of it that in parts of the Fox River a single patch might cover a space five miles by two, so thick that sometimes passage for a canoe had to be chopped through it. Often, in spite of its value as a food supply, the luxuriant growth became a mere nuisance.

Neither the Indians nor the waterfowl could eat enough to exhaust the endless grain supply, for one small lake could produce enough to feed two thousand people. Jolliet and Marquette found the tall stalks swaying above the water, "still full of grain, though it was now late spring and the new growth was ready to begin."

Father Marquette described the "wild oats" as "a kind of grass which grows spontaneously in little rivers with slimy bottoms, and in marshy places; they are very like the wild oats that grow up among our wheat. The ears are on stalks knotted at intervals; they rise above the water about the month of June, and keep rising till they float about two feet above it. The grain is not thicker than our oats, but is as long again, so that the meal is much more abundant."

Wilderness ways change slowly. The exploring priest describes, in 1673, exactly the way in which to this very day the Ojibway Indians of Minnesota and Ontario still gather their wild rice harvest: "In the month of September, which is the proper time for this harvest, they go in canoes across these fields of wild oats, and shake the ears on their right and left into the canoe as they advance; the grain falls easily if it is ripe, and in a little while their provision is made." The Indians then trod out the grain with moccasined feet, winnowed away the chaff, and dried the rice over a fire, after which they pounded it into meal—a practice horrifying to the modern epicure, who now pays large prices for it at a "fancy" grocery and boils it whole, as the perfect accompaniment to fowl or game.

The worthy father also paused to investigate a marvellous herb whose root, "very hot," with "the taste of powder when crushed between the teeth," was supposed to be a specific against snake bite—as it probably was in Canada, where poisonous serpents are practically non-existent. Snakes were said to flee the presence of anyone rubbed with this wonderful plant, and some ambitious annotator has added the information that "if two or three drops are put into a snake's mouth, it immediately dies." One wonders if anyone was ever foolish enough to pry open the mouth of a rattler or a copperhead, to try it!

Before leaving the Fox River, they made a short halt at a village of the Maskouten, or "Fire Indians." The view from the village, Père Marquette noted, "is beautiful and very picturesque, for from the eminence on which it is perched, the eye discovers on every side prairies spreading away beyond its reach, interspersed with thickets or groves of lofty trees."

Beyond this agreeable campsite, Jolliet and Marquette reached the flat, swampy watershed—a "drowned prairie," La Salle later called it—between the Fox and Wisconsin rivers, too late for the spring floods and therefore had to portage. A little earlier, they might have had the unique experience of paddling over a watershed; for here, when the streams were highest, there was a queer temporary lake, whose waters covered the divide and flowed in two directions, part going down the Fox, into the Great Lakes, and part down the Wisconsin, into the Mississippi. Jolliet and Marquette found the high water gone, but the ground still so wet that their portage was "cut up by marshes and little lakes."

They did not, however, find this portage in such bad condition as did Pierre Le Sueur, a former Jesuit donné, or lay assistant, who had become an active trader much interested in mining possibilities and who in September, 1700, found half of it "un pays tremblant"—one of those dreadful muskegs, where the traveler leaps from one sinking hummock to another, trying never to stay on any one quite long enough to be overwhelmed by mud and water.

Parts of Michigan and Wisconsin were then much more broken up by small lakes, ponds and marshes than they are today, after much artificial drainage. In this they resembled Ohio, Indiana, and Illinois.

In winter, as La Salle discovered a few years later, this could be rather a grim landscape. An early nineteenth century traveler describes how his way "led through oak openings of rolling land, called 'the Short Hills,' which I can best assimilate to a collection of enormous graves—the tombs of households, if you choose—thrown confusedly together upon a perfectly level surface; where a patch of wild meadowland, a cranberry marsh, or a bog that looked like the desolated bed of a lake, and frequently, indeed, the shallow lake itself, filled up the intervals. The huge oaks that crowned the summits of these formal mounds were the only objects that relieved the dreariness of the landscape." One might, in winter, travel thus for miles without seeing more than a raven, the deer and moose having "yarded up," the bears having hibernated, and most birds having fled southward. At other times even the winter woods might be rather lively, large flocks of snowbirds twittering among the burr-oaks, jays screaming here and there, and "packs of grouse," sometimes taking wing in the openings—probably hens and their grown broods which had not yet separated.

In spring, the season which Jolliet and Marquette wisely chose for the start of their dangerous journey, luxuriance burst out again.

A portage of only a mile and a half brought them over to the upper waters of the Wisconsin River, "very broad, with a sandy bottom, forming many shallows"—the kind of water to which the light Indian birchbark is perfectly adapted. The stream was full of "fine-clad islets" (Marquette, like all the other French explorers, however intent he might be on holy things, had already noted that "good wine could be made"), while around them lay open prairies, hills, and woodland, with practically no small game, but with "deer and moose in considerable numbers" along the stream.

The game animals were staying close to the river, as they love to do in hot weather. Even today, in the wilder Canadian woodlands, you sometimes have to stop your canoe to chase the moose away. Deer are more timorous creatures, likely to bolt at the first sight of man. But a moose, comfortable among the lily pads of a wilderness stream, is often quite fearless and reluctant to move at all. When he does at length throw back his mighty antlers and lift his great nostrils haughtily in the air, he gives the abashed intruder the impression of a proud proprietor, disturbed without warrant on his own land, but too well-bred a gentleman to make a fuss about it.

After something more than a hundred miles of easy paddling down the Wisconsin amid delightful scenery, with food to be had for the killing whenever they wanted it, Jolliet and Marquette turned into the clear, limpid main current of the upper Mississippi on June 17. The Mississippi at the mouth of the Wisconsin was, then as now, relatively small, compared to the tremendous river into which it is transformed after the Missouri and Ohio have poured in their floods. Nevertheless, the Frenchmen were delighted and impressed when, on sounding, they found a depth of ten fathoms, or sixty feet. This must have been in one of the narrow places where the whole Mississippi current is compressed into a little more than two hundred yards. Elsewhere they found a

width of about two miles, with "very high mountains" on the right
(west) bank and "fine lands" on the left, with many islands. Nowhere
was there any sign of humanity.

The banks of the upper and middle Mississippi were edged with
sycamore, white and black oak, white and black ash, elm, gumtree,
hickory, black walnut, and dogwood, the latter much larger than that
of the northern states, though the trees thinned out and even disappeared in many places as one went downstream.

As they floated down the wild, silent stream, between the empty
lands of Iowa and Illinois, they noted how the woodlands of the upper
river were changing to prairie country, though they could not guess at
the incredible richness of the future farm lands through which they
were passing. A much later settler remarked of the soil around "Kekala-
mazoo," in Michigan, that it was "so fat that it will grease your
fingers"; and as they left Michigan and Wisconsin behind, Jolliet
and Marquette were coming into country more fertile still. Iowa, past
which they paddled, is credited with one fourth of the Class A farm
land in the whole United States. Only in a few favored areas of Europe,
is there anything to match it.

"There is now almost no wood or mountain, the islands are more
beautiful and covered with finer trees," noted Père Marquette. There
were still deer and moose, but as yet no buffalo, along the banks,
together with waterfowl—also "bustards" (probably wild geese) and
"wingless swans, for they shed their plumes in this country." Their
failure to find buffalo was probably accidental, for another priest going
downstream in 1699 remarks that "from Chikagou to the Akanseas
(Arkansas River) in the Mississipi (sic), the bison and cows are so
numerous that you cannot lack provisions if you have powder and ball."
This party found bear and deer numerous and so fearless that they killed
several with swords!

The travelers had seen no fish in the Wisconsin River, probably
because they spent no time trying to catch them; but they soon
noticed the "monstrous fish" of the Mississippi, which could not be
ignored even when no one wanted to catch them. One of these, according to Marquette, "struck so violently against our canoes that I
took it for a large tree about to knock us to pieces."

Most modern writers assume that this was one of the huge Mississippi catfish; but it may quite as easily have been a sturgeon, drowsing
in the sun near the surface until startled by the passing canoes when,
naturally, it bolted—a hundred pounds or so of muscle—for the safety
of deep water.

If the immense creature really was a Mississippi catfish, it is just as well that it got away, for it took French explorers some time to realize how formidably the American catfish was armed. Iberville, who a few years later explored the lower reaches of the great river, remarks that in it swam "fishes that have a sting." One of his sailors was so badly hurt by catfish spines that the loss of his leg was feared and he was not able to stand for two months—no doubt mainly because the wound became infected.

Jolliet and Marquette met with less painful ichthyological surprises. Casting their nets, the French newcomers took sturgeon and spadefish, the latter "a very extraordinary kind of fish; it resembles a trout with this difference, that it has a larger mouth, but smaller eyes and snout. Near the latter is a large bone, like a woman's busk, three fingers wide, and a cubit long; the end as circular and as wide as the hand. In leaping out of the water the weight of this often throws it back." This was "le spatule" of the later French voyagers and *Polyodon spatula* of Linnaeus and modern ichthyologists, which both De Soto and Radisson had already seen. It is a rare creature today, but with its bony shovel nose is still startling as ever to the twentieth century fishermen who occasionally take one or two.

"A woman's busk" was the flat bone used by ladies of the time for stays; and persons who think such a comparison unlikely to occur to the saintly Marquette have tried to persuade themselves that this passage must be an excerpt from Jolliet's lost journals.

Once the voyagers saw "a monster with the head of a tiger, a pointed snout like a wild-cat's, a beard and ears erect, a grayish head and neck all black"—obviously either a lynx or a melanic form of the ordinary American cougar, or mountain lion, which, so long as the deer supply held out, ranged all of the United States. It is true that the cougar has no beard but it has the stiff bristling whiskers common to all cats. Does not Shakespeare say "bearded like the pard"?

Farther down the Mississippi, near Natchez, what must have been the same animal was called a "spotted tiger." Even in 1810, a traveler says, "Although not numerous, yet of late years they are frequently met with."

Near modern Rock Island, Jolliet and Marquette noticed that moose and deer began to grow less frequent, while they saw more and more buffalo ("pisikous, or wild cattle") and more wild turkeys.

For one stretch of 280 miles, Jolliet and Marquette saw game every fifteen minutes.

On their left they passed the mouth of the wild Rock River, running through high, undulating land, rather sparsely wooded, named for the rocks over which its current tumbled, and with water so clear that idlers on the banks could see "the minutest object that lies upon its bottom, including pike and catfish up to 150 pounds, redhorse and perch that ranged between three feet and ten." The springs which fed it were so cold that it hurt to dip the hands in them for more than half a minute.

They had to take considerable risks in hunting buffalo on foot. "When attacked," wrote Père Marquette, "they take a man with their horns, if they can, lift him up, and then dash him on the ground, trample on him, and kill him. When you fire at them from a distance with gun or bow, you must throw yourself on the ground as soon as you fire, and hide in the grass; for, if they perceive the one who fired, they rush on him and attack." There were no horses in this part of the plains country yet and hunting buffalo on foot, with bow and arrow or clumsy muzzle-loading firearms, was very different from hunting on trained ponies with powerful rifles. A herd of four hundred seemed remarkably large to these early travelers, who had no idea how huge the western buffalo herds could be. This small herd created an amusing sensation when it was reported at Quebec, and its supposedly huge size was relayed to the royal government in Paris again and again. La Salle was equally naive in reporting buffalo along the Illinois and Wabash, "in prodigious quantities," in numbers "greater than can be believed."

Thus far, Jolliet and Marquette had seen no Indians nor even Indian sign. Now, on the west bank, probably nearly opposite Quincy, Illinois, they saw "footprints of men by the water-side, and a beaten path entering a beautiful prairie." Clearly there was a village somewhere inland. Leaving their men in safety in the canoes, Jolliet and Marquette themselves set out to hunt for it—a risky business since strangers, however peaceful in their intentions, were likely to be killed out of hand. By good luck they reached the first village undiscovered and approached so near that they could hear the Indians talking. Farther on they could see two other villages.

To prove their friendly attitude, they now shouted with all their might, and then stood where they were in full view—no enemy does that. Indians came rushing from the lodges. The explorers must have held their breath, for the next few minutes meant life or death. Then four old men slowly approached bearing peace-pipes. The danger was over. These were Illinois Indians, whose Algonkian dialect resembled other Algonkian languages known to Father Marquette closely enough so that he could make himself understood. As they seemed perfectly friendly, Jolliet and Marquette remained with them for a few days and then "about the end of June, at three o'clock in the afternoon," started down the river again.

They now had open prairies on their right, and precipitous rocky shores on the east bank, with forests growing on them. These woodlands were immensely picturesque. A wandering German artist describes them in the mid-nineteenth century—still much as Jolliet and Marquette had seen them—vine-hung oaks, elms, poplars, nut trees, locusts, maples, and persimmons: "What distinguishes these native forests from others is the rank growth of creepers and climbing plants and the dead trees. . . .

"As soon as the foliage is in full leaf, the mighty trunks themselves are hidden from view by rank luxuriance of creepers and twining plants.

"Interlacing with one another and intertwining about the trees these vines made a sylvan decoration the richest as well as the most graceful that one can imagine. The festoons sway with the gentlest breeze and loosen themselves from the support of the twigs. Sometimes, under a gust of wind, garlands as thick as a man's arm are detached and hang suspended from the boughs to the ground like the rope of a sail."

As the Frenchmen approached steep cliffs on the east bank, near Alton, Illinois, they "saw two monsters painted on one of these rocks, which startled us at first, and on which the boldest Indian dare not gaze long. They are as large as a calf, with horns on the head like a deer, a fearful look, red eyes, bearded like a tiger, the face somewhat like a man's, the body covered with scales, and the tail so long that it twice makes the turn of the body, passing over the head and down between the legs, and ending at last in a fish's tail. Green, red, and a kind of black, are the colors employed. On the whole, these two monsters are so well painted, that we could not believe any Indian to have been the designer, as good painters in France would find it hard to do as well; besides this, they are so high upon the rock that it is hard to get conveniently at them to paint them."

These were simply Indian rock paintings of a not unusual sort, though of more than usual size. The larger figure was about eight feet long and five feet high, while the other figure—which, by the seventeenth century had been reduced to a mere head—had probably at one time been of about the same dimensions. They commemorated the slaying, by the hero Wassatogo and his warriors, of an enormous mythological animal, half-beast, half-bird, which lived on human flesh—a legend which may have some remote kind of basis in fact, since a cave filled several feet deep with human bones was discovered far up the cliff in the latter nineteenth century.

A Trip on the St. John River in Florida

THE ORANGE GROVE is but narrow, betwixt the river banks and ancient Indian fields, where there are evident traces of the habitations of the ancients, surrounded with groves of live oak, laurel magnolia, zanthoxylon, liquidambar, and others.

How harmonious and soothing is this native sylvan music now at still evening! inexpressibly tender are the responsive cooings of the innocent dove, in the fragrant zanthoxylon groves, and the variable and tuneful warblings of the nonpareil, with the more sprightly and elevated strains of the blue linnet and golden icterus: this is indeed harmony, even amidst the incessant croaking of the frogs: the shades of silent night are made more cheerful, with the shrill voice of the whip-poor-will and active mock-bird.

My situation high and airy: a brisk and cool breeze steadily and incessantly passing over the clear waters of the lake, and fluttering over me through the surrounding groves, wings its way to the moon-light savannas, while I repose on my sweet and healthy couch of the soft tillandsia usnea-adscites, and the latter gloomy and still hours of night pass rapidly away as it were in a moment. I arose, strengthened and cheerful, in the morning. Having some repairs to make in the tackle of my vessel, I paid my first attention to them; which being accomplished, my curiosity prompted me to penetrate the grove and view the illuminated plains. . . .

My morning excursion finished, I returned to my camp, breakfasted, then went on board my boat, gently descended the noble river, and passed by several openings of extensive plains and meadows, environing the east lake, charming beyond compare. At evening I came to at a good harbour, under the high banks of the river, and rested during the night amidst the fragrant groves, exposed to the constant breezes from the river: here I made ample collections of specimens and growing roots of curious vegetables, which kept me fully employed the greatest part of the day; and in the evening arrived at a charming spot on the east bank, which I had marked on my ascent up the river, where I made some addition to my collections; and the next day I employed myself in the same manner, putting into shore frequently at convenient places, which I had noticed; and in the evening arrived again at the upper store, where I had the pleasure of finding my old friend, the trader, in good health and cheerful, and his affairs in a prosperous way. There were also a small party of Indians here, who had lately arrived with their hunts to purchase goods. I continued a few days at this post, searching its environs for curious vegetable productions, collecting seeds and planting growing roots in boxes, to be transported to the lower trading house.

Now, having procured necessaries to accommodate me on my voyage down to the lower store, I bid adieu to my old friend and benefactor, Mr. Job Wiggens, embarked alone on board my little fortunate vessel, and set sail. I chose to follow the easternmost channel of the river to the Great Lake, because it ran by high banks and bluffs of the eastern main the greatest part of the distance, which afforded me an opportunity of observing a far greater variety of natural subjects, than if I had taken the western or middle channel, which flowed through swamps and marshes.

At evening I arrived at Cedar Point, my former safe and pleasant harbour, at the east cape of the Great Lake, where I had noticed some curious shrubs and plants; here I rested, and on the smooth and gentle current launch again into the little ocean of Lake George, meaning now, on my return, to coast his western shores in search of new beauties in the bounteous kingdom of Flora.

I was however induced to deviate a little from my intended course, and touch at the inchanting little Isle of Palms. This delightful spot, planted by nature, is almost an entire grove of Palms, with a few pyramidal Magnolias, Live Oaks, golden Orange, and the animating Zanthoxylon. What a beautiful retreat is here! blessed unviolated spot of earth, rising from the limpid waters of the lake: its fragrant groves and blooming lawns invested and protected by encircling ranks of the Yucca gloriosa. A fascinating atmosphere surrounds this blissful garden; the balmy Lantana, ambrosial Citra, perfumed Crinum, perspiring their mingled odors, wafted through Zanthoxylon groves. I at last broke away from the enchanting spot, and stepped on board my boat, hoisted sail, and soon approached the coast of the main, at the cool eve of day; then traversing a capacious semicircular cove of the lake, verged by low, extensive grassy meadows, I at length by dusk made a

View on the St. John River, Florida, 1878.

safe harbour, in a little lagoon, on the sea shore or strand of a bold sandy point which descended from the surf of the lake. This was a clean sandy beach, hard and firm by the beating surf, when the wind sets from the east coast. I drew up my light vessel on the sloping shore, that she might be safe from the beating waves in case of a sudden storm of wind in the night. A few yards back the land was a little elevated, and over-grown with thickets of shrubs and low trees. . . . These groves were but low, yet sufficiently high to shelter me from the chilling dews; and being but a few yards distance from my vessel, here I fixed my encampment. A brisk wind arising from the lake, drove away the clouds of musquitoes into the thickets. I now, with difficulty and industry, collected a sufficiency of dry wood to keep up a light during the night, and to roast some trout which I had caught when descending the river: their heads I stewed in the juice of Oranges, which, with boiled rice, afforded me a wholesome and delicious supper: I hung the remainder of my broiled fish on the snags of some shrubs over my head. I at last, after reconnoitring my habitation, returned, spread abroad my skins and blanket upon the clean sands by my fire-side, and betook myself to repose.

How glorious the powerful sun, minister of the Most High in the rule and government of this earth, leaves our hemisphere, retiring from our sight beyond the western forests! I behold with gratitude his departing smiles, tinging the fleecy roseate clouds, now riding far away on the eastern horizon; behold they vanish from sight in the azure skies!

All now silent and peaceable, I suddenly fell asleep. At midnight I awake; when, raising my head erect, I find myself alone in the wilderness of Florida, on the shores of Lake George. Alone indeed, but under the care of the Almighty, and protected by the invisible hand of my guardian angel.

When quite awake, I started at the heavy tread of some animal; the dry limbs of trees upon the ground crack under his feet; the close shrubby thickets part and bend under him as he rushes off.

I rekindle my sleepy fire; lay in contact the exfoliated smoking brands damp with the dew of heaven.

The bright flame ascends and illuminates the ground and groves around me.

When looking up, I found my fish carried off, though I had thought them safe on the shrubs, just over my head; but their scent, carried to a great distance by the damp nocturnal breezes, I suppose were too powerful attractions to resist.

Perhaps it may not be time lost, to rest a while here, and reflect on the unexpected and unaccountable incident, which however pointed out to me an extraordinary deliverance or protection of my life, from the rapacious wolf that stole my fish from over my head.

How much easier and more eligible might it have been for him to have leaped upon my breast in the dead of sleep, and torn my throat, which would have instantly deprived me of life, and then glutted his stomach for the present with my warm blood, and dragged off my body, which would have made a feast afterwards for him and his howling associates! I say, would not this have been a wiser step, than to have made protracted and circular approaches, and then after, by chance, espying the fish over my head, with the greatest caution and silence rear up, and take them off the snags one by one, then make off with them, and that so cunningly as not to waken me until he had fairly accomplished his purpose?

The morning being clear, I set sail with a favourable breeze, coasting along the shores; when on a sudden the waters became transparent, and discovered the sandy bottom, and the several nations of fish, passing and repassing each other. Following this course I was led to the cape of the little river, descending from Six Mile Springs, and meandering six miles from its source through green meadows. I entered this pellucid stream, sailing over the heads of innumerable squadrons of fish, which, although many feet deep in the water, were distinctly to be seen. I passed by charming islets of flourishing trees, as Palm, Red Bay, Ash, Maple, Nyssa, and others. As I approached the distant high forest on the main, the river widened, floating fields of the green Pistia surrounded me, the rapid stream winding through them. What an alluring scene was now before me! A vast bason or little lake of crystal waters, half encircled by swelling hills, clad with Orange and odoriferous Illicium groves, the towering Magnolia, itself a grove, and the exalted Palm, as if conscious of their transcendent glories, tossed about their lofty heads, painting, with mutable shades, the green floating fields beneath. The social prattling coot enrobed in blue, and the squealing water-hen, with wings half expanded, tripped after each other, over the watery mirrour.

I put in at an ancient landing place, which is a sloping ascent to a level grassy plain, an old Indian field. As I intended to make my most considerable collections at this place, I proceeded immediately to fix my encampment but a few yards from my safe harbour, where I securely fastened my boat to a Live Oak, which overshadowed my port.

The Ohio

W HEN MY WIFE, my eldest son (then an infant), and myself were
returning from Pennsylvania to Kentucky, we found it expedient,
the waters being unusually low, to provide ourselves with a *skiff*, to
enable us to proceed to our abode at Henderson. I purchased a large,
commodious, and light boat of that denomination. We procured a
mattress, and our friends furnished us with ready prepared viands. We
had two stout negro rowers, and in this trim we left the village of
Shippingport, in expectation of reaching the place of our destination
in a very few days.

It was in the month of October. The autumnal tints already decorated the shores of that queen of rivers, the Ohio. Every tree was hung
with long and flowing festoons of different species of vines, many
loaded with clustered fruits of varied brilliancy, their rich bronzed
carmine mingling beautifully with the yellow foliage, which now pre-
dominated over the yet green leaves, reflecting more lively tints from
the clear stream than ever landscape painter portrayed, or poet imagined.

The days were yet warm. The sun had assumed the rich and glowing
hue which at that season produces the singular phenomenon called
there the "Indian Summer." The moon had rather passed the meridian
of her grandeur. We glided down the river, meeting no other ripple of
the water than that formed by the propulsion of our boat. Leisurely we
moved along, gazing all day on the grandeur and beauty of the wild
scenery around us.

Now and then a large catfish rose to the surface of the water, in
pursuit of a shoal of fry, which, starting simultaneously from the liquid
element like so many silver arrows, produced a shower of light, while
the pursuer with open jaws seized the stragglers, and, with a splash of
his tail, disappeared from our view. Other fishes we heard, uttering
beneath our bark a rumbling noise, the strange sound of which we discovered to proceed from the white perch, for on casting our net from

the bow, we caught several of that species, when the noise ceased for a time.

Nature, in her varied arrangements, seems to have felt a partiality towards this portion of our country. As the traveller ascends or descends the Ohio, he cannot help remarking that alternately, nearly the whole length of the river, the margin, on one side, is bounded by lofty hills and a rolling surface, while on the other, extensive plains of the richest alluvial land are seen as far as the eye can command the view. Islands of varied size and form rise here and there from the bosom of the water, and the winding course of the stream frequently brings you to places where the idea of being on a river of great length changes to that of floating on a lake of moderate extent. Some of these islands are of considerable size and value; while others, small and insignificant, seem as if intended for contrast, and as serving to enhance the general interest of the scenery. These little islands are frequently overflowed during great freshets or floods, and receive at their heads prodigious heaps of drifted timber. We foresaw with great concern the alterations that cultivation would soon produce along those delightful banks.

As night came, sinking in darkness the broader portions of the river, our minds became affected by strong emotions, and wandered far beyond the present moments. The tinkling of bells told us that the cattle which bore them were gently roving from valley to valley in search of food, or returning to their distant homes. The hooting of the Great Owl, or the muffled noise of its wings, as it sailed smoothly over the stream, were matters of interest to us; so was the sound of the boatman's horn, as it came winding more and more softly from afar. When daylight returned, many songsters burst forth with echoing notes, more and more mellow to the listening ear. Here and there the lonely cabin of a squatter struck the eye, giving note of commencing civilization. The crossing of the stream by a Deer foretold how soon the hills would be covered with snow.

Many sluggish flatboats we overtook and passed; some laden with produce from the different head-waters of the small rivers that pour their tributary streams into the Ohio; others, of less dimensions, crowded with emigrants from distant parts, in search of a new home. Purer pleasures I never felt; nor have you, reader, I ween, unless indeed you have felt the like, and in such company.

The margins of the shores and of the river were, at this season, amply supplied with game. A Wild Turkey, a Grouse, or a Blue-winged Teal, could be procured in a few moments; and we fared well, for, whenever we pleased we landed, struck up a fire, and provided as we were with the necessary utensils, procured a good repast.

Several of these happy days passed, and we neared our home, when, one evening, not far from Pigeon Creek (a small stream which runs into the Ohio from the State of Indiana), a loud and strange noise was heard, so like the yells of Indian warfare, that we pulled at our oars, and made for the opposite side as fast and as quietly as possible. The sounds increased, we imagined we heard cries of "murder;" and as we knew that some depredations had lately been committed in the country by dissatisfied parties of aborigines, we felt for a while extremely uncomfortable. Ere long, however, our minds became more calmed, and we plainly discovered that the singular uproar was produced by an enthusiastic set of Methodists, who had wandered thus far out of the common way for the purpose of holding one of their annual camp-meetings, under the shade of a beech forest. Without meeting with any other interruption, we reached Henderson, distant from Shippingport, by water, about two hundred miles.

When I think of these times, and call back to my mind the grandeur and beauty of those almost uninhabited shores; when I picture to myself the dense and lofty summits of the forests, that everywhere spread along the hills and overhung the margins of the stream, unmolested by the axe or the settler; when I know how dearly purchased the safe navigation of that river has been, by the blood of many worthy Virginians; when I see that no longer any aborigines are to be found there, and that the vast herds of Elk, Deer, and Buffaloes which once pastured on these hills, and in these valleys, making for themselves great roads to the several salt-springs, have ceased to exist; when I reflect that all this grand portion of our Union, instead of being in a state of nature, is now more or less covered with villages, farms, and towns, where the din of hammers and machinery is constantly; that the woods are fast disappearing under the axe by day, and the fire by night; that hundreds of steamboats are gliding to and fro, over the whole length of the majestic river, forcing commerce to take root and to prosper at every spot; when I see the surplus population of Europe coming to assist in the destruction of the forest, and transplanting civilization into its darkest recesses; when I remember that these extraordinary changes have all taken place in the short period of twenty years, I pause, wonder, and although I know all to be fact, can scarcely believe its reality.

Whether these changes are for the better or for the worse, I shall not pretend to say; but in whatever way my conclusion may incline, I feel with regret that there are on record no satisfactory accounts of the state of that portion of the country, from the time when our people first settled in it. This has not been because no one in America is able

View on the Great Miami near Cleves, Ohio, 1857.

to accomplish such an undertaking. Our Irvings and our Coopers have proved themselves fully competent for the task. It has more probably been because the changes have succeeded each other with such rapidity as almost to rival the movements of their pens. However, it is not too late yet; and I sincerely hope that either or both of them will ere long furnish the generations to come with those delightful descriptions which they are so well qualified to give, of the original state of a country that has been so rapidly forced to change her form and attire under the influence of increasing population. Yes, I hope to read, ere I close my earthly career, accounts from those delightful writers of the progress of civilization in our Western Country. They will speak of the Clarks, the Croghans, the Boones, and many other men of great and daring enterprise. They will analyze, as it were, into each component part, the country as it once existed, and will render the picture, as it ought to be, immortal.

Hospitality in the Woods

HOSPITALITY IS A virtue the exercise of which, although always agreeable to the stranger, is not always duly appreciated. The traveller
who has acquired celebrity is not unfrequently received with a species
of hospitality which is much alloyed by the obvious attention of the
host to his own interest; and the favor conferred upon the stranger
must have less weight when it comes mingled with almost interminable
questions as to his perilous adventures. Another receives hospitality at
the hands of persons who, possessed of all the comforts of life, receive
the way-worn wanderer with pomposity, lead him from one part of their
spacious mansion to another and bidding him good-night, leave him
to amuse himself in his solitary apartment, because he is thought unfit
to be presented to a party of friends. A third stumbles on a congenial
spirit, who receives him with open arms, offers him servants, horses,
perhaps even his purse, to enable him to pursue his journey, and parts
from him with regret. In all these cases the traveller feels more or less
under obligation, and is accordingly grateful. But, kind reader, the
hospitality received from the inhabitant of the forest, who can offer
only the shelter of his humble roof and the refreshment of his homely
fare, remains more deeply impressed on the memory of the bewildered
traveller than any other. This kind of hospitality I have myself frequently experienced in our woods, and now proceed to relate an instance of it.

I had walked several hundred miles, accompanied by my son, then a
stripling, and, coming upon a clear stream, observed a house on the
opposite shore. We crossed in a canoe, and finding that we had arrived at a tavern, determined upon spending the night there. As we
were both greatly fatigued, I made an arrangement with our host to be
conveyed in a light Jersey wagon a distance of a hundred miles, the
period of our departure to be determined by the rising of the moon.
Fair Cynthia, with her shorn beams, peeped over the forest about two
hours before dawn, and our conductor, provided with a long twig of
hickory, took his station in the fore-part of the wagon. Off we went at
a round trot, dancing in the cart like peas in a sieve. The road, which
was just wide enough to allow us to pass, was full of deep ruts, and
covered here and there with trunks and stumps, over all which we were
hurried. Our conductor, Mr. Flint, the landlord of the tavern, boasting
of his perfect knowledge of the country, undertook to drive us by a
short cut, and we willingly confided ourselves to his management. So
we jogged along, now and then deviating to double the fallen timber.

Day commenced with promise of fine weather, but several nights of white frost having occurred, a change was expected. To our sorrow, the change took place long before we got to the road again. The rain fell in torrents; the thunder bellowed; the lightning blazed. It was now evening, but the storm had brought perfect night, black and dismal. Our cart had no cover. Cold and wet, we sat silent and melancholy, with no better expectation than that of passing the night under the little shelter the cart could afford us.

To stop was considered worse than to proceed. So we gave the reins to the horses, with some faint hope that they would drag us out of our forlorn state. Of a sudden the steeds altered their course, and soon after we perceived the glimmer of a faint light in the distance, and almost at the same moment heard the barking of dogs. Our horses stopped by a high fence and fell a-neighing, while I hallooed at such a rate that an answer was speedily obtained. The next moment a flaming pine torch crossed the gloom, and advanced to the spot where we stood. The negro boy who bore it, without waiting to question us, enjoined us to follow the fence, and said that Master had sent him to show the strangers to the house. We proceeded, much relieved, and soon reached the gate of a little yard, in which a small cabin was perceived.

A tall, fine-looking young man stood in the open door, and desired us get out of the cart and walk in. We did so, when the following conversation took place. "A bad night this, strangers; how came you to be along the fence? You certainly must have lost your way, for there is no public road within twenty miles." "Ay," answered Mr. Flint, "sure enough we lost our way; but, thank God! we have got to a house; and thank you for your reception." "Reception!" replied the woodsman; "no very great thing after all; you are all here safe, and that's enough. Eliza," turning to his wife, "see about some victuals for the strangers, and you, Jupiter," addressing the negro lad, "bring some wood and mend the fire. Eliza, call the boys up, and treat the strangers the best way you can. Come, gentlemen, pull off your wet clothes, and draw to the fire. Eliza, bring some socks and a shirt or two."

For my part, kind reader, knowing my countrymen as I do, I was not much struck at all this; but my son, who had scarcely reached the age of thirteen, drew near to me, and observed how pleasant it was to have met with such good people. Mr. Flint bore a hand in getting his horses put under a shed. The young wife was already stirring with so much liveliness that to have doubted for a moment that all she did was a pleasure to her would have been impossible. Two negro lads made their appearance, looked at us for a moment, and going out, called the dogs. Soon after the cries of the poultry informed us that good cheer was at hand. Jupiter brought more wood, the blaze of which illumined the cottage. Mr. Flint and our host returned, and we already began to feel the comforts of hospitality. The woodsman remarked that it was a pity we had not chanced to come that day three weeks; "for," said he, "it was our wedding-day, and father gave us a good house-warming, and you might have fared better; but, however, if you can eat bacon and eggs, and a broiled chicken, you shall have that. I have no whiskey in the house, but father has some capital cider, and I'll go over and bring a keg of it." I asked how far off his father lived. "Only three miles, sir, and I'll be back before Eliza has cooked your supper." Off he went accordingly, and the next moment the galloping of his horse was heard. The rain fell in torrents, and now I also became struck with the kindness of our host.

To all appearance the united ages of the pair under whose roof we had found shelter did not exceed two score. Their means seemed barely sufficient to render them comfortable, but the generosity of their young hearts had no limits. The cabin was new. The logs of which it was formed were all of the tulip-tree, and were nicely pared. Every part was beautifully clean. Even the coarse slabs of wood that formed the floor looked as if newly washed and dried. Sundry gowns and petticoats of substantial homespun hung from the logs that formed one of the sides of the cabin, while the other was covered with articles of male attire. A large spinning-wheel, with rolls of wool and cotton, occupied one corner. In another was a small cupboard, containing the little stock of new dishes, cups, plates, and tin pans. The table was small also, but quite new, and as bright as polished walnut could be. The only bed that I saw was of domestic manufacture, and the counterpane proved how expert the young wife was at spinning and weaving. A fine rifle ornamented the chimney-piece. The fireplace was of such dimensions that it looked as if it had been purposely constructed for holding the numerous progeny expected to result from the happy union.

The black boy was engaged in grinding some coffee. Bread was prepared by the fair hands of the bride, and placed on a flat board in front of the fire. The bacon and eggs already murmured and spluttered in the frying-pan, and a pair of chickens puffed and swelled on a gridiron over the embers, in front of the hearth. The cloth was laid, and everything arranged, when the clattering of hoofs announced the return of the husband. In he came, bearing a two-gallon keg of cider. His eyes sparkled with pleasure as he said, "Only think, Eliza; father wanted to rob us of the strangers, and was for coming here to ask them to his own house, just as if we could not give them enough ourselves; but here's the drink. Come, gentlemen, sit down and help yourselves." We did so, and I, to enjoy the repast, took a chair of the husband's making, in preference to one of those called *Windsor*, of which there were six in the cabin. This chair was bottomed with a piece of Deer's skin tightly stretched, and afforded a very comfortable seat.

The wife now resumed her spinning, and the husband filled a jug with the sparkling cider, and, seated by the blazing fire, was drying his clothes. The happiness he enjoyed beamed from his eye, as at my request he proceeded to give us an account of his affairs and prospects, which he did in the following words: "I shall be twenty-two next Christmas-day," said our host. "My father came from Virginia when young, and settled on the large tract of land where he yet lives, and where with hard working he has done well. There were nine children of us. Most of them are married and settled in the neighborhood. The old man has divided his lands among some of us, and bought others for the rest. The land where I am he gave me two years ago, and a finer piece is not easily to be found. I have cleared a couple of fields, and planted an orchard. Father gave me a stock of cattle, some hogs, and four horses, with two negro boys. I camped here for most of the time when clearing and planting; and when about to marry the young woman you see at the wheel, father helped me in raising this hut. My wife, as luck would have it, had a negro also, and we have begun the world as well off as most folks, and, the Lord willing, may—But, gentlemen, you don't eat; do help yourselves. Eliza, maybe the strangers would like some milk." The wife stopped her work, and kindly asked if we preferred sweet or sour milk; for you must know, reader, that sour milk is by some of our farmers considered a treat. Both sorts were produced, but, for my part, I chose to stick to the cider.

Supper over, we all neared the fire, and engaged in conversation. At length our kind host addressed his wife as follows: "Eliza, the gentlemen would like to lie down, I guess. What sort of bed can you fix for them?" Eliza looked up with a smile, and said, "Why, Willy, we will divide the bedding, and arrange half on the floor, on which we can sleep very well, and the gentlemen will have the best we can spare them." To this arrangement I immediately objected, and proposed lying on a blanket by the fire; but neither Willy nor Eliza would listen. So they arranged a part of their bedding on the floor, on which, after some debate, we at length settled. The negroes were sent to their own cabin, the young couple went to bed, and Mr. Flint lulled us all asleep with a long story intended to show us how passing strange it was that he should have lost his way.

"Tired nature's sweet restorer, balmy sleep," and so forth. But Aurora soon turned her off. Mr. Speed, our host, rose, went to the door, and returning assured us that the weather was too bad for us to attempt proceeding. I really believe he was heartily glad of it; but anxious to continue our journey, I desired Mr. Flint to see about his horses. Eliza by this time was up too, and I observed her whispering to her husband, when he immediately said aloud, "To be sure, the gentlemen will eat breakfast before they go, and I will show them the way to the road." Excuses were of no avail. Breakfast was prepared and eaten. The weather brightened a little, and by nine we were under way. Willy, on horseback, headed us. In a few hours our cart arrived at a road, by following which we at length got to the main one, and parted from our woodsman with the greater regret that he would accept nothing from any of us. On the contrary, telling Mr. Flint, with a smile, that he hoped he might some time again follow the longest track for a short cut, he bade us adieu, and trotted back to his fair Eliza and his happy home.

Night hunting, a forest scene, 1853.

Breaking the Ice

EMERGING FROM THE mud-holes of Westport, we pursued our way for some time along the narrow track, in the checkered sunshine and shadow of the woods, till at length, issuing into the broad light, we left behind us the farthest outskirts of the great forest, that once spread from the western plains to the shore of the Atlantic. Looking over an intervening belt of bushes, we saw the green, ocean-like expanse of prairie, stretching swell beyond swell to the horizon.

It was a mild, calm spring day; a day when one is more disposed to musing and revery than to action, and the softest part of his nature is apt to gain the upper hand. I rode in advance of the party, as we passed through the bushes, and, as a nook of green grass offered a strong temptation, I dismounted and lay down there. All the trees and saplings were in flower, or budding into fresh leaf; the red clusters of the maple-blossoms and the rich flowers of the Indian apple were there in pro-fusion; and I was half inclined to regret leaving behind the land of gardens for the rude and stern scenes of the prairie and the mountains.

Meanwhile the party came in sight out of the bushes. Foremost rode Henry Chatillon, our guide and hunter, a fine athletic figure, mounted on a hardy gray Wyandot pony. He wore a white blanket-coat, a broad hat of felt, moccasons, and trousers of deer-skin, ornamented along the seams with rows of long fringes. His knife was stuck in his belt; his bullet-pouch and powder-horn hung at his side, and his rifle lay before him, resting against the high pommel of his saddle, which, like all his equipments, had seen hard service, and was much the worse for wear. Shaw followed close, mounted on a little sorrel horse, and leading a larger animal by a rope. His outfit, which resembled mine, had been provided with a view to use rather than ornament. It consisted of a plain, black Spanish saddle, with holsters of heavy pistols, a blanket rolled up behind, and the trail-rope attached to his horse's neck hanging coiled in front. He carried a double-barrelled smooth-bore, while I had a rifle of some fifteen pounds' weight. At that time our attire, though far from elegant, bore some marks of civilization, and offered a very favorable contrast to the inimitable shabbiness of our appearance on the return journey. A red flannel shirt, belted around the waist like a frock, then constituted our upper garment; moccasons had supplanted our failing boots; and the remaining essential portion of our attire consisted of an extraordinary article, manufactured by a squaw out of smoked buckskin. Our muleteer, Deslauriers, brought up the rear with his cart, wading ankle-deep in the mud, alternately puffing at his pipe, and ejaculating in his prairie patois, "*sacré enfant de garce!*" as one of the mules would seem to recoil before some abyss of unusual profundity. The cart was of the kind that one may see by scores around the market-place at Quebec, and had a white covering to protect the articles within. These were our provisions and a tent, with ammunition, blankets, and presents for the Indians.

We were in all four men with eight animals; for besides the spare horses led by Shaw and myself, an additional mule was driven along with us as a reserve in case of accident.

After this summing up of our forces, it may not be amiss to glance at the characters of the two men who accompanied us.

Deslauriers was a Canadian, with all the characteristics of the true Jean Baptiste. Neither fatigue, exposure, nor hard labor could ever impair his cheerfulness and gayety, or his politeness to his *bourgeois;* and when night came, he would sit down by the fire, smoke his pipe, and tell stories with the utmost contentment. The prairie was his element. Henry Chatillon was of a different stamp. When we were at St. Louis, several gentlemen of the Fur Company had kindly offered to procure for us a hunter and guide suited for our purposes, and on coming one afternoon to the office we found there a tall and exceedingly well dressed man, with a face so open and frank that it attracted our notice at once. We were surprised at being told that it was he who wished to guide us to the mountains. He was born in a little French town near St. Louis, and from the age of fifteen years had been constantly in the neighborhood of the Rocky Mountains, employed for the most part by the company, to supply their forts with buffalo meat. As a hunter, he had but one rival in the whole region, a man named Simoneau, with whom, to the honor of both of them, he was on terms of the closest friendship. He had arrived at St. Louis the day before, from the mountains, where he had been for four years; and he now asked only to go and spend a day with his mother, before setting out on another expedition. His age was about thirty; he was six feet high, and very powerfully and gracefully moulded. The prairies had been his school; he could neither read nor write, but he had a natural refinement and delicacy of mind, such as is rare even in women. His manly face was a mirror of uprightness, simplicity, and kindness of heart; he had, moreover, a keen perception of character, and a tact that would preserve him from flagrant error in any society. Henry had not the restless energy of an Anglo-American. He was content to take things as he found them; and his chief fault arose from an excess of easy generosity, not conducive to thriving in the world. Yet it was commonly remarked of him, that whatever he might choose to do with what belonged to himself, the property of others was always safe in his hands. His bravery was as much celebrated in the mountains as his skill in hunting; but it is characteristic of him that in a country where the rifle is the chief arbiter between man and man, he was very seldom involved in quarrels. Once or twice, indeed, his quiet good-nature had been mistaken and presumed upon, but the consequences of the error were such that no one was ever known to repeat it. No better evidence of the intrepidity of his temper could be asked, than the common report that he had killed more than thirty grizzly bears. He was a proof of what unaided nature will sometimes do. I have never, in the city or in the wilderness, met a better man than my true-hearted friend, Henry Chatillon.

We were soon free of the woods and bushes, and fairly upon the broad prairie. Now and then a Shawanoe passed us, riding his little shaggy pony at a "lope"; his calico shirt, his gaudy sash, and the gay handkerchief bound around his snaky hair, fluttering in the wind. At noon we stopped to rest not far from a little creek, replete with frogs and young turtles. There had been an Indian encampment at the place, and the framework of the lodges still remained, enabling us very easily to gain a shelter from the sun, by merely spreading one or two blankets over them. Thus shaded, we sat upon our saddles, and Shaw for the first time lighted his favorite Indian pipe; while Deslauriers was squatted over a hot bed of coals, shading his eyes with one hand, and holding a little stick in the other, with which he regulated the hissing contents of the frying-pan. The horses were turned to feed among the scattered bushes of a low oozy meadow. A drowsy spring-like sultriness pervaded the air, and the voices of ten thousand young frogs and insects, just awakened into life, rose in varied chorus from the creek and the meadows. . . .

A few hours' ride brought us to the banks of the river Kanzas. Traversing the woods that lined it, and ploughing through the deep sand, we encamped not far from the bank, at the Lower Delaware crossing. Our tent was erected for the first time, on a meadow close to the woods, and the camp preparations being complete, we began to think of supper. An old Delaware woman, of some three hundred pounds' weight, sat on the porch of a little log-house, close to the water, and a very pretty half-breed girl was engaged, under her super-intendence, in feeding a large flock of turkeys that were fluttering and gobbling about the door. But no offers of money, or even of tobacco, could induce her to part with one of her favorites: so I took my rifle, to see if the woods or the river could furnish us anything. A multitude of quails were plaintively whistling in the meadows; but nothing appro-priate to the rifle was to be seen, except three buzzards, seated on the spectral limbs of an old dead sycamore, that thrust itself out over the river from the dense sunny wall of fresh foliage. Their ugly heads were drawn down between their shoulders, and they seemed to luxuriate in the soft sunshine that was pouring from the west. As they offered no epicurean temptations, I refrained from disturbing their enjoyment; but contented myself with admiring the calm beauty of the sunset,—for the river, eddying swiftly in deep purple shadows between the impend-ing woods, formed a wild but tranquillizing scene.

When I returned to the camp, I found Shaw and an old Indian seated on the ground in close conference passing the pipe between them. The old man was explaining that he loved the whites, and had an especial partiality for tobacco. Deslauriers was arranging upon the ground our service of tin cups and plates; and as other viands were not to be had, he set before us a repast of biscuit and bacon, and a large pot of coffee. Unsheathing our knives, we attacked it, disposed of the greater part, and tossed the residue to the Indian. Meanwhile our horses, now hobbled for the first time, stood among the trees, with their fore-legs tied together, in great disgust and astonishment. They seemed by no means to relish this foretaste of what awaited them. Mine, in particular, had conceived a mortal aversion to the prairie life. One of them, christened Hendrick, an animal whose strength and hardihood were his only merits, and who yielded to nothing but the cogent arguments of the whip, looked toward us with an indignant countenance, as if he meditated avenging his wrongs with a kick. The other, Pontiac, a good horse, though of plebeian lineage, stood with his head drooping and his mane hanging about his eyes, with the grieved and sulky air of a lubberly boy sent off to school. His forebod-ings were but too just; for when I last heard from him, he was under the lash of an Ogillallah brave, on a war-party against the Crows.

As it grew dark and the voices of the whippoorwills succeeded the whistle of the quails, we removed our saddles to the tent to serve as pillows, spread our blankets upon the ground, and prepared to bivouac for the first time that season. Each man selected the place in the tent which he was to occupy for the journey. To Deslauriers, however, was assigned the cart into which he could creep in wet weather, and find a much better shelter than his *bourgeois* enjoyed in the tent.

The river Kanzas at this point forms the boundary-line between the country of the Shawanoes and that of the Delawares. We crossed it on the following day, rafting over our horses and equipments with much difficulty, and unlading our cart in order to make our way up the steep ascent on the farther bank. It was a Sunday morning; warm, tranquil, and bright; and a perfect stillness reigned over the rough enclosures and neglected fields of the Delawares, except the ceaseless hum and chirruping of myriads of insects. Now and then an Indian rode past on his way to the meeting-house, or, through the dilapidated entrance of some shattered log-house, an old woman might be discerned enjoying all the luxury of idleness. There was no village bell, for the Delawares have none; and yet upon that forlorn and rude settlement was the same spirit of Sabbath repose and tranquillity as in some New England village among the mountains of New Hampshire, or the Vermont woods.

A military road led from this point to Fort Leavenworth, and for many miles the farms and cabins of the Delawares were scattered at short intervals on either hand. The little rude structures of logs erected usually on the borders of a tract of woods made a picturesque feature in the landscape. But the scenery needed no foreign aid. Nature had done enough for it; and the alternation of rich green prairies and groves that stood in clusters, or lined the banks of the numerous little streams, had all the softened and polished beauty of a region that had been for centuries under the hand of man. At that early season, too, it was in the height of its freshness. The woods were flushed with the red buds of the maple; there were frequent flowering shrubs unknown in the east; and the green swells of the prairie were thickly studded with blossoms. . . .

Jumping Off

S HOULD ANY ONE of my readers ever be impelled to visit the prairies, and should he choose the route of the Platte (the best, perhaps, that can be adopted), I can assure him that he need not think to enter at once upon the paradise of his imagination. A dreary preliminary, a protracted crossing of the threshold, awaits him before he finds himself fairly upon the verge of the "great American desert,"—those barren wastes, the haunts of the buffalo and the Indian, where the very shadow of civilization lies a hundred leagues behind him. The intervening country, the wide and fertile belt that extends for several hundred miles beyond the extreme frontier, will probably answer tolerably well to his preconceived ideas of the prairie; for this it is from which picturesque tourists, painters, poets, and novelists, who have seldom penetrated farther, have derived their conceptions of the whole region. If he has a painter's eye, he may find his period of probation not wholly void of interest. The scenery, though tame, is graceful and pleasing. Here are level plains, too wide for the eye to measure; green undulations, like motionless swells of the ocean; abundance of streams, followed through all their windings by lines of woods and scattered groves. But let him be as enthusiastic as he may, he will find enough to damp his ardor. His wagons will stick in the mud; his horses will break loose; harness will give way; and axle-trees prove unsound. His bed will be a soft one, consisting often of black mud of the richest consistency. As for food, he must content himself with biscuit and salt provisions; for, strange as it may seem, this tract of country produces very little game. As he advances, indeed, he will see, mouldering in the grass by his path, the vast antlers of the elk, and farther on the whitened skulls of the buffalo, once swarming over this now deserted region. Perhaps, like us, he may journey for a fortnight, and see not so much as the hoof-print of a deer; in the spring, not even a prairie-hen is to be had.

Yet, to compensate him for this unlooked-for deficiency of game, he will find himself beset with "varmints" innumerable. The wolves will entertain him with a concert at night, and skulk around him by day, just beyond rifle-shot; his horse will step into badger-holes; from every marsh and mud-puddle will arise the bellowing, croaking, and trilling of legions of frogs, infinitely various in color, shape, and dimensions. A profusion of snakes will glide away from under his horse's feet, or quietly visit him in his tent at night; while the pertinacious humming of unnumbered mosquitoes will banish sleep from his eyelids. When, thirsty with a long ride in the scorching sun over some boundless reach of prairie, he comes at length to a pool of water, and alights to drink, he discovers a troop of young tadpoles sporting in the bottom of his cup. Add to this, that, all the morning, the sun beats upon him with a sultry, penetrating heat, and that, with provoking regularity, at about four o'clock in the afternoon, a thunderstorm rises and drenches him to the skin.

One day, after a protracted morning's ride, we stopped to rest at noon upon the open prairie. No trees were in sight; but close at hand a little dribbling brook was twisting from side to side through a hollow; now forming holes of stagnant water, and now gliding over the mud in a scarcely perceptible current, among a growth of sickly bushes, and great clumps of tall rank grass. The day was excessively hot and oppressive. The horses and mules were rolling on the prairie to refresh themselves, or feeding among the bushes in the hollow. We had dined; and Deslauriers, puffing at his pipe, lay in the shade, under the cart, to rest for a while before the word should be given to "catch up." Henry Chatillon, before lying down, was looking about for signs of snakes, the only things that he feared, and uttering various ejaculations of disgust at finding several suspicious-looking holes close to the cart. I sat leaning against the wheel in a scanty strip of shade, making a pair of hobbles to replace those which my contumacious steed Pontiac had broken the night before. The camp of our friends, a rod or two distant, presented the same scene of lazy tranquility.

"Hallo!" cried Henry, looking up from his inspection of the snake-holes, "here comes the old captain."

The captain approached, and stood for a moment contemplating us in silence.

"I say, Parkman," he began, "look at Shaw there, asleep under the cart, with the tar dripping off the hub of the wheel on his shoulder."

At this Shaw got up, with his eyes half opened, and feeling the part indicated, found his hand glued fast to his red flannel shirt.

"He'll look well, when he gets among the squaws, won't he?" observed the captain, with a grin.

He then crawled under the cart, and began to tell stories, of which his stock was inexhaustible. Yet every moment he would glance nervously at the horses. At last he jumped up in great excitement. "See that horse! There—that fellow just walking over the hill! By Jove! he's off. It's your big horse, Shaw; no, it isn't, it's Jack's. Jack! Jack! hallo, Jack!" Jack, thus invoked, jumped up and stared vacantly at us.

"Go and catch your horse, if you don't want to lose him," roared the captain.

Jack instantly set off at a run through the grass, his broad trousers flapping about his feet. The captain gazed anxiously till he saw that the horse was caught; then he sat down, with a countenance of thoughtfulness and care.

"I tell you what it is," he said, "this will never do at all. We shall lose every horse in the band some day or other, and then a pretty plight we should be in! Now I am convinced that the only way for us is to have every man in the camp stand horse-guard in rotation whenever we stop. Supposing a hundred Pawnees should jump up out of that ravine, all yelling and flapping their buffalo robes, in the way they do! Why, in two minutes, not a hoof would be in sight." We reminded the captain that a hundred Pawnees would probably demolish the horse-guard if he were to resist their depredations.

"At any rate," pursued the captain, evading the point, "our whole system is wrong; I'm convinced of it; it is totally unmilitary. Why, the way we travel, strung out over the prairie for a mile, an enemy might attack the foremost men, and cut them off before the rest could come up."

"We are not in an enemy's country yet," said Shaw; "when we are, we'll travel together."

"Then," said the captain, "we might be attacked in camp. We've no sentinels; we 'camp in disorder; no precautions at all to guard against surprise. My own convictions are, that we ought to 'camp in a hollow-square, with the fires in the centre; and have sentinels, and a regular password appointed for every night. Beside, there should be videttes, riding in advance, to find a place for the camp and give warning of an enemy. These are my convictions. I don't want to dictate to any man. I give advice to the best of my judgment, that's all; and then let people do as they please."

His plan of sending out videttes seemed particularly dear to him; and as no one else was disposed to second his views on this point, he took it into his head to ride forward that afternoon himself.

"Come, Parkman," said he, "will you go with me?"

We set out together, and rode a mile or two in advance. The captain, in the course of twenty years' service in the British army, had seen something of life; and being naturally a pleasant fellow, he was a very entertaining companion. He cracked jokes and told stories for an hour or two; until, looking back, we saw the prairie behind us stretching away to the horizon, without a horseman or a wagon in sight.

"Now," said the captain, "I think the videttes had better stop till the main body comes up."

I was of the same opinion. There was a thick growth of woods just before us, with a stream running through them. Having crossed this, we found on the other side a level meadow, half encircled by the trees; and, fastening our horses to some bushes, we sat down on the grass, while, with an old stump of a tree for a target, I began to display the superiority of the renowned rifle of the backwoods over the foreign innovation borne by the captain. At length voices could be heard in the distance, behind the trees.

"There they come," said the captain; "let's go and see how they get through the creek."

We mounted and rode to the bank of the stream, where the trail crossed it. It ran in a deep hollow, full of trees. As we looked down, we saw a confused crowd of horsemen riding through the water; and among the dingy habiliments of our party glittered the uniforms of four dragoons.

Shaw came whipping his horse up the bank, in advance of the rest, with a somewhat indignant countenance. The first word he spoke was a blessing fervently invoked on the head of R——, who was riding, with a crestfallen air, in the rear. Thanks to the ingenious devices of this gentleman, we had missed the track entirely, and wandered, not towards the Platte, but to the village of the Iowa Indians. This we learned from the dragoons, who had lately deserted from Fort Leavenworth. They told us that our best plan now was to keep to the northward until we should strike the trail formed by several parties of Oregon emigrants, who had that season set out from St. Joseph, in Missouri.

In extremely bad temper, we encamped on this ill-starred spot, while the deserters, whose case admitted of no delay, rode rapidly forward. On the day following, striking the St. Joseph's trail, we turned our horses' heads towards Fort Laramie, then about seven hundred miles to the westward.

The Passes

"A T THE Big Tuolumne Meadows I remained more than a month sketching, botanizing, and climbing among the surrounding mountains. The mountaineer with whom I then happened to be camping was one of those remarkable men one so frequently meets in California, the hard angles and bosses of whose characters have been brought into relief by the grinding excitements of the gold period, until they resemble glacial landscapes. But at this late day, my friend's activities had subsided, and his craving for rest caused him to become a gentle shepherd and literally to lie down with the lamb.

Recognizing the unsatisfiable longings of my Scotch Highland instincts, he threw out some hints concerning Bloody Cañon, and advised me to explore it. "I have never seen it myself," he said, "for I never was so unfortunate as to pass that way. But I have heard many a strange story about it, and I warrant you will at least find it wild enough."

Then of course I made haste to see it. Early next morning I made up a bundle of bread, tied my notebook to my belt, and strode away in the bracing air, full of eager, indefinite hope. The plushy lawns that lay in my path served to soothe my morning haste. The sod in many places was starred with daisies and blue gentians, over which I lingered. I traced the paths of the ancient glaciers over many a shining pavement, and marked the gaps in the upper forests that told the power of the winter avalanches. Climbing higher, I saw for the first time the gradual dwarfing of the pines in compliance with climate, and on the summit discovered creeping mats of the arctic willow overgrown with silky catkins, and patches of the dwarf vaccinium with its round flowers sprinkled in the grass like purple hail; while in every direction the landscape stretched sublimely away in fresh wilderness—a manuscript written by the hand of Nature alone.

At length, as I entered the pass, the huge rocks began to close around in all their wild, mysterious impressiveness, when suddenly, as I was

Marble Cañon, Colorado, 1888.

gazing eagerly about me, a drove of gray hairy beings came in sight, lumbering toward me with a kind of boneless, wallowing motion like bears.

I never turn back, though often so inclined, and in this particular instance, amid such surroundings, everything seemed singularly unfavorable for the calm acceptance of so grim a company. Suppressing my fears, I soon discovered that although as hairy as bears and as crooked as summit pines, the strange creatures were sufficiently erect to belong to our own species. They proved to be nothing more formidable than Mono Indians dressed in the skins of sage-rabbits. Both the men and the women begged persistently for whisky and tobacco, and seemed so accustomed to denials that I found it impossible to convince them that I had none to give. Excepting the names of these two products of civilization, they seemed to understand not a word of English; but I afterward learned that they were on their way to Yosemite Valley to feast awhile on trout and procure a load of acorns to carry back through the pass to their huts on the shore of Mono Lake.

Occasionally a good countenance may be seen among the Mono Indians, but these, the first specimens I had seen, were mostly ugly, and some of them altogether hideous. The dirt on their faces was fairly stratified, and seemed so ancient and so undisturbed it might almost possess a geological significance. The older faces were, moreover, strangely blurred and divided into sections by furrows that looked like the cleavage-joints of rocks, suggesting exposure on the mountains in a castaway condition for ages. Somehow they seemed to have no right place in the landscape, and I was glad to see them fading out of sight down the pass.

Then came evening, and the somber cliffs were inspired with the ineffable beauty of the alpenglow. A solemn calm fell upon everything. All the lower portion of the cañon was in gloaming shadow, and I crept into a hollow near one of the upper lakelets to smooth the ground in a sheltered nook for a bed. When the short twilight faded, I kindled a sunny fire, made a cup of tea, and lay down to rest and look at the stars. Soon the night-wind began to flow and pour in torrents among the jagged peaks, mingling strange tones with those of the waterfalls sounding far below; and as I drifted toward sleep I began to experience an uncomfortable feeling of nearness to the furred Monos. Then the full moon looked down over the edge of the cañon wall, her countenance seemingly filled with intense concern, and apparently so near as to produce a startling effect as if she had entered my bedroom, forgetting all the world, to gaze on me alone.

The night was full of strange sounds, and I gladly welcomed the morning. Breakfast was soon done, and I set forth in the exhilarating freshness of the new day, rejoicing in the abundance of pure wildness so close about me. The stupendous rocks, hacked and scarred with centuries of storms, stood sharply out in the thin early light, while down in the bottom of the cañon grooved and polished bosses heaved and glistened like swelling sea-waves, telling a grand old story of the ancient glacier that poured its crushing floods above them.

Here for the first time I met the arctic daisies in all their perfection of purity and spirituality,—gentle mountaineers face to face with the stormy sky, kept safe and warm by a thousand miracles. I leaped lightly from rock to rock, glorying in the eternal freshness and sufficiency of Nature, and in the ineffable tenderness with which she nurtures her mountain darlings in the very fountains of storms. Fresh beauty appeared at every step, delicate rock-ferns, and groups of the fairest flowers. Now another lake came to view, now a waterfall. Never fell light in brighter spangles, never fell water in whiter foam. I seemed to float through the cañon enchanted, feeling nothing of its roughness, and was out in the Mono levels before I was aware.

Looking back from the shore of Moraine Lake, my morning ramble seemed all a dream. There curved Bloody Cañon, a mere glacial furrow 2000 feet deep, with smooth rocks projecting from the sides and braided together in the middle, like bulging, swelling muscles. Here the lilies were higher than my head, and the sunshine was warm enough for palms. Yet the snow around the arctic willows was plainly visible only four miles away, and between were narrow specimen zones of all the principal climates of the globe.

On the bank of a small brook that comes gurgling down the side of the left lateral moraine, I found a camp-fire still burning, which no doubt belonged to the gray Indians I had met on the summit, and I listened instinctively and moved cautiously forward, half expecting to see some of their grim faces peering out of the bushes.

Passing on toward the open plain, I noticed three well-defined terminal moraines curved gracefully across the cañon stream, and joined by long splices to the two noble laterals. These mark the halting-places of the vanished glacier when it was retreating into its summit shadows on the breaking-up of the glacial winter.

Five miles below the foot of Moraine Lake, just where the lateral moraines lose themselves in the plain, there was a field of wild rye, growing in magnificent waving bunches six to eight feet high, bearing heads from six to twelve inches long. Rubbing out some of the grains, I found them about five eighths of an inch long, dark-colored, and sweet. Indian women were gathering it in baskets, bending down large handfuls, beating it out, and fanning it in the wind. They were quite picturesque, coming through the rye, as one caught glimpses of them here and there, in winding lanes and openings, with splendid tufts arching above their heads, while their incessant chat and laughter showed their heedless joy.

2

Years of Spacious Living

WITHIN THE PAGES of this section there will be found no polemical slant. There is nothing here but enchanting reading, a good deal of it from the pens of authors who are less well known than they deserve to be. Read here to be entertained, and if what you read inspires you to pick up the gauntlet which I have flung down, so much the better.

I need make no comment on the individual selections; they will speak for themselves. But I should like to mention that Thoreau's "hogshead of molasses or brandy directed to John Smith, Cuttingsville, Vermont," was consigned to a village not far from Landgrove, and I like to believe that the consignee was a forebear of my dear friend Willard Smith who lives in that place, as did his ancestors before him. And Audubon's Great Egg Harbour is a part of my background too, for here a friend of mine kept his motor boat, and from this river port we explored the broad reaches of Barnegat Bay.

I have summered with my family when I was a kid in just such a boarding house as that maintained by Miss Locke; although my adventures took place in the Adirondacks, and I came from near New York, not Boston, the two scenes are almost identical. And more recently, I have sailed the waters of Merrick's Lake Champlain on the forty-foot ketch Windlass.

There are very few scenes delineated within these pages with which I am not lovingly familiar, and it is with deep affection for them that I now turn them over to you.

Great Egg Harbor

SOME YEARS AGO, after having spent the spring in observing the habits of the migratory Warblers and other land birds, which arrived in vast numbers in the vicinity of Camden in New Jersey, I prepared to visit the sea shores of that State, for the purpose of making myself acquainted with their feathered inhabitants. June had commenced, the weather was pleasant, and the country seemed to smile in the prospect of bright days and gentle gales. Fishermen-gunners passed daily between Philadelphia and the various small seaports, with Jersey wagons, laden with fish, fowls, and other provisions, or with such articles as were required by the families of those hardy boatmen; and I bargained with one of them to take myself and my baggage to Great Egg Harbor.

One afternoon, about sunset, the vehicle halted at my lodgings, and the conductor intimated that he was anxious to proceed as quickly as possible. A trunk, a couple of guns, and such other articles as are found necessary by persons whose pursuits are similar to mine, were immediately thrust into the wagon, and were followed by their owner. The conductor whistled to his steeds, and off we went at a round pace over the loose and deep sand that in almost every part of this State forms the basis of the roads. After a while we overtook a whole caravan of similar vehicles, moving in the same direction, and when we got near them our horses slackened their pace to a regular walk, the driver leaped from his seat, I followed his example, and we presently found ourselves in the midst of a group of merry wagoners, relating their adventures of the week, it being now Saturday night. One gave intimation of the number of "Sheep-heads" he had taken to town, another spoke of the Curlews which yet remained on the sands, and a third boasted of having gathered so many dozens of Marsh Hens' eggs. I inquired if the Fish Hawks were plentiful near Great Egg Harbor, and was answered by an elderly man, who with a laugh asked if I had ever seen the "Weak fish" along the coast without the bird in question.

Not knowing the animal he had named, I confessed my ignorance, when the whole party burst into a loud laugh, in which, there being nothing better for it, I joined.

About midnight the caravan reached a half-way house, where we rested a while. Several roads diverged from this spot, and the wagons separated, one only keeping us company. The night was dark and gloomy, but the sand of the road indicated our course very distinctly. Suddenly the galloping of horses struck my ear, and looking back we perceived that our wagon must in an instant be in imminent danger. The driver leaped off, and drew his steeds aside, barely in time to allow the runaways to pass without injuring us. Off they went at full speed, and not long after their owner came up panting, and informed us that they had suddenly taken fright at some noise proceeding from the woods, but hoped they would soon stop. Immediately after we heard a crack; then for a few moments all was silent; but the neighing of horses presently assured us that they had broken loose. On reaching the spot we found the wagon upset, and a few yards farther on were the horses, quietly browsing by the roadside.

The first dawn of morn in the Jerseys in the month of June is worthy of a better description than I can furnish, and therefore I shall only say that the moment the sunbeams blazed over the horizon, the loud and mellow notes of the Meadow Lark saluted our ears. On each side of the road were open woods, on the tallest trees of which I observed at intervals the nest of a Fish Hawk, far above which the white-breasted bird slowly winged its way, as it commenced its early journey to the sea, the odor of which filled me with delight. In half an hour more we were in the centre of Great Egg Harbor.

There I had the good fortune to be received into the house of a thoroughbred fisherman-gunner, who, besides owning a comfortable cot only a few hundred yards from the shore, had an excellent woman for a wife, and a little daughter as playful as a kitten, though as wild as a Sea-Gull. In less than half an hour I was quite at home, and the rest of the day was spent in devotion.

Oysters, though reckoned out of season at this period, are as good as ever when fresh from their beds, and my first meal was of some as large and white as any I have eaten. The sight of them placed before me on a clean table, with an honest and industrious family in my company, never failed to afford more pleasure than the most sumptuous fare under different circumstances; and our conversation being simple and harmless, gayety shone in every face. As we became better acquainted, I had to answer several questions relative to the object of my visit. The good man rubbed his hands with joy, as I spoke of shooting and fishing, and of long excursions through the swamps and marshes around.

My host was then, and I hope still is, a tall, strong-boned, muscular man, of dark complexion, with eyes as keen as those of the Sea-Eagle. He was a tough walker, laughed at difficulties, and could pull an oar with any man. As to shooting, I have often doubted whether he or Mr. Egan, the worthy pilot of Indian Isle, was best; and rarely indeed have I seen either of them miss a shot.

At daybreak on Monday, I shouldered my double-barrelled gun, and my host carried with him a long fowling-piece, a pair of oars, and a pair of oyster-tongs, while the wife and daughter brought along a seine. The boat was good, the breeze gentle, and along the inlets we sailed for parts well known to my companions. To such naturalists as are qualified to observe many different objects at the same time, Great Egg Harbor would probably afford as ample a field as any part of our coast, excepting the Florida Keys. Birds of many kinds are abundant, as are fishes and testaceous animals. The forests shelter many beautiful plants, and even on the driest sand-bar you may see insects of the most brilliant tints. Our principal object, however, was to procure certain birds known there by the name of Lawyers, and to accomplish this we entered and followed for several miles a winding inlet or bayou, which led us to the interior of a vast marsh, where after some search we found the birds and their nests. Our seine had been placed across the channel, and when we returned to it the tide had run out, and left in it a number of fine fish, some of which we cooked and ate on the spot. One, which I considered as a curiosity, was saved, and transmitted to Baron Cuvier. Our repast ended, the seine was spread out to dry, and we again betook ourselves to the marshes to pursue our researches until the return of the tide. Having collected enough to satisfy us, we took up our oars, and returned to the shore in front of the fisherman's house, where we dragged the seine several times with success.

In this manner I passed several weeks along those delightful and healthy shores, one day going to the woods, to search the swamps in which the herons bred, passing another amid the joyous cries of the Marsh Hens, and on a third carrying slaughter among the White-breasted Sea-Gulls; by way of amusement sometimes hauling the fish called the Sheep's-head from an eddy along the shore, or watching the gay Terns as they danced in the air, or plunged into the waters to seize the tiny fry. Many a drawing I made at Great Egg Harbor, many a pleasant day I spent along its shores; and much pleasure would it give me once more to visit the good and happy family in whose house I resided there.

The Profits of Idleness

SATURDAY, AUGUST 13TH.—My life, at this time, is more like that of a boy, externally, than it has been since I was really a boy. It is usually supposed that the cares of life come with matrimony; but I seem to have cast off all care, and live on with as much easy trust in Providence as Adam could possibly have felt before he had learned that there was a world beyond Paradise. My chief anxiety consists in watching the prosperity of my vegetables, in observing how they are affected by the rain or sunshine, in lamenting the blight of one squash and rejoicing at the luxurious growth of another. It is as if the original relation between man and Nature were restored in my case, and as if I were to look exclusively to her for the support of my Eve and myself—to trust to her for food and clothing, and all things needful, with the full assurance that she would not fail me. The fight with the world—the struggle of a man among men—the agony of the universal effort to wrench the means of living from a host of greedy competitors—all this seems like a dream to me. My business is merely to live and to enjoy; and whatever is essential to life and enjoyment will come as naturally as the dew from heaven. This is, practically at least, my faith. And so I awake in the morning with a boyish thoughtlessness as to how the outgoings of the day are to be provided for, and its incomings rendered certain. After breakfast, I go forth into my garden, and gather whatever the bountiful Mother has made fit for our present sustenance; and of late days she generally gives me two squashes and a cucumber, and promises me green corn and shell-beans very soon. Then I pass down through our orchard to the river-side, and ramble along its margin in search of flowers. Usually I discern a fragrant white lily, here and there along the shore, growing, with sweet prudishness, beyond the grasp of mortal arm. But it does not escape me so. I know what is its fitting destiny better than the silly flower knows for itself; so I wade in, heedless of wet trousers, and seize the shy lily by its slender stem. Thus I make prize of five or six, which are as many as usually blossom within my reach in a single morning—some of them partially worm-eaten or blighted, like virgins with an eating sorrow at the heart; others as fair and perfect as Nature's own idea was, when she first imagined this lovely flower. A perfect pond-lily is the most satisfactory of flowers. Besides these, I gather whatever else of beauty chances to be growing in the moist soil by the river-side—an amphibious tribe, yet with more richness and grace than the wild-flowers of the deep and dry woodlands and hedgerows—sometimes the white arrow-head, always the blue spires and broad green leaves of the pickerel-flower, which contrast and harmonize so well with the white lilies. For the last two or three days, I have found scattered stalks of the cardinal-flower, the gorgeous scarlet of which it is a joy even to remember. The world is made brighter and sunnier by flowers of such a hue. Even perfume, which otherwise is the soul and spirit of a flower, may be spared when it arrays itself in this scarlet glory. It is a flower of thought and feeling, too; it seems to have its roots deep down in the hearts of those who gaze at it. Other bright flowers sometimes impress me as wanting sentiment; but it is not so with this.

Well, having made up my bunch of flowers, I return home with them. . . . Then I ascend to my study, and generally read, or perchance scribble in this journal, and otherwise suffer Time to loiter onward at his own pleasure, till the dinner-hour. In pleasant days, the chief events of the afternoon, and the happiest one of the day, is our walk. . . . So comes the night; and I look back upon a day spent in what the world would call idleness, and for which I myself can suggest no more appropriate epithet, but which, nevertheless, I cannot feel to have been spent amiss. True, it might be a sin and shame, in such a world as ours, to spend a lifetime in this manner; but for a few summer weeks it is good to live as if this world were heaven. And so it is, and so it shall be, although, in a little while, a flitting shadow of earthly care and toil will mingle itself with our realities.

Monday, August 15th.—George Hillard and his wife arrived from Boston in the dusk of Saturday evening, to spend Sunday with us. It was a pleasant sensation, when the coach rumbled up our avenue, and wheeled round at the door; for I felt that I was regarded as a man with a household—a man having a tangible existence and locality in the world—when friends came to avail themselves of our hospitality. It was a sort of acknowledgment and reception of us into the corps of married people—a sanction by no means essential to our peace and well-being, but yet agreeable enough to receive. So we welcomed them cordially at the door, and ushered them into our parlor, and soon into the supper-room. . . . The night flitted over us all, and passed away, and up rose a gray and sullen morning, . . . and we had a splendid breakfast of flapjacks, or slapjacks, and whortleberries, which I gathered on a neighboring hill, and perch, bream, and pout, which I hooked out of the river the evening before. About nine o'clock, Hillard and I set out for a walk to Walden Pond, calling by the way at Mr. Emerson's, to obtain his guidance or directions, and he accompanied us in his own illustrious person. We turned aside a little from our way, to visit Mr. ——, a yeoman, of whose homely and self-acquired wisdom Mr. Emerson has a very high opinion. We found him walking in his fields, a short and stalwart and sturdy personage of middle age, with a face of shrewd and kind expression, and manners of natural courtesy. He had a very free flow of talk; for, with a little induction from Mr. Emerson, he began to discourse about the state of the nation, agriculture, and business in general, uttering thoughts that had come to him at the plough, and which had a sort of flavor of the fresh earth about them. His views were sensible and characteristic, and had grown in the soil where we found them; . . . and he is certainly a man of intellectual and moral substance, a sturdy fact, a reality, something to be felt and touched, whose ideas seem to be dug out of his mind as he digs potatoes, beets, carrots, and turnips out of the ground.

After leaving Mr. ——, we proceeded through woodpaths to Walden Pond, picking blackberries of enormous size along the way. The pond itself was beautiful and refreshing to my soul, after such long and exclusive familiarity with our tawny and sluggish river. It lies embosomed among wooded hills—it is not very extensive, but large enough for waves to dance upon its surface, and to look like a piece of blue firmament, earth-encircled. The shore has a narrow, pebbly strand, which it was worth a day's journey to look at, for the sake of the contrast between it and the weedy, oozy margin of the river. Farther within its depths, you perceive a bottom of pure white sand, sparkling through the transparent water, which, methought, was the very purest liquid in the world. After Mr. Emerson left us, Hillard and I bathed in the pond, and it does really seem as if my spirit, as well as corporeal person, were refreshed by that bath. A good deal of mud and river slime had accumulated on my soul; but these bright waters washed them all away.

We returned home in due season for dinner. . . . To my misfortune, however, a box of Mediterranean wine proved to have undergone the acetous fermentation; so that the splendor of the festival suffered some diminution. Nevertheless, we ate our dinner with a good appetite, and afterwards went universally to take our several siestas.

Meantime there came a shower, which so besprinkled the grass and shrubbery as to make it rather wet for our after-tea ramble. The chief result of the walk was the bringing home of an immense burden of the trailing clematis-vine, now just in blossom, and with which all our flower-stands and vases are this morning decorated. On our return we found Mr. and Mrs. S——, and E. H——, who shortly took their leave, and we sat up late, telling ghost-stories. This morning, at seven, our friends left us. We were both pleased with the visit, and so, I think, were our guests.

Sounds

I LOVE A BROAD MARGIN to my life. Sometimes, in a summer morning, having taken my accustomed bath, I sat in my sunny doorway from sunrise till noon, rapt in a revery, amidst the pines and hickories and sumachs, in undisturbed solitude and stillness, while the birds sang around or flitted noiseless through the house, until by the sun falling in at my west window, or the noise of some traveler's wagon on the distant highway, I was reminded of the lapse of time. I grew in those seasons like corn in the night, and they were far better than any work of the hands would have been. They were not time subtracted from my life, but so much over and above my usual allowance. I realized what the Orientals mean by contemplation and the forsaking of works. For the most part, I minded not how the hours went. The day advanced as if to light some work of mine; it was morning, and lo, now it is evening, and nothing memorable is accomplished. Instead of singing like the birds, I silently smiled at my incessant good fortune. As the sparrow had its trill, sitting on the hickory before my door, so had I my chuckle or suppressed warble which he might hear out of my nest. My days were not days of the week, bearing the stamp of any heathen deity, nor were they minced into hours and fretted by the ticking of a clock; for I lived like the Puri Indians, of whom it is said that "for yesterday, to-day, and to-morrow they have only one word, and they express the variety of meaning by pointing backward for yesterday, forward for to-morrow, and overhead for the passing day." This was sheer idleness to my fellow-townsmen, no doubt; but if the birds and flowers had tried me by their standard, I should not have been found wanting. A man must find his occasions in himself, it is true. The natural day is very calm, and will hardly reprove his indolence.

I had this advantage, at least, in my mode of life, over those who were obliged to look abroad for amusement, to society and the theatre, that my life itself was become my amusement and never ceased to be novel. It was a drama of many scenes and without an end. If we were always indeed getting our living, and regulating our lives according to the last and best mode we had learned, we should never be troubled with ennui. Follow your genius closely enough, and it will not fail to show you a fresh prospect every hour. Housework was a pleasant pastime. When my floor was dirty, I rose early, and, setting all my furniture out of doors on the grass, bed and bedstead making but one budget, dashed water on the floor, and sprinkled white sand from the pond on it, and then with a broom scrubbed it clean and white; and by the time the villagers had broken their fast the morning sun had dried my house sufficiently to allow me to move in again, and my meditations were almost uninterrupted. It was pleasant to see my whole household effects out on the grass, making a little pile like a gypsy's pack, and my three-legged table, from which I did not remove the books and pen and ink, standing amid the pines and hickories. They seemed glad to get out themselves, and as if unwilling to be brought in. I was sometimes tempted to stretch an awning over them and take my seat there. It was worth the while to see the sun shine on these things, and hear the free wind blow on them; so much more interesting most familiar objects look out doors than in the house. A bird sits on the next bough, life-everlasting grows under the table, and blackberry vines run round its legs; pine cones, chestnut burs, and strawberry leaves are strewn about. It looked as if this was the way these forms came to be transferred to our furniture, to tables, chairs, and bedstead,—because they once stood in their midst.

My house was on the side of a hill, immediately on the edge of the larger wood, in the midst of a young forest of pitch pines and hickories, and half a dozen rods from the pond, to which a narrow footpath led down the hill. In my front yard grew the strawberry, blackberry, and life-everlasting, johnswort and goldenrod, shrub-oaks and sand-cherry, blueberry and groundnut. Near the end of May, the sand-cherry (*cerasus pumila*) adorned the sides of the path with its delicate flowers arranged in umbels cylindrically about its short stems, which last, in the fall, weighed down with good-sized and handsome cherries, fell over in wreaths like rays on every side. I tasted them out of compliment to Nature, though they were scarcely palatable. The sumach (*rhus glabra*) grew luxuriantly about the house, pushing up through the embankment which I had made, and growing five or six feet the first season. Its broad pinnate tropical leaf was pleasant though strange to look on. The large buds, suddenly pushing out late in the spring from dry sticks which had seemed to be dead, developed themselves as by magic

Mill Creek near Cincinnati, Ohio, 1887.

into graceful green and tender boughs, an inch in diameter; and sometimes, as I sat at my window, so heedlessly did they grow and tax
their weak joints, I heard a fresh and tender bough suddenly fall like
a fan to the ground, when there was not a breath of air stirring, broken
off by its own weight. In August, the large masses of berries, which,
when in flower, had attracted many wild bees, gradually assumed their
bright velvety crimson hue, and by their weight again bent down and
broke the tender limbs.

*   *   *

As I sit at my window this summer afternoon, hawks are circling about
my clearing; the tantivy of wild pigeons, flying by twos and threes
athwart my view, or perching restless on the white-pine boughs behind
my house, gives a voice to the air; a fishhawk dimples the glassy surface
of the pond and brings up a fish; a mink steals out of the marsh before
my door and seizes a frog by the shore; the sedge is bending under
the weight of the reed-birds flitting hither and thither; and for the last
half hour I have heard the rattle of railroad cars, now dying away and
then reviving like the beat of a partridge, conveying travellers from
Boston to the country. For I did not live so out of the world as that
boy who, as I hear, was put out to a farmer in the east part of the
town, but erelong ran away and came home again, quite down at the
heel and homesick. He had never seen such a dull and out-of-the-way
place; the folks were all gone off; why, you couldn't even hear the
whistle! I doubt if there is such a place in Massachusetts now:—

> "In truth, our village has become a butt
> For one of those fleet railroad shafts, and o'er
> Our peaceful plain its soothing sound is—Concord."

The Fitchburg Railroad touches the pond about a hundred rods
south of where I dwell. I usually go to the village along its causeway,
and am, as it were, related to society by this link. The men on the
freight trains, who go over the whole length of the road, bow to me
as to an old acquaintance, they pass me so often, and apparently they
take me for an employee; and so I am. I too would fain be a track-
repairer somewhere in the orbit of the earth.

The whistle of the locomotive penetrates my woods summer and
winter, sounding like the scream of a hawk sailing over some farmer's
yard, informing me that many restless city merchants are arriving
within the circle of the town, or adventurous country traders from the
other side. As they come under one horizon, they shout their warning
to get off the track to the other, heard sometimes through the circles

of two towns. Here come your groceries, country; your rations, country-men! Nor is there any man so independent on his farm that he can say them nay. And here's your pay for them! screams the countryman's whistle; timber like long battering rams going twenty miles an hour against the city's walls, and chairs enough to seat all the weary and heavy laden that dwell within them. With such huge and lumbering civility the country hands a chair to the city. All the Indian huckle-berry hills are stripped, all the cranberry meadows are raked into the city. Up comes the cotton, down goes the woven cloth; up comes the silk, down goes the woollen; up come the books, but down goes the wit that writes them.

When I meet the engine with its train of cars moving off with planetary motion,—or, rather like a comet, for the beholder knows not if with that velocity and with that direction it will ever revisit this system, since its orbit does not look like a returning curve,—with its steam cloud like a banner streaming behind in golden and silver wreaths, like many a downy cloud which I have seen, high in the heavens, unfolding its masses to the light,—as if this travelling demigod, this cloud-compeller, would erelong take the sunset sky for the livery of his train; when I hear the iron horse make the hills echo with his snort like thunder, shaking the earth with his feet, and breathing fire and smoke from his nostrils (what kind of winged horse or fiery dragon they will put into the new Mythology I don't know), it seems as if the earth had got a race now worthy to inhabit it. If all were as it seems, and men made the elements their servants for noble ends! If the cloud that hangs over the engine were the perspiration of heroic deeds, or as beneficent as that which floats over the farmer's fields, then the elements and Nature herself would cheerfully accompany men on their errands and be their escort.

I watch the passage of the morning cars with the same feeling that I do the rising of the sun, which is hardly more regular. Their train of clouds stretching far behind and rising higher and higher, going to heaven while the cars are going to Boston, conceals the sun for a minute and casts my distant field into the shade, a celestial train beside which the petty train of cars which hugs the earth is but the barb of the spear. The stabler of the iron horse was up early this winter morn-ing by the light of the stars amid the mountains, to fodder and harness his steed. Fire, too, was awakened thus early to put the vital heat in him and get him off. If the enterprise were as innocent as it is early! If the snow lies deep, they strap on his snowshoes, and with the giant plough plough a furrow from the mountains to the seaboard, in which the cars, like a following drill-barrow, sprinkle all the restless men and floating merchandise in the country for seed. All day the fire-steed flies over the country, stopping only that his master may rest, and I am awakened by his tramp and defiant snort at midnight, when in some remote glen in the woods he fronts the elements incased in ice and snow; and he will reach his stall only with the morning star, to start once more on his travels without rest or slumber. Or perchance, at evening, I hear him in his stable blowing off the superfluous energy of the day, that he may calm his nerves and cool his liver and brain for a few hours of iron slumber. If the enterprise were as heroic and commanding as it is protracted and unwearied!

Far through unfrequented woods on the confines of towns, where once only the hunter penetrated by day, in the darkest night dart these bright saloons without the knowledge of their inhabitants; this moment stopping at some brilliant station-house in town or city, where a social crowd is gathered, the next in the Dismal Swamp, scaring the owl and fox. The startings and arrivals of the cars are now the epochs in the village day. They go and come with such regularity and precision, and their whistle can be heard so far, that the farmers set their clocks by them, and thus one well-conducted institution regulates a whole country. Have not men improved somewhat in punctuality since the railroad was invented? Do they not talk and think faster in the depot than they did in the stage-office? There is something electrifying in the atmosphere of the former place. I have been astonished at the miracles it has wrought; that some of my neighbors, who, I should have prophesied, once for all, would never get to Boston by so prompt a conveyance, are on hand when the bell rings. To do things "railroad fashion" is now the by-word; and it is worth the while to be warned so often and so sincerely by any power to get off its track. There is no stopping to read the riot act, no firing over the heads of the mob, in this case. We have constructed a fate, an *Atropos*, that never turns aside. (Let that be the name of your engine.) Men are advertised that at a certain hour and minute these bolts will be shot toward particular points of the compass; yet it interferes with no man's business, and the children go to school on the other track. We live the steadier for it. We are all educated thus to be sons of Tell. The air is full of invisible bolts. Every path but your own is the path of fate. Keep on your own track, then.

What recommends commerce to me is its enterprise and bravery. It does not clasp its hands and pray to Jupiter. I see these men every day go about their business with more or less courage and content, doing more even than they suspect, and perchance better employed than they could have consciously devised. I am less affected by their heroism who stood up for half an hour in the front line at Buena Vista, than by the steady and cheerful valor of the men who inhabit the snow-plough for their winter quarters; who have not merely the three o'clock in the morning courage, which Bonaparte thought was the rarest, but whose courage does not go to rest so early, who go to sleep only when the storm sleeps or the sinews of their iron steed are frozen. On this morning of the Great Snow, perchance, which is still raging and chilling men's blood, I hear the muffled tone of their engine bell from out the fog bank of their chilled breath, which announces that the cars are coming, without long delay, notwithstanding the veto of a New England northeast snow storm, and I behold the ploughmen covered with snow and rime, their heads peering above the mouldboard which is turning down other than daisies and the nests of field-mice, like boulders of the Sierra Nevada, that occupy an outside place in the universe.

Commerce is unexpectedly confident and serene, alert, adventurous, and unwearied. It is very natural in its method withal, far more so than many fantastic enterprises and sentimental experiments, and hence its singular success. I am refreshed and expanded when the freight train rattles past me, and I smell the stores which go dispensing their odors all the way from Long Wharf to Lake Champlain, reminding me of foreign parts, of coral reefs, and Indian oceans, and tropical climes, and the extent of the globe. I feel more like a citizen of the world at the sight of the palm-leaf which will cover so many flaxen New England heads the next summer, the Manila hemp and cocoanut husks, the old junk, gunny bags, scrap iron, and rusty nails. This carload of torn sails is more legible and interesting now than if they should be wrought into paper and printed books. Who can write so graphically the history of the storms they have weathered as these rents have done? They are proof-sheets which need no correction. Here goes lumber from the Maine woods, which did not go out to sea in the last freshet, risen four dollars on the thousand because of what did go out or was split up: pine, spruce, cedar,—first, second, third, and fourth qualities, so lately all of one quality, to wave over the bear, and moose, and caribou. Next rolls Thomaston lime, a prime lot, which will get far among the hills before it gets slacked. These rags in bales, of all hues and qualities, the lowest condition to which cotton and linen descend, the final result of dress,—of patterns which are now no longer cried up, unless it be in Milwaukee, as those splendid articles, English, French, or American prints, ginghams, muslins, &c., gathered from all quarters both of fashion and poverty, going to become paper of one color or a few shades only, on which forsooth will be written tales of real life, high and low, and founded on fact! This closed car smells of salt fish, the strong New England and commercial scent, reminding me of the Grand Banks and the fisheries. Who has not seen a salt fish, thoroughly cured for this world, so that nothing can spoil it, and putting the perseverance of the saints to the blush? with which you may sweep or pave the streets, and split your kindlings, and the teamster shelter himself and his lading against sun, wind, and rain behind it,— and the trader, as a Concord trader once did, hang it up by his door for a sign when he commences business, until at last his oldest customer cannot tell surely whether it be animal, vegetable, or mineral, and yet it shall be as pure as a snowflake, and if it be put into a pot and boiled, will come out an excellent dun fish for a Saturday's dinner. Next Spanish hides, with the tails still preserving their twist and the angle of elevation they had when the oxen that wore them were careering over the pampas of the Spanish main—a type of all obstinacy, and evincing how almost hopeless and incurable are all constitutional vices. I confess that, practically speaking, when I have learned a man's real disposition, I have no hopes of changing it for the better or worse in this state of existence. As the Orientals say, "A cur's tail may be warmed, and pressed, and bound round with ligatures, and after a twelve years' labor bestowed upon it, still it will retain its natural form." The only effectual cure for such inveteracies as these tails exhibit is to make glue of them, which I believe is what is usually done with them, and then they will stay put and stick. Here is a hogshead of molasses or of brandy directed to John Smith, Cuttingsville, Vermont, some trader among the Green Mountains, who imports for the farmers near his clearing, and now perchance stands over his bulkhead and thinks of the last arrivals on the coast, how they may affect the price for him, telling his customers this moment, as he has told them twenty times before this morning, that he expects some by the next train of prime quality. It is advertised in the Cuttingsville Times.

While these things go up other things come down. Warned by the whizzing sound, I look up from my book and see some tall pine, hewn on far northern hills, which has winged its way over the Green Mountains and the Connecticut, shot like an arrow through the township within ten minutes, and scarce another eye beholds it; going

> "to be the mast
> Of some great ammiral."

And hark! here comes the cattle-train bearing the cattle of a thousand hills, sheepcots, stables, and cow-yards in the air, drovers with their sticks, and shepherd boys in the midst of their flocks, all but the mountain pastures, whirled along like leaves blown from the mountains by the September gales. The air is filled with the bleating of calves and sheep, and the hustling of oxen, as if a pastoral valley were going by. When the old bell-wether at the head rattles his bell, the mountains do indeed skip like rams and the little hills like lambs. A carload of drovers, too, in the midst, on a level with their droves now, their vocation gone, but still clinging to their useless sticks as their badge of office. But their dogs, where are they? It is a stampede to them; they are quite thrown out; they have lost the scent. Methinks I hear them barking behind the Peterboro' Hills, or panting up the western slope of the Green Mountains. They will not be in at the death. Their vocation, too, is gone. Their fidelity and sagacity are below par now. They will slink back to their kennels in disgrace, or perchance run wild and strike a league with the wolf and the fox. So is your pastoral life whirled past and away. But the bell rings, and I must get off the track and let the cars go by:—

> What's the railroad to me?
> I never go to see
> Where it ends.
> It fills a few hollows,
> And makes banks for the swallows,
> It sets the sand a-blowing,
> And the blackberries a-growing,

but I cross it like a cart-path in the woods. I will not have my eyes put out and my ears spoiled by its smoke and steam and hissing.

*   *   *

Now that the cars are gone by and all the restless world with them, and the fishes in the pond no longer feel their rumbling, I am more alone than ever. For the rest of the long afternoon, perhaps, my meditations are interrupted only by the faint rattle of a carriage or team along the distant highway.

Sometimes, on Sundays, I heard the bells, the Lincoln, Acton, Bedford, or Concord bell, when the wind was favorable, a faint, sweet, and, as it were, natural melody, worth importing into the wilderness. At a sufficient distance over the woods this sound acquires a certain vibratory hum, as if the pine needles in the horizon were the strings of a harp which it swept. All sound heard at the greatest possible distance produces one and the same effect, a vibration of the universal lyre, just as the intervening atmosphere makes a distant ridge of earth interesting to our eyes by the azure tint it imparts to it. There came to me in this case a melody which the air had strained, and which had conversed with every leaf and needle of the wood, that portion of the sound which the elements had taken up and modulated and echoed from vale to vale. The echo is, to some extent, an original sound, and therein is the magic and charm of it. It is not merely a repetition of what was worth repeating in the bell, but partly the voice of the wood; the same trivial words and notes sung by a wood-nymph.

At evening, the distant lowing of some cow in the horizon beyond the woods sounded sweet and melodious, and at first I would mistake it for the voices of certain minstrels by whom I was sometimes serenaded, who might be straying over hill and dale; but soon I was not unpleasantly disappointed when it was prolonged into the cheap and natural music of the cow. I do not mean to be satirical, but to express my appreciation of those youths' singing, when I state that I perceived clearly that it was akin to the music of the cow, and they were at length one articulation of Nature.

Regularly at half-past seven, in one part of the summer, after the evening train had gone by, the whippoorwills chanted their vespers for half an hour, sitting on a stump by my door, or upon the ridge pole of the house. They would begin to sing almost with as much precision as a clock, within five minutes of a particular time, referred to the setting of the sun, every evening. I had a rare opportunity to become acquainted with their habits. Sometimes I heard four or five at once in different parts of the wood, by accident one a bar behind another, and so near me that I distinguished not only the cluck after each note, but often that singular buzzing sound like a fly in a spider's web, only proportionally louder. Sometimes one would circle round and round me in the woods a few feet distant as if tethered by a string, when probably I was near its eggs. They sang at intervals throughout the night, and were again as musical as ever just before and about dawn.

When other birds are still the screech owls take up the strain, like mourning women their ancient u-lu-lu. Their dismal scream is truly Ben Jonsonian. Wise midnight hags! It is no honest and blunt tu-whit tu-who of the poets, but, without jesting, a most solemn graveyard ditty, the mutual consolations of suicide lovers remembering the pangs and delights of supernal love in the infernal groves. Yet I love to hear their wailing, their doleful responses, trilled along the woodside; reminding me sometimes of music and singing birds; as if it were the dark and tearful side of music, the regrets and sighs that would fain be sung. They are the spirits, the low spirits and melancholy forebodings, of fallen souls that once in human shape nightwalked the earth and did the deeds of darkness, now expiating their sins with their wailing hymns or threnodies in the scenery of their transgressions. They give me a new sense of the variety and capacity of that nature which is our common dwelling. *Oh-o-o-o-o- that I never had been bor-r-r-n!* sighs one on this side of the pond, and circles with the restlessness of despair to some new perch on the gray oaks. Then—*that I never had been bor-r-r-n!* echoes another on the farther side with tremulous sincerity, and—*bor-r-r-n!* comes faintly from far in the Lincoln woods.

I was also serenaded by a hooting owl. Near at hand you could fancy it the most melancholy sound in Nature, as if she meant by this to stereotype and make permanent in her choir the dying moans of a human being,—some poor weak relic of mortality who has left hope behind, and howls like an animal, yet with human sobs, on entering the dark valley, made more awful by a certain gurgling melodiousness,—I find myself beginning with the letters gl when I try to imitate it,—expressive of a mind which has reached the gelatinous mildewy stage in the mortification of all healthy and courageous thought. It reminded me of ghouls and idiots and insane howlings. But now one answers from far woods in a strain made really melodious by distance,—*Hoo hoo hoo hoorer hoo;* and indeed for the most part it suggested only pleasing associations, whether heard by day or night, summer or winter.

I rejoice that there are owls. Let them do the idiotic and maniacal hooting for men. It is a sound admirably suited to swamps and twilight woods which no day illustrates, suggesting a vast and undeveloped nature which men have not recognized. They represent the stark twilight and unsatisfied thoughts which all have. All day the sun has shone on the surface of some savage swamp, where the single spruce stands hung with usnea lichens, and small hawks circulate above, and the chickadee lisps amid the evergreens, and the partridge and rabbit skulk beneath; but now a more dismal and fitting day dawns, and a different race of creatures awakes to express the meaning of Nature there.

Late in the evening I heard the distant rumbling of wagons over bridges,—a sound heard farther than almost any other at night,— the baying of dogs, and sometimes again the lowing of some disconsolate cow in a distant barn-yard. In the meanwhile all the shore rang with the trump of bullfrogs, the sturdy spirits of ancient wine-bibbers, and wassailers, still unrepentant, trying to sing a catch in their Stygian lake, —if the Walden nymphs will pardon the comparison, for though there are almost no weeds, there are frogs there,—who would fain keep up the hilarious rules of their old festal tables, though their voices have waxed hoarse and solemnly grave, mocking at mirth, and the wine has lost its flavor, and become only liquor to distend their paunches, and sweet intoxication never comes to drown the memory of the past, but mere saturation and waterloggedness and distention. The most aldermanic, with his chin upon a heart-leaf, which serves for a napkin to his drooling chaps, under this northern shore quaffs a deep draught of the once scorned water, and passes round the cup with the ejaculation *tr-r-r-oonk, tr-r-r-oonk, tr-r-r-oonk!* and straightway comes over the water from some distant cove the same password repeated, where the next in seniority and girth has gulped down to his mark; and when this observance has made the circuit of the shores, then ejaculates the master of ceremonies, with satisfaction, *tr-r-r-oonk!* and each in his turn repeats the same down to the least distended, leakiest, and flabbiest-paunched, that there be no mistake; and then the bowl goes round again and again, until the sun disperses the morning mist, and only the patriarch is not under the pond, but vainly bellowing *troonk* from time to time, and pausing for a reply.

I am not sure that I ever heard the sound of cock-crowing from my clearing, and I thought that it might be worth the while to keep a cockerel for his music merely, as a singing bird. The note of this once wild Indian pheasant is certainly the most remarkable of any bird's, and if they could be naturalized without being domesticated, it would soon become the most famous sound in our woods, surpassing the clangor of the goose and the hooting of the owl; and then imagine the cackling of the hens to fill the pauses when their lords' clarions rested! No wonder that man added this bird to his tame stock,—to say nothing of the eggs and the drumsticks. To walk in a winter morning in a wood where these birds abounded, their native woods, and hear the wild cockerels crow on the trees, clear and shrill for miles over the resounding earth, drowning the feebler notes of other birds,—think of it! It would put nations on the alert. Who would not be early to rise, and rise earlier and earlier every successive day of his life, till he became unspeakably healthy, wealthy, and wise? This foreign bird's note is celebrated by the poets of all countries along with the notes of their native songsters. All climates agree with brave Chanticleer. He is more indigenous even than the natives. His health is ever good, his lungs are sound, his spirits never flag. Even the sailor on the Atlantic and Pacific is awakened by his voice; but its shrill sound never roused me from my slumbers. I kept neither dog, cat, cow, pig, nor hens, so that you would have said there was a deficiency of domestic sounds; neither the churn, nor the spinning-wheel, nor even the singing of the kettle, nor the hissing of the urn, nor children crying, to comfort one. An old-fashioned man would have lost his senses or died of ennui before this. Not even rats in the wall, for they were starved out, or rather were never baited in,—only squirrels on the roof and under the floor, a whippoorwill on the ridge pole, a blue-jay screaming beneath the window, a hare or woodchuck under the house, a screech-owl or a cat-owl behind it, a flock of wild geese or a laughing loon on the pond, and a fox to bark in the night. Not even a lark or an oriole, those mild plantation birds, ever visited my clearing. No cockerels to crow nor hens to cackle in the yard. No yard! but unfenced Nature reaching up to your very sills. A young forest growing up under your windows, and wild sumachs and blackberry vines breaking through into your cellar; sturdy pitch-pines rubbing and creaking against the shingles for want of room, their roots reaching quite under the house. Instead of a scuttle or a blind blown off in the gale,—a pine tree snapped off or torn up by the roots behind your house for fuel. Instead of no path to the front-yard gate in the Great Snow,—no gate—no front-yard,—and no path to the civilized world!

Quincy

BOYS ARE WILD ANIMALS, rich in the treasures of sense, but the New England boy had a wider range of emotions than boys of more equable climates. He felt his nature crudely, as it was meant. To the boy Henry Adams, summer was drunken. Among senses, smell was the strongest—smell of hot pine-woods and sweet-fern in the scorching summer noon; of new-mown hay; of ploughed earth; of box hedges; of peaches, lilacs, syringas; of stables, barns, cow-yards; of salt water and low tide on the marshes; nothing came amiss. Next to smell came taste, and the children knew the taste of everything they saw or touched, from pennyroyal and flagroot to the shell of a pignut and the letters of a spelling-book—the taste of A-B, AB, suddenly revived on the boy's tongue sixty years afterwards. Light, line, and color as sensual pleasures, came later and were as crude as the rest. The New England light is glare, and the atmosphere harshens color. The boy was a full man before he ever knew what was meant by atmosphere; his idea of pleasure in light was the blaze of a New England sun. His idea of color was a peony, with the dew of early morning on its petals. The intense blue of the sea, as he saw it a mile or two away, from the Quincy hills; the cumuli in a June afternoon sky; the strong reds and greens and purples of colored prints and children's picture-books, as the American colors then ran; these were ideals. The opposites or antipathies, were the cold grays of November evenings, and the thick, muddy thaws of Boston winter. With such standards, the Bostonian could not but develop a double nature. Life was a double thing. After a January blizzard, the boy who could look with pleasure into the violent snow-glare of the cold white sunshine, with its intense light and shade, scarcely knew what was meant by tone. He could reach it only by education.

Winter and summer, then, were two hostile lives, and bred two separate natures. Winter was always the effort to live; summer was tropical license. Whether the children rolled in the grass, or waded in the brook, or swam in the salt ocean, or sailed in the bay, or fished for smelts in the creeks, or netted minnows in the salt-marshes, or took to the pine-woods and the granite quarries, or chased musk-rats and hunted snapping-turtles in the swamps, or mushrooms or nuts on the autumn hills, summer and country were always sensual living, while winter was always compulsory learning. Summer was the multiplicity of nature; winter was school.

The bearing of the two seasons on the education of Henry Adams was no fancy; it was the most decisive force he ever knew: it ran through life, and made the division between its perplexing, warring, irreconcilable problems, irreducible opposites, with growing emphasis to the last year of study. From earliest childhood the boy was accustomed to feel that, for him, life was double. Winter and summer, town and country, law and liberty, were hostile, and the man who pretended they were not, was in his eyes a schoolmaster—that is, a man employed to tell lies to little boys. Though Quincy was but two hours' walk from Beacon Hill, it belonged in a different world. For two hundred years, every Adams, from father to son, had lived within sight of State Street, and sometimes had lived in it, yet none had ever taken kindly to the town, or been taken kindly by it. The boy inherited his double nature. He knew as yet nothing about his great-grandfather, who had died a dozen years before his own birth: he took for granted that any great-grandfather of his must have always been good, and his enemies wicked; but he divined his great-grandfather's character from his own. Never for a moment did he connect the two ideas of Boston and John Adams; they were separate and antagonistic; the idea of John Adams went with Quincy. He knew his grandfather John Quincy Adams only as an old man of seventy-five or eighty who was friendly and gentle with him, but except that he heard his grandfather always called "the President," and his grandmother "the Madam," he had no reason to suppose that his Adams grandfather differed in character from his Brooks grandfather who was equally kind and benevolent. He liked the Adams side best, but for no other reason than that it reminded him of the country, the summer, and the absence of restraint. Yet he felt also that Quincy was in a way inferior to Boston, and that socially Boston looked down on Quincy. The reason was clear enough even to a five-year-old child. Quincy had no Boston style. Little enough style had either; a simpler manner of life and thought could hardly exist, short of cave-dwelling. The flint-and-steel with which his grandfather Adams used to light his own fires in the early morning was still on the mantelpiece of his study. The idea of a livery or even a dress for servants, or of an evening toilette, was next to blasphemy. Bathrooms, water-supplies, lighting, heating, and the whole array of domestic comforts, were unknown at Quincy. Boston had already a bathroom, a water-supply, a furnace, and gas. The superiority of Boston was evident, but a child liked it no better for that. . . .

My First Visit to New England

I WONDER IF there is a stage that still runs between Lowell and Concord, past meadow walls, and under the caressing boughs of way-side
elms, and through the bird-haunted gloom of woodland roads, in the
freshness of the summer morning? By a blessed chance I found that
there was such a stage in 1860, and I took it from my hotel, instead
of going back to Boston and up to Concord as I must have had to do
by train. The journey gave me the intimacy of the New England
country as I could have had it in no other fashion, and for the first time
I saw it in all the summer sweetness which I have often steeped my
soul in since. The meadows were newly mown, and the air was fragrant
with the grass, stretching in long windrows among the brown bowlders,
or capped with canvas in the little haycocks it had been gathered into
the day before. I was fresh from the affluent farms of the Western
Reserve, and this care of the grass touched me with a rude pity, which
I also bestowed on the meagre fields of corn and wheat; but still the
land was lovelier than any I had ever seen, with its old farmhouses,
and brambled gray stone walls, its stony hillsides, its staggering
orchards, its wooded tops, and its thick-brackened valleys. From West
to East the difference was as great as I afterwards found it from America to Europe, and my impression of something quaint and strange
was no keener when I saw Old England the next year than when I saw
New England now. I had imagined the landscape bare of trees, and
I was astonished to find it almost as full of them as at home, though
they all looked very little, as they well might to eyes used to the
primeval forests of Ohio. The road ran through them from time to
time, and took their coolness on its smooth hard reaches, and then
issued again in the glisten of the open fields. . . .

Prairie Farm

THE COUNTRY SCHOOLHOUSE was three miles from my uncle's farm. It stood in a clearing in the woods and would hold about twenty-five boys and girls. We attended the school with more or less regularity once or twice a week, in summer, walking to it in the cool of the morning by the forest paths and back in the gloaming at the end of the day. All the pupils brought their dinners in baskets—corn dodger, buttermilk and other good things—and sat in the shade of the trees at noon and ate them. It is the part of my education which I look back upon with the most satisfaction. My first visit to the school was when I was seven. A strapping girl of fifteen, in the customary sunbonnet and calico dress, asked me if I "used tobacco"—meaning did I chew it. I said no. It roused her scorn. She reported me to all the crowd and said:

"Here is a boy seven years old who can't chaw tobacco."

By the looks and comments which this produced I realized that I was a degraded object; I was cruelly ashamed of myself. I determined to reform. But I only made myself sick; I was not able to learn to chew tobacco. I learned to smoke fairly well but that did not conciliate anybody and I remained a poor thing and characterless. I longed to be respected but I never was able to rise. Children have but little charity for one another's defects.

As I have said, I spent some part of every year at the farm until I was twelve or thirteen years old. The life which I led there with my cousins was full of charm, and so is the memory of it yet. I can call back the solemn twilight and mystery of the deep woods, the earthy smells, the faint odors of the wild flowers, the sheen of rain-washed foliage, the rattling clatter of drops when the wind shook the trees, the far-off hammering of woodpeckers and the muffled drumming of wood pheasants in the remoteness of the forest, the snapshot glimpses of disturbed wild creatures scurrying through the grass—I can call it all back and make it as real as it ever was, and as blessed. I can call back

73

the prairie, and its loneliness and peace, and a vast hawk hanging motionless in the sky, with his wings spread wide and the blue of the vault showing through the fringe of their end feathers. I can see the woods in their autumn dress, the oaks purple, the hickories washed with gold, the maples and the sumachs luminous with crimson fires, and I can hear the rustle made by the fallen leaves as we plowed through them. I can see the blue clusters of wild grapes hanging among the foliage of the saplings, and I remember the taste of them and the smell. I know how the wild blackberries looked, and how they tasted, and the same with the paw-paws, the hazelnuts, and the persimmons; and I can feel the thumping rain, upon my head, of hickory nuts and walnuts when we were out in the frosty dawn to scramble for them with the pigs, and the gusts of wind loosed them and sent them down. I know the stain of blackberries, and how pretty it is, and I know the stain of walnut hulls, and how little it minds soap and water, also what grudged experience it had of either of them. I know the taste of maple sap, and when to gather it, and how to arrange the troughs and the delivery tubes, and how to boil down the juice, and how to hook the sugar after it is made, also how much better hooked sugar tastes than any that is honestly come by, let bigots say what they will.

I know how a prize watermelon looks when it is sunning its fat rotundity among pumpkin vines and "simblins"; I know how to tell when it is ripe without "plugging" it; I know how inviting it looks when it is cooling itself in a tub of water under the bed, waiting; I know how it looks when it lies on the table in the sheltered great floor space between house and kitchen, and the children gathered for the sacrifice and their mouths watering; I know the crackling sound it makes when the carving knife enters its end, and I can see the split fly along in front of the blade as the knife cleaves its way to the other end; I can see its halves fall apart and display the rich red meat and the black seeds, and the heart standing up, a luxury fit for the elect; I know how a boy looks behind a yard-long slice of that melon, and I know how he feels; for I have been there. I know the taste of the watermelon which has been honestly come by, and I know the taste of the watermelon which has been acquired by art. Both taste good, but the experienced know which tastes best. I know the look of green apples and peaches and pears on the trees, and I know how entertaining they are when they are inside of a person. I know how ripe ones look when they are piled in pyramids under the trees, and how pretty they are and how vivid their colors. I know how a frozen apple looks, in a barrel down cellar in the wintertime, and how hard it is to bite, and how the frost makes the teeth ache, and yet how good it is, notwithstanding. I know the disposition of elderly people to select the speckled apples for the children, and I once knew ways to beat the game. I know the look of an apple that is roasting and sizzling on a hearth on a winter's evening, and I know the comfort that comes of eating it hot, along with some sugar and a drench of cream. I know the delicate art and mystery of so cracking hickory nuts and walnuts on a flatiron with a hammer that the kernels will be delivered whole, and I know how the nuts, taken in conjunction with winter apples, cider, and doughnuts, make old people's old tales and old jokes sound fresh and crisp and enchanting, and juggle an evening away before you know what went with the time. I know the look of Uncle Dan'l's kitchen as it was on the privileged nights, when I was a child, and I can see the white and black children grouped on the hearth, with the firelight playing on their faces and the shadows flickering upon the walls, clear back toward the cavernous gloom of the rear, and I can hear Uncle Dan'l telling the immortal tales which Uncle Remus Harris was to gather into his books and charm the world with, by and by; and I can feel again the creepy joy which quivered through me when the time for the ghost story of the "Golden Arm" was reached—and the sense of regret, too, which came over me, for it was always the

last story of the evening and there was nothing between it and the un-
welcome bed.

I can remember the bare wooden stairway in my uncle's house, and
the turn to the left above the landing, and the rafters and the slanting
roof over my bed, and the squares of moonlight on the floor, and the
white cold world of snow outside, seen through the curtainless window.
I can remember the howling of the wind and the quaking of the house
on stormy nights, and how snug and cozy one felt, under the blankets,
listening; and how the powdery snow used to sift in, around the sashes,
and lie in little ridges on the floor and make the place look chilly in
the morning and curb the wild desire to get up—in case there was
any. I can remember how very dark that room was, in the dark of the
moon, and how packed it was with ghostly stillness when one woke up
by accident away in the night, and forgotten sins came flocking out
of the secret chambers of the memory and wanted a hearing; and how
ill chosen the time seemed for this kind of business; and how dismal
was the hoo-hooing of the owl and the wailing of the wolf, sent
mourning by on the night wind.

I remember the raging of the rain on that roof, summer nights, and
how pleasant it was to lie and listen to it, and enjoy the white splendor
of the lightning and the majestic booming and crashing of the thunder.
It was a very satisfactory room, and there was a lightning rod which
was reachable from the window, an adorable and skittish thing to climb
up and down, summer nights, when there were duties on hand of a
sort to make privacy desirable.

I remember the 'coon and 'possum hunts, nights, with the Negroes,
and the long marches through the black gloom of the woods, and the
excitement which fired everybody when the distant bay of an experienced dog announced that the game was treed; then the wild scram-
blings and stumblings through briers and bushes and over roots to get
to the spot; then the lighting of a fire and the felling of the tree, the
joyful frenzy of the dogs and the Negroes, and the weird picture it all
made in the red glare—I remember it all well, and the delight that
everyone got out of it, except the 'coon.

I remember the pigeon seasons, when the birds would come in millions and cover the trees and by their weight break down the branches.
They were clubbed to death with sticks; guns were not necessary and
were not used. I remember the squirrel hunts, and prairie-chicken
hunts, and wild-turkey hunts, and all that; and how we turned out,
mornings, while it was still dark, to go on these expeditions, and how
chilly and dismal it was, and how often I regretted that I was well
enough to go. A toot on a tin horn brought twice as many dogs as

were needed, and in their happiness they raced and scampered about, and knocked small people down, and made no end of unnecessary noise. At the word, they vanished away toward the woods, and we drifted silently after them in the melancholy gloom. But presently the gray dawn stole over the world, the birds piped up, then the sun rose and poured light and comfort all around, everything was fresh and dewy and fragrant, and life was a boon again. After three hours of tramping we arrived back wholesomely tired, overladen with game, very hungry, and just in time for breakfast.

A Judicial Wedding

IN LEAVING Gallup behind, my spirits rose. I wished that Zulime might have shared this strange landscape with me. On the right a distant, dimly-blue wall of mountains ran, while to the west rolled high, treeless hills, against which an occasional native hut showed like a wolf's den, half-hid among dwarf piñon trees and surrounded by naked children and savage dogs.

At intervals we came upon solitary shepherds tending their piebald flocks, as David and Abner guarded their father's sheep in Judea. That these patient shepherds, watching their lean herds, these Deborahs weaving their bright blankets beneath gnarled branches of sparse cedar trees, should be living less than forty-eight hours from Chicago, was incredible, and yet here they were! Their life and landscape, though of a texture with that of Arabia, were as real as Illinois, and every mile carried me deeper into the silence and serenity of their tribal home.

Brown boys, belted with silver and wearing shirts of gay calico, met us, riding their wiry little ponies with easy grace. Children, naked, shy as foxes, arrested their play beside dry clumps of sage-brush and stared in solemn row, whilst their wrinkled, leathery grand-sires hobbled out, cupping their thin brown hands in prayer for tobacco.

There was something Oriental, fictive in it all, and when at the end of the day I found myself a guest in a pleasant cottage at the Agency, I was fully awake to the contrasts of my "material." My ears, as well as my eyes, were open to the drama of this land whose prehistoric customs were about to pass. For the moment I was inclined to rest there and study my surroundings, but as the real objective of my journey was Ganado, about thirty miles to the west of the Fort, I decided to go on.

Ganado was the home of a famous Indian trader named Hubbell, whose store was known to me as a center of Navajo life. Toward this point I set forth a few days later, attended by a young Navajo whose hogan was in that direction, and who had promised to put me on my trail.

He was a fine, athletic youth of pleasant countenance, mounted upon a spotted pony and wearing a shirt of purple calico. With a belt of silver disks around his waist and a fillet of green cloth binding his glossy black hair, he was distinctly and delightfully colorful.

Our way rose at once to the level of a majestic plateau, sparsely set with pines and cedars, a barren land from which the grass and shrubs had long since been cropped by swarms of sheep and goats. Nevertheless, it was lovely to the eye, and as we rode forward we came upon a party of Navajo girls gathering piñon nuts, laughing and singing in happy abandon, untroubled by the white man's world. They greeted my guide with jests, but became very grave as he pointed out a fresh bear-track in the dust of the trail.

"Heap bears," he said to me. "Injun no kill bears. Bears big medicine," and as we rode away he laughed back at the panic-stricken girls, who were hurriedly collecting their nuts in order to flee the spot.

At last my guide halted. "I go here," he signed with graceful hand. "You keep trail; bimeby you come deep valley—stream. On left white man's house. You stop there." All of which was as plain as if in spoken words.

As I rode on alone, the peace, the poetry, the suggestive charm of that silent, lonely, radiant land took hold upon me with compelling power. Here in the midst of busy, commonplace America it lay, a section of the Polished Stone Age, retaining the most distinctive customs, songs and dances of the past. Here was a people going about its immemorial pursuits, undisturbed by the railway and the telephone. Its shepherds, like Hittites, who wandered down from the hills upon the city of Babylon two thousand years before the Christian Era, were patriarchal and pastoral. They asked but a tent, a piece of goat's flesh, and a cool spring.

Late in the afternoon (I loitered luxuriously) I came to the summit of a long ridge which overlooked a broad, curving valley, at the far-away western rim of which a slender line of water gleamed. How beautiful it all was, but how empty! No furrow, no hut, no hint of human habitation appeared, a land which must ever be lonely, for it is without rains, and barren of streams for irrigation.

An hour later I rode up to the door of a long, low, mud-walled building, and was met by the trader, a bush-bearded, middle-aged man with piercing gray eyes and sturdy, upright figure. This was Lorenzo Hubbell, one of the best-known citizens of New Mexico, living here alone, a day's ride from a white settler.

Though hairy and spectacled he was a comparatively young man, but his mixed blood had already given him a singular power over his dark-skinned neighbors of the territory.

His wife and children were spending the summer in Albuquerque, and in the intimacy of our long days together I spoke of my approaching marriage. "I want to buy some native blankets and some Navajo silver for our new home."

His interest was quick. "Let me send your wife a wedding present. How would she like some Hopi jars?"

The off-hand way in which he used the words, "your wife," startled me—reminded me that in less than two weeks I was due at Professor Taft's home to claim my bride. I accepted his offer of the vases and began to collect silver and turquoise ornaments, in order that I might carry back to Zulime some part of the poetry of this land and its people.

"The more I think about it," I wrote to her, "the more I want you to share my knowledge of 'the High Country.' Why not put our wedding a week earlier and let me take you into the mountains? If you will advance the date to the eighteenth of November we can have an eight-day trip in Colorado and still reach mother and the Homestead in time for Thanksgiving. I want to show you my best beloved valleys and peaks."

Though addressing the letter to her Chicago home, I knew that she was about to leave for Kansas; therefore I added a postscript: "I am planning to meet you in your father's house about the eighteenth of the month, and I hope you will approve my scheme."

In the glow of my plan for a splendid Colorado wedding journey, I lost interest in Ganado and its Indians. Making arrangements for the shipment of my treasures, I saddled my horse one morning, waved Hubbell a joyous farewell, and started back toward the Agency in the hope of finding there a letter from my girl.

In this I was not disappointed. She wrote: "I shall leave for Kansas on the Burlington, Sunday night. You can write me at Hanover." It was plain she had not received my latest word.

I began to figure. "If I leave here to-morrow forenoon, and catch the express at Gallup to-morrow night, I can make the close connection at Topeka, and arrive in St. Joseph just half an hour before Zulime's train comes in on Monday morning. I shall surprise her—and delight myself—by having breakfast with her!"

However, I could not get away till morning, and with an evening to wear away I accepted the Agent's invitation to witness a native dance which had been announced to him by one of the young Navajo policemen. I had never seen a Navajo dance, and gladly accepted the opportunity to do so.

It was a clear, crisp November evening as we started out, the clerk, his sister, one of the teachers and myself riding in a two-seated open wagon, drawn by a pair of spirited horses. The native village was some ten miles to the north, and all the way up hill, so that before we came in sight of it darkness had fallen, and in the light of a bonfire the dancers were assembling.

Of the village, if there was a village, I could see little, but a tall old man (the town crier) was chanting an invitation or command of some sort, and dark forms were moving to and fro among the shadows of the piñon trees. How remote it all was from the white man's world, how self-sufficing and peaceful—how idyllic!

The master of ceremonies met us and gave us seats, and for three hours we sat in the glow of the fire, watching the youthful, tireless dancers circle and leap in monotonous yet graceful evolutions. Here was love and courtship, and jealousy and faithful friendship, just as among the white dancers of Neshonoc. Roguish black eyes gleamed in the light of the fire, small feet beat the earth in joyous rhythm, and the calm faces of the old men lent dignity and a kind of religious significance to the scene. They were dreaming of the past, when no white man had entered their world.

The young people were almost equally indifferent to us, and as the night deepened we who were white merged more and more indistinguishably with the crowd of dusky onlookers. It was easy to imagine ourselves back in the sixteenth century, looking upon this scene from the wondering viewpoint of the Spanish explorers. Whence came these people, these dances, these ceremonials?

At last the time came for us to set forth upon our long ride back to the Agency, and so, silently, we rose and slipped away into the darkness, leaving the dancers to end their immemorial festival without the aliens' presence. They had no need of us, no care for us. At a little distance I turned and looked back. The songs, interrupted by shrill, wolfish howlings and owl-like hootings, rang through the night with singular savage charm, a chant out of the past, a chorus which was carrying forward into an individualistic white man's world the voices of the indeterminate tribal past.

The sky was moonless, the air frosty, and after we had entered the narrow cañon, which was several miles long and very steep, the clerk, who was not very skilled with horses, turned the reins over to me, and for an hour or more I drove with one foot on the brake, trusting mainly to the horses to find their way. It was bitter cold in the cañon, and my cramped right leg became lame—so lame that I could hardly get out of the wagon after we reached the Agency. Excruciating pain developed in the sciatic nerve, and though I passed a sleepless night

I was determined to leave next morning. "I shall go if I have to be carried to my horse," I said grimly to the clerk, who begged me to stay in bed.

Fortunately, the trader was going to the railway and kindly offered to take me with him; and so, laden with Navajo silver (bracelets, buckles and rings), I started out so lame that I dragged one leg with a groan, hoping that with the warmth of the sun my pain would pass away.

Reaching Gallup at noon I spent the afternoon sitting in the sun, waiting for the train. At six o'clock it came, and soon I was washed and shaved and eating dinner on the dinner-car of the Continental Limited.

All that night and all the next day and far into the second night I rode, my fear of missing connections at Topeka uniting with my rheumatism to make the hours seem of interminable length. It seemed at times a long, long "shot"—but I made it! I reached the station at Topeka just in time to catch the connecting train, and I was on the platform at St. Joseph at sun-rise, a full half-hour before the Burlington coaches from Chicago were due.

As I walked up and down, I smiled with anticipation of the surprise I had in store. "If she keeps her schedule I shall see her step from the Pullman car without the slightest suspicion that I am within six hundred miles of her," I thought, doing my best to walk the kink out of my leg, which was still painful. "She is coming! My wife is coming!" I repeated, incredulous of the fact.

At eight o'clock the engine came nosing in, and while watching the line of passengers descend, I lost hope. It was too much to expect!

She was there! I saw her as she stepped down from the rear Pullman, and just as she was about to take her valise from the porter, I touched her on the shoulder and said, "I'll take charge of that."

She started and turned with a look of alarm, a look which changed to amazement, to delight. "Oh!" she gasped. "Where did you come from?"

"From the Navajo reservation," I replied calmly.

"But how did you get here?"

"By train, like yourself."

"But when—how long ago?"

"About thirty minutes," I laughed. "I'm a wizard at making close connections." Then, seeing that she must know all about it at once, I added, "Come into the station restaurant, and while we are eating breakfast I will tell you where I have been and what brought me back so soon."

While waiting for our coffee I took from my valise a bracelet of silver, a broad band shaped and ornamented by some Navajo silversmith. "Hold out your arm," I commanded. She obeyed, and I clasped the barbaric gyve about her wrist. "That is a sign of your slavery," I said gravely.

Smilingly, meditatively, she fingered it, realizing dimly the grim truth which ran beneath my jesting. She was about to take on a relationship which must inevitably bring work and worry as well as joy.

(That silver has never left her wrist for a moment. For twenty-two years she has worn it, keeping it bright with service for me, for her children and for her friends. There is something symbolic in the fact that it has never lost its clear luster and that it has never tarnished the arm it adorns.)

Her joy in this present, her astonishment at my unexpected appearance on the railway platform, amused and delighted me. I could scarcely convince her that at six o'clock on Saturday night I was in a New Mexico town, waiting for the eastern express. It was all a piece of miraculous adventure on my part, but her evident pleasure in its successful working out made me rich—and very humble. "What did you do it for?" she asked; then, with a look of dismay, she added, "What am I going to do with you in Hanover?"

The Frontier of Indiana

To ME, THEREFORE, this region was holy Ganges—Mecca, Medina—
the blessed isles of the West. In approaching Bowling Green, Ohio,
I was saying to myself how strange it will be to see H—— again,
should he chance to be there! What an interesting talk I will have
with him! And after Bowling Green how interesting to pass through
Grand Rapids, even though there was not a soul whom I would wish
to greet again! Toledo was too far north to bother about.

When we entered Bowling Green, however, by a smooth macadam
road under a blazing sun, it was really not interesting at all; indeed it
was most disappointing. The houses were small and low and everything
was still, and after one sees town after town for eight hundred or a
thousand miles, all more or less alike, one town must be different and
possessed of some intrinsic merit not previously encountered to attract
attention.

I persuaded Franklin to stop at the office of the principal newspaper,
in order that I might make inquiry as to the present whereabouts of
H——. He had written me, about four years before, to say that he was
connected with a paper here. He wanted me to teach him how to write
short stories! It was a dull room or store, facing the principal street,
like a bank. In it were a young, reporterish looking boy, very trig
and brisk and curious as to his glance, and a middle aged man, bald,
red faced, roundly constructed like a pigeon, and about as active.

"Do you happen to recall a man by the name of H——who used
to work here in Bowling Green?" I inquired of the elder, not willing to
believe that he had controlled a paper, though I had understood from
someone that he had.

"B—— H——?" he replied, looking me over.

"Yes, that's the man."

"He did work here on the other paper for a while," he replied with
what seemed to me a faint look of contempt, though it may not have
been. "He hasn't been here for four or five years at the least. He's

up in Michigan now, I believe—Battle Creek, or Sheboygan, or some such place as that. They might tell you over at the other office." He waved his hand toward some outside institution—the other paper.

"You didn't happen to know him personally, I presume?"

"No, I saw him a few times. He was their general utility man, I believe."

I went out, uncertain whether to bother any more or not. Twenty-three years is a long time. I had not seen him in all of that. I started to walk toward the other newspaper office, but the sight of the bare street, with a buggy or two and an automobile, and the low, quiet store buildings, deterred me.

"What's the use?" I asked myself. "This is a stale, impossible atmosphere. There isn't an idea above hay and feed in the whole place."

I climbed back in the car and we fled.

It was not much better for some distance beyond here until we began to draw near Napoleon, Ohio. The country for at least twenty miles was dreadfully flat and uninteresting—houses with low fences and prominent chicken coops, orchards laden with apples of a still greenish yellow color, fields of yellowing wheat or green corn—oh, so very flat. Not a spire of an interesting church anywhere, not a respectable piece of architecture, nothing. Outside of one town, where we stopped for a glass of water, we did encounter a brick and plaster mausoleum—the adjunct, I believe, of a crematory—set down at the junction of two macadam crossroads, and enclosed by a most offensive wooden fence. Although there were some wide fields and some patches of woods, which might have been utilized to give an institution of this kind a little grace—it had none, not the faintest trace. The ground was grassless, or only patched in spots with it. The stained glass windows which ornamented its four sides were botches—done by some wholesale stained glass window company, very likely of Peoria, Illinois.

"Kind heaven," I exclaimed, on sight of it, "what is the matter with a country where such things can be? What's the trouble with their minds anyhow? What a deadly yearning for the commonplace and crude and offensive possesses them!"

"Yes, and they slave to do it," replied Franklin. "You haven't any idea how people will toil for years under a hot sun or in cold or snow to be able to build a thing like that"—and he pointed to a new yellow house of the most repulsive design.

"You're right! You're right!" I replied.

"This country isn't so bad, perhaps, but the intellectual or tempera-mental condition of the people spoils it—their point of view. I feel a kind of chicken raising mind to be dominant here. If another kind of creature lived on this soil it would be lovely, I'm sure of it."

We sank into a deep silence. The car raced on. Once Franklin, seeing some fine apples on a tree, stopped the car, climbed a fence, and helped himself to a dozen. They were better to look at than to eat.

It was only when we reached the region of the Maumee that things began to brighten up again. We were entering a much fairer land—a region extending from the Maumee here at Grand Rapids, Ohio, to Fort Wayne, Warsaw and North Manchester, Indiana, and indeed, nearly all the rest of our journey. We were leaving the manufacturing section of Ohio and the East, and entering the grain growing, rural life loving middle West. The Maumee, when we reached it again, revivified all my earliest and best impressions of it. It was a beautiful stream, dimpling smoothly between raised banks of dark earth and fringed for the most of the way by lines of poplar, willow, and syca-more. Great patches of the parasite gold thread flourished here— more gold thread than I ever saw in my life before—look like flames of light on a grey day, and covering whole small islands and steep banks for distances of thirty or forty feet or more at a stretch. We might have ridden into and through Grand Rapids, but I thought it scarcely worth while. What would I see anyhow? Another town like Bowling Green, only smaller, and the farm of H——'s parents, perhaps, if I could find it. All this would take time, and would it be worth while? I decided not. The Maumee, once we began to skirt its banks, was so poetic that I knew it could not be better nor more reminiscent of those older days, even though I followed it into Toledo.

But truly, this section, now that we were out of the cruder, coarser manufacturing and farming region which lay to the east of it, appealed to me mightily. I was beginning to feel as if I were in good company again—better company than we had been in for some time. Perhaps the people were not so pushing, so manufacturing,—for which heaven be praised. We encountered three towns, Napoleon, Defiance and Hicksville, before nightfall, which revived all the happiest days and ideals of my youth. Indeed, Napoleon was Warsaw over again, with its stone and red brick courthouse,—surmounted by a statue of Napo-leon Bonaparte (gosh!)—and its O.N.G. Armory, and its pretty red brick Methodist and brownstone Presbyterian Churches and its iron bridges over the Maumee. The river here was as wide and shallow a thing as had been the Tippecanoe at home, at its best, with a few small boat houses at one place, and lawns or gardens which came down to the water's edge at others. The principal street was crowded with ramshackle buggies and very good automobiles (exceedingly fancy ones, in many instances) and farmers and idlers in patched brown coats and baggy, shapeless trousers—delightful pictures, every one of them. We eventually agreed to stop, and got out and hung about, while Speed went back to a garage which we had seen and treated himself to oil and gas.

Truly, if I were a poet, I would now attempt a "Rubaiyat of a Middle West Town," or I would compose "The Ballad of Napoleon, Ohio," or "Verses on Hicksville," or "Rondels of Warsaw." You have no idea what a charm these places have—what a song they sing—to one who has ever been of them and then gone out into the world and changed and cannot see life any more through the medium—the stained glass medium, if you will—of the time and the mood which we call our youth.

Here, as at Warsaw, the railroad station of an older day was hidden away in a side street, where possibly six trains a day may have stopped. At Warsaw we had the village bus, which took passengers to the one hotel. Here they had a Ford, by heck!

"None o' your cheap busses for us any more!"

And in the plain red brick business street was this motley and yet charming collection of people. I have indicated farmers and farmers' wives in (the equivalent of) homespun and linen. Behold, now, your town dandy, bustling into the bank or bookstore at two P.M. of this fine afternoon, a veritable village Beau Brummell, very conscious of his charms. He is between twentyone and twentythree and very likely papar owns the book or the clothing store and is proud of his son's appearance. In my day son would have had a smart runabout, with red or yellow wheels, in which he would have arrived, picking up a very pretty girl by the way. Now he has an automobile—even if it is only a Buick—and he feels himself to be the most perfect of youths.

And here come three girls, arm in arm, village belles, so pretty in their bright, summery washdresses. Do you think New York can teach them anything—or Paris? Tush! Not so fast. Look at our skirts, scarcely below the knees, with pointed ruffles, and flaring flounces, and our bright grey kid slippers, and the delicate frills about our necks, and the soft bloomy gaiety of our "sport" hats. New York teach us anything? We teach New York, rather! We are down for mail, or stationery, or an ice cream soda, and to see and be seen. Perhaps Beau Brummell will drive us home in his car, or we may refuse and just laugh at him.

And, if you please, here is one of the town's young scarlet women. No companionship for her. She is dressed like the others, only more so, but to emphasize the difference she is rouged as to cheeks and lips. Those eager, seeking eyes! No woman will openly look at her, nor any girl. But the men—these farmers and lawyers and town politicians! Which one of them will seek her out first tonight, do you suppose— the lawyer, the doctor, or the storekeeper?

How good it all tasted after New York! And what a spell it cast. I can scarcely make you understand, I fear. Indiana is a world all unto itself, and this extreme western portion of Ohio is a part of it, not by official, but rather by natural arrangement. The air felt different—the sky and trees and streets here were sweeter. They really were. The intervening years frizzled away and once more I saw myself quite clearly in this region, with the ideas and moods of my youth still dominant. I was a "kid" again, and these streets and stores were as familiar to me as though I had lived in them all my life.

Franklin and I were looking in at the window of the one combined music and piano store, to see what they sold. All the popular songs were there—"I Didn't Raise My Boy To Be a Soldier," "It's a Long, Long Way to Tipperary," "He's a Devil in His Own Home Town," and others such as "Goodbye, Goodbye" and "Though We Should Never Meet Again." As I looked at these things, so redolent of small town love affairs and of calling Wednesdays and Saturdays, my mind went back to all the similar matters I had known (not my own—I never had any) and the condition of the attractive girl and the average young men in a town like this. How careful is their upbringing—supposedly. How earnestly is the Sunday School and the precept and the maxim invoked, and how persistently so many of them go their own way. They do not know what it is all about, all this talk about religion and morality and duty. In their blood is a certain something which responds to the light of the sun and the blue of the sky.

Growing up Along the Brandywine

I HAVE MENTIONED several times the curiously emotional influences of the Brandywine. The tender-minded never speak of it without sentiment, and on the romantic imagination it has had the same unfortunate effect as a glass of wine upon the neurotic genius of a Poe. Yet the chief quality of its influence is healthier, and can best be described as affection. I have never known a river, except the upper Thames, to be held by those who know it well in such affectionate regard. Washington cannot have loved it, since its inconveniently numerous fords upset his strategy, and General Sullivan must have hated the sound of its name. But even the early millers, who worked all day hip-deep in cold water trying to save their races in floodtime, speak of it in their journals with a mingling of respect for its sudden bursts of excess power and a proprietary affection for its never-failing amber waters. While they built their mills like cliffs over its first tidewater pool, they kept the race-ways below their houses like water gardens. The beautiful canyon from which their power came was never stripped of its fine forest. There are trees today within the boundaries of Wilmington's Brandywine Park that must have been once owned by inhabitants of New Sweden.

All rivers seem personal by comparison with plains, or even mountains, as I have said in the first chapter of this book. The most personal are those which fall and twist and slide from noisy rapid to quiet pool, and follow, like a living creature, the contours of the land. They change from year to year, like a man who changes his clothes or a woman who redoes her hair. When you get to know such a river well, you will note new cuts into grassy banks, new channels through meadowlands, a maple bending farther down until its branches ripple the current, a sycamore dropped into a pool, its roots parched, its arms a hiding place for fish instead of birds. And, on the banks, sun and Quaker ladies where there had been shade, or shade and beds of Brandywine blue-

bells where there had been sun. Therefore I make no apology for con-
cluding this book with an interweaving of my own personal memories
with what has always seemed to me the very real personality of the
Brandywine.

I was born on a hill above the dams and races of the lower stream,
just where Washington's army camped before they moved toward the
Battle of the Brandywine. Two or three squares (as we called them
then) brought me to the end of streets and to an open field, bordered
by the high forest of Brandywine Park. Beyond the line of woods was
a steep and stony descent to the races and the river, two hundred feet
below. My first memories are of glimpses of fast-running water near
which children were not allowed to go. My next is of an adventurous
party of little boys and girls—we barelegged, the girls with petticoats
and drawers bunched up between their legs—wading and stumbling
across the rapids just above the old Colonial ford. Some fell in, some
were spanked, but not I.

My next clear Brandywine memory is of age ten or eleven, in winter,
when the old Barley Mill dam was frozen solid, something that seldom
happened in our mild climate. To me, with my skates, scrambling down
the wooded slopes, all the world seemed gathered on the ice. There
were big girls with red, woolen mufflers streaming, big boys with
"shinny sticks" knocking wooden blocks over the ice, grownups skating
hand in hand. It was a fête. And in one corner, where the ice was
smoother, a little old man, white-haired, with a velvet cap, velvet knick-
erbockers, and a tight-fitting jacket, was spinning and twisting in con-
temptuously beautiful curves while the careless throng clicked and slid
around his reservation. Everyone else was laughing or shouting, but he
had a look withdrawn and self-centered, as if he were actor and critic
both. It was probably the first time that I had seen an artist at work.

It may have been that summer when I was taken up to a farm in
middle Brandywine where, for weeks each year, I learned country life—
how to plant corn, four grains to a hill, how to make tunnels in the
hay, how to swim. For this last we were allowed a shallow pool on the
Pocopson, where the worst possible disaster was a belly scratched on
the rocky bottom. In the meadows beside the stream, we raced naked
with the calves, and painted ourselves with the yellow mud of the
valley. But soon, following older boys on a Sunday, we came to the
cool, deep-flowing Brandywine. I remember the bank, and the pool,
into which I first ventured in deep-running waters—and the nettles
which stung me as I dressed.

This initiation was a preliminary to many a happy Saturday later in
the gorge of the lower Brandywine where, with young du Ponts and

their relatives, we had Hagley dam—its deep waters with a sycamore overhanging for a diving place, its steep rising forests, and its grand slope of swift-breaking current—all a secluded playground of our own. There, all morning, and often all afternoon, we splashed and dove and explored the cool contributory streams. In an old flatboat we dared the racing waters of the dam, bringing up halfway down on a rock with a crash that threw us all overboard; then, with a crowbar, pried our craft up the rocky wall of the race for another ride. Such sunburn! Or we waded precariously down the dam slope, looking for bass to tickle in the crevices, or slid into the great pothole, where, standing shoulder-deep, one's toes felt for nicely rounded stones.

Before this, I had become acquainted with the full length of the river on its western branch up to its retreat in the Welsh Hills. Yet this was only from a window in a car on the Wilmington and Northern, which followed the crooked stream as closely as it could. It was said that at the horseshoe curve at Granogue the two ends of a freight train passed each other so close that the fireman on the engine could hand the morning paper to a brakeman on the caboose! I felt sympathetic with the twitching tail of the train; since, as a small boy, I usually got ill as we entered the Honeybrook hills, and welcomed the sight of the broad valley of the Schuylkill on the other side of the Welsh Hills.

And once I camped, with three other boys equally ignorant of wood-craft, on a meadow below Point Lookout. We shot squirrels, chip-munks, and, I regret to say, robins, with an old muzzle-loading shotgun, which dribbled its shot or knocked us over backward according to the way in which we charged it. Yet we got some game, having brought no other food except some bread, and cooked the fragments in a lard pail until the bottom fell out and quenched our fire. We came nearest then to seeing the Brandywine as young Indians saw it—a larder and place of adventure.

But my intimate knowledge of the whole extent of the middle Brandywine came much later when, with other young men and girls, fond, like Joseph Townsend, of new things, I put a canoe on the Brandywine, at Rockland. Our first canoe house was an old stone barn, where the canoes rested on beams above a manure pile. On an early morning, the obliging farmer would haul them up to a station of the Wilmington and Northern, and by ten o'clock, we accompanying, they would be dumped off at Northbrook, well up on the west branch.

It was the beginning of a good day, to slide the green bodies of the canoes across the soft grass of spring or the slippery autumn turf, and launch them in the little river, which here ran quick and free around sharp meadow curves. At first the skill was to balance nicely as we shot under overhanging banks. But soon the real rapids began, where steering was an art. We know each by name. There was the tree rapid, in which the only solution was to shove powerfully toward a dark tunnel by the right bank where the current had bored a way under the heavy arms of a half-fallen maple. You aimed, you pushed, and then flattened down in the canoe under whips and strokings of the branches. And there was the fish-dam rapid farther down—that very V in which the Indians used to spear their shad. Here there was only one course, and that through the opening at the point of the V; but twenty feet above a cross rock made straight running impossible, even in high water. The knowing canoeist swung right, swung left, and darted through the middle. But often someone overturned.

The day ended with a drift at dusk down Rockland dam between high, wild woods and soft, misty meadows; and, last, a night walk over steep Rockland hill to the waiting trolley. A time for youth!

It was later that I discovered how much the Brandywine had meant to maturer imaginations than those of our canoeists. A descriptive chapter much longer than this one could be written on what might well be called the du Pont Brandywine, which has been kept rural, arboriferous, and beautiful out of love for the land and the stream. And another on the river and woodland reservation left in trust by William Bancroft, which I have already mentioned. But I seem always to have known that the Brandywine was a stream to love. On Sunday afternoons, when I was a child, my father, who was born in sound of the old Great Falls, would take me to our family house, called "Brandywine," and it was part of the ritual to go down through the gardens to the race bank, and try to discover the ruins of the old First Dam. Or if not to "Brandywine," then to the park below our hill, and the dizzy suspension footbridge that crossed to the then wild north bank, where, later, I went bird-nesting on my own. He had some story to tell me of every race, and dam, and fall.

I left the Brandywine country for New England even before my canoeing days, and my later knowledge of the river was a vacation knowledge only. Yet, though I have lived in the Connecticut hills longer than on the Brandywine, I still feel a stir of familiar content when I set foot on the meadows without boulders, see the hills without sharp New England angles, and the deep soil and high, straight hardwood groves of the Brandywine valley. Not England and Scotland are more truly dissimilar than Connecticut and Delaware.

I was translated into New England too early to write the book which, I fear, no one in our time will write about the Brandywine. Someone, someday, I hope, will supplement this history of mine with a book like

White's *Selborne*, or that unassembled one of Thoreau's on Concord, to be found scattered through his Journal. In Thoreau, the rough, tough Concord country, and the soft and languorous Concord River, both so different from the Brandywine, have been given a lifetime of observation and infinite detail. The Brandywine deserves this kind of natural history. Someone will have to spend his days and nights with nature on the river to do it, and both observer and reader will be well rewarded. My task has been both broader and briefer. I offer what could be done by one who, at least, has the river in his imagination, knows all of it a little, much of it well, and has read its records wherever he can find them.

Summer on the Old Farm

SOMETIME IN June, each summer that we lived at the mill, a little furniture, some bedding, clothes, cooking utensils, and the family were loaded onto the lumber wagon, the cow was hitched behind, and we were off to spend six weeks at the old farm on the hill. Many things to live with were left in the old house the year around, so moving to the farm and back was not too great an inconvenience.

I remember, well, the old cord bedsteads with corn-husk filled mattresses and featherbeds on top on which the children slept. The beds were bumpy and uneven, but I do not remember that they were uncomfortable. The bottom tick was filled with carefully dried corn husks and I have heard of mice getting into them with rather exciting results. The beautiful, plump pillows and featherbeds were filled with down and carefully selected feathers plucked from live geese and hens. These tediously prepared items of bedding had been at the old farmhouse for more than one generation, for when carefully cared for, they lasted for years.

Father planted a garden and some crops on the farm and went down to Snowsville every day or two to take care of business at the mill.

At the mill, with so much teaming and log-handling, Mother had to keep a constant lookout for the safety of her children, but on the old farm we could run wild. I am not quite sure why, "Green apples and cherries, look out for your bellies," always brings to mind the cherry tree that grew south of the house, but maybe it is because I "et too many." Wild strawberries on long stems grew in the fields, red and black raspberries covered the stone walls, and large fuzzy cap-like berries, which we called mulberries, were found on our explorations up the road that led over the mountain to Connecticut Corners.

There was a big yard east of the house which was cropped close by the sheep pastured there, and this was the place of baseball games and horseshoe pitching when the relatives came for picnics. There must have been excitement to watch and hear, for I remember being cautioned that the words, "By Gosh!" were too big for a boy of my size to use. In the center of the yard was a flat rock where Father touched off the Fourth-of-July fireworks.

Almost every summer, Mother's sisters and their families came to stay for short vacations. The older children never tired of exploring the old house and the most daring used to get into the space between the partitions and the big square chimney and go completely around it. Walter Kerwin got wedged in there once and Aunt Cassie, his mother, nearly had hysterics before he finally wriggled loose.

A long time before we lived there, the highway had passed directly by the house, and parallel stone walls led down the hill to the brook. The nursery rhyme, "Baa, baa, black sheep," has always had a special appeal to me, for this old road with the stone walls was the "lane," the sheep were there even to the "black one," and I was the "little boy."

Several times during the summer an all-day trip was made to Grandfather Butterfield's home in Roxbury. This meant extra hustling around in the morning, for the ten mile trip over Cram Hill required about three hours each way. Father was up early to do the chores and to feed and curry the horses so that they would be ready to hitch to the surrey right after breakfast. Helen and Leonard, who were the oldest, took turns sitting in front with Father and the smaller children rode in the middle, for their short legs didn't reach the floor and at the steep or bumpy places they needed help to stay on the slippery leather seats. These were happy days, for going to Roxbury to see Grandfather and Aunt Mary and to watch the trains rushing through Roxbury was one of the high spots of our simple way of life.

The steep hill down to West Brookfield from the farm had to be taken at a walk, but when almost at the bottom Father would let the horses trot down the last little grade, across the stone bridge that spanned the brook and up the rise at the other side. We always sang a big bumpy "Ah-h-h-h," as the horses started to trot and this reached a shout as we crossed the bridge with the horses almost at a run.

The road turns left toward the mountain just beyond the bridge and for a few rods follows the brook where it babbles through a sunny level pasture. Then the valley narrows abruptly and the road becomes more steep and the brook more noisy. But, as the woods grow dense farther up the mountain, the brook seems to gradually grow more quiet as if awed by the towering trees, until at the summit there is neither brook nor its music.

The slow pace of the farm horses was ideal for observation and quick young eyes could see many of Mother Nature's smaller folk who made their homes on Cram Hill. Robins and woodpeckers and crows were friendly, and there was an old owl that roosted on a dead tree at the top of the mountain. Red squirrels and chipmunks scampered across the road ahead of the horses and sometimes we would catch a glimpse of a weasel or a fox. Woodchucks ran for their holes as we approached and once or twice we saw hedgehogs waddling off into the brush at the side of the road.

The thunder of a partridge taking to the air from a spot close to the wagon was startling and we were a little frightened by the cry of the hawk soaring high above, for Mother told us that he was flying up there until his keen eyes saw some small thing that he could pounce upon for his dinner. A pretty sight that we watched from a little distance was a mother skunk and her babies moving in a little procession up the ditch at the side of the road.

Halfway up the hill, Father stopped to water his horses at the same water-trough where I met Mr. and Mrs. Cram so many years afterward. The water came from a spring above the road and we would hold a cup under the wooden spout and each take his turn at drinking the sparkling cold water. I wonder if anyone who has not held a cup under such a primitive spout has a full appreciation of the gift of running water. I am sure that we were aware of the beauty that was all around us as we crossed the hill, for there was a little song that we used to sing every time we passed under a tree that bent over the road. All that I remember of it now are the final words, "red and gold and purple arching overhead."

When the summit was reached, we knew that it would not be too long before we reached Grandfather's for the descent to the Roxbury valley was quickly made. From Johnnycake Flat to the village the road was almost beside the railroad, and sometimes we had to wait for a train at one of the crossings. We must have gone that way to Grandfather's for Thanksgiving at least once, for the picture brought to me by, "over the white and drifted snow," is a gray horse hitched to a sleigh waiting at the railroad crossing at Johnnycake Flat.

When we finally reached Grandfather's house, Aunt Mary's pantry was the first attraction. There was a round wooden box where Aunt Mary kept her cookies, sometimes ginger snaps, sometimes white cookies with caraway seeds in them, but the best ones were the light brown cookies with a hump in the middle filled with jelly. My wife, who is an excellent cook, laughs at me when I tell her that the texture of Aunt Mary's filled cookies was different than that of any cookie I have tasted since. I wish that I had the recipe so that I could share it with you.

We all had been well coached in regard to eating at Grandfather Butterfield's for he was a stern disciplinarian and expected children to behave at all times, and at the table, perfectly. We were to sit with folded hands until everyone was served, say, "Please," and "Thank you," nicely and eat without slobbering. Conversation at the table was for grown-ups and a child was not to speak unless he was addressed directly.

At home, Mother used an oil-cloth on the table for "every day" and bibs were tied around our necks, but at Aunt Mary's the table was covered with a beautiful linen tablecloth that hung off the edges of the table into our laps, and napkins two feet square were pinned around our necks, covering us almost completely. Aunt Mary had a set of big blue dinner plates with pictures of important government and historical buildings, the Capitol, White House, Independence Hall, and the others, a full dozen, and I learned to recognize and name them all long before I ever went to school, in fact we used to ask Aunt Mary to put special plates at our places at the table. I remember, too, that cranberry sauce and honey were served in fancy round glass dishes. These were excellent meals, for Aunt Mary as a cook left little to be desired, but it was always a big relief to hear the words, "Children, you may be excused."

We loved Aunt Mary, Mother's old maid sister who kept house for Grandfather, for she was fat and jolly and always made a special effort to entertain us. There were toys stored away that she would bring out for us to play with, including a big box of blocks and a double-twelve set of dominoes that had been there since Uncle Henry's boyhood. Aunt Mary's hair was thin and she pulled it back tightly into a pug on the back of her head, and when she rubbed her face against yours it pricked, for she had a heavy black beard and had to shave every day like a man.

Aunt Mary was always talking about some new project that she was going into to make a lot of money, like raising chickens or squabs or Chinchilla rabbits. But these ideas never came to anything, for when, her housework done and the house in spotless order, she sat down in her rocking chair by the sunny window in the sitting room to read or sew, in a very few minutes the paper or sewing would fall to the floor, her head would go back against the cushion of the high-backed chair, her mouth would fall loosely open, and she would start quietly to snore.

After dinner, Mother would make a few calls on old neighbors and Father would go to the depot with Grandfather to see what was going on and to listen to talk about current happenings on the railroad. But long before sunset, Aunt Mary would give us milk and bread and jam sandwiches, Father would hitch up the horses and we would be off for home. Sometimes we went by way of the four-mile-woods, where the road was just a wood-road with grass in the middle all the way, and one time we were caught in a thunder-storm and stopped under the shed of an old logging camp until the rain was over.

By the time we reached West Brookfield it was dark, and the chatter which had been kept up all day was silent. As the horses climbed the hill up to the farm, there was only the muffled sound of their hoofs in the soft dirt, with now and then a quiet word from Father or Mother as the children slept, snuggling against them. Arriving at the farm, Father lifted down those who were awake enough to walk, and carried the others into the house where Mother soon had us all in bed and fast asleep.

Mill and Village

THE LOCATION OF East Braintree was determined by the falls in Ayer's Brook which provided power for the mill. A wooden dam was thrown across the brook, and at the time of my earliest recollection a good-sized pond extended several hundred feet upstream. A heavily timbered flume, large enough to permit a man to go through it, carried the water from the pond, under the road and the millyard to the turbine. I remember about the flume in particular, for once the pond was drained for inspection and repair of the flume. When Father and a helper went into the tunnel, they gathered up big pails of suckers which had been left stranded when the water drained out.

Included in purchase of the East Braintree mill was the abandoned, tumbledown mill at West Brookfield with its site and water rights. I once went there with Father and saw the old overshot water wheel and the up-and-down saw, and I remember how he pointed out that the saw marks on boards sawed here would be straight instead of the curved marks made by the circular saw of the East Braintree mill. In Aunt Jane Wellington's house were pine floor boards more than twenty inches wide which were sawed, without doubt, by the up-and-down saw at the Meadow.

When the farmers brought their milk each morning to the creamery which was across the road from the mill, they brought yellow flint corn, oats and barley to be ground. Provender, made from corn and oats ground together, was a standard horse feed, and ground barley was used in dairy rations and as a hog feed. The grain was poured into a huge square hopper above the granite millstones and a series of elevators and chutes carried the ground grain to bins for storage or bagging.

There was a bolt, a large eight-sided cloth covered drum, for making flour, but I doubt if father ever used it for making wheat flour. India wheat flour, however, was made at this mill as late as 1910. Father packed his winter apples in barrels with India Wheat hulls, a practice that approached modern insulating and refrigeration. In the grist mill were a small hand-operated corn sheller and special machines for making cracked corn and corn-cob meal in which the cobs were ground with the kernels.

Grinding was paid for in money or by giving the miller a share of the grain. The miller's portion of the grain was stored and sold with bran, cottonseed meal and other commercial feeds. The grist mill was operated on a year-around basis for little water was required for power, but the saw mill needed a good pond full of water and the heaviest part of this work was done in the spring freshet period.

Father bought some logs outright and took others as pay for sawing. His biggest customer was the partnership of Mann and Richmond who owned a large acreage in the Four Mile Woods area. With the first good sledding the logs started to arrive, and before spring they were piled high entirely around the house, with only a roadway left to drive into the barn and a walk from the road to the front door. A half-million board feet was considered a good spring's sawing.

In this enterprise, Mother was the bookkeeper and attended to all financial matters including paying bills and paying the help. Some men didn't like the idea of dealing with a woman, but when Father said that "The Mrs." would take care of a matter, it was handled that way. "Bert" Farnsworth built a reputation for honest dealing and from many sources in later years I heard the comment, "His word was as good as his bond."

It was necessary to extend some credit. There were some bills that were not paid promptly, but these were owed by Father's neighbors and he did not press them too hard for settlement, for he knew their circumstances.

There was one barn at Randolph Center that Mother said belonged partly to her because the lumber was never paid for in full. Another bill was paid many years afterward by one farmer because he knew that mother needed the money to raise her family. But the strangest episode was when mother received, in 1937, a letter from Henry Hyzer, who was then in Florida, reading as follows, "I have joined Father Devine's cult and his first requirement is that we pay every bill that we owe. I never quite finished paying Bert for those shingles and enclose money order for five dollars in settlement." More than thirty years had elapsed since the purchase of the shingles, and if Mr. Hyzer remembered the bill after all those years, how often in the interim he must have been troubled by the thought of this small obligation.

Mother was a busy woman, even with a hired girl to help when work was heaviest. Her four sons were born, Leonard in 1897, Russell in 1900, Alton in 1902 and Everett in 1904. Still there was time to enjoy life in the simple, unsophisticated way of the rural village of those days before the automobile came. The neighbors were good folks, intelligent and for the most part, thrifty. There were the Blanchards, the Flints, the Hutchinsons, the Thayers, the Dibbles, the Stowes, the Manns and the Martins, each name bringing to mind some particular characteristic or anecdote, people of a common background and common purpose, good neighbors.

George Thayer was a plumber, if I remember correctly, Mr. McIntire

The Notch House in the White Mountains, New Hampshire, 1853.

was the village blacksmith and required a helper in his shop. There were quite a number of the village men who worked out by the day, changing occupations with the seasons, lumbering in the winter, working at the mill in the spring, doing farm work during the haying and threshing seasons, sometimes just playing checkers. One dollar, with dinner furnished, was good pay for a ten hour day. George Sumner was the buttermaker in the creamery and Byron Wakefield was a harnessmaker in addition to being the village undertaker.

This reminds me that in a small building just beyond the church was kept the town hearse. This was an ornamental vehicle with two sets of undercarriages, wheels for summer and light sleds for winter. Due to lack of use or lack of care on the part of the selectmen, a minor catastrophe occurred one day, when on the way to the cemetery following the funeral for a resident, the sleds collapsed and a box sleigh had to be pressed into service to complete the trip.

There were a half-dozen Blanchard families and it was said that when it was desirable for the entire clan to get together, Wallace Blanchard would go up on the hill back of his place and make the announcement to the Blanchards within the sound of his voice. Such was his vocal equipment that at the appointed hour every Blanchard from up and down the valley would show up at the rendezvous.

Watson Banister was a man who peppered his cider and after more than moderate indulgence was said to have explained that, "he didn't care so much about the cider as he did about the pepper, 'Twas kinda warmin'." Though not a recognized member of the bar, Mr. Banister was known as a practical adviser in legal matters and a champion of the under-dog, quite a man for digging up facts that were helpful to a man in a tight place. His clients, if such you could call them, paid him little for his service, but many sought him for his homely, practical advice.

Uncle Guy Clough organized a group of citizens and built the Clough telephone line, and from that day communication was no longer dependent upon the legs of a man or a horse. Each telephone subscriber was required to build and maintain a mile of poles and wire in addition to a monthly fee. Mail was brought from Randolph once each day by two-horse stage. Wallace Peavey, who drove the stage when I first knew about it, delivered the mail to post offices at East Braintree and West Brookfield, carried passengers and some lighter freight. For carrying the mail on the route from Randolph to West Brookfield, he received approximately ten dollars a week, additional income depending upon his own enterprise.

Eusebe Simonds was Wallace Peavey's mother-in-law and was an old lady when I was born. Mrs. Simonds had married when she was very young and was widowed within a year or two after her marriage, leaving her with a daughter. She was a school teacher and greatly admired by all who knew her and although her hand was sought by many men who would have wed her, she remained true to her deceased young husband to the end of her days. I remember the story of one of her admirers even though I shall have to substitute a name instead of the true one. In going " 'cross lots" over the mountain from the Roxbury valley, where he lived, to East Braintree to call on the lady, this man became lost in the woods and a searching party was sent out to find him. It is related that his rescuer finally reached him by following the sound of the suitor's voice, shouting again and again,

> "I'm lost, Oh, I'm lost,
> My name is Myron Freeman
> And I'm courtin' Seeby Simonds,
> And I'm lost!"

Across the bridge from the mill stood the home of George Flagg, Civil War veteran, ex-professional wrestler, and proprietor of the sales and livery stable that served very much the same purpose at that time as the automobile salesroom and service station do today, for away from the railroad, horses provided the only means of travel and transportation.

Mr. Flagg was a giant of a man with a great booming voice, and one of my earliest memories is his greeting heard through half of the village, "Here come the boys from across the bridge!" In his stables were fine Clydesdales and Percherons, brought from the West in carload lots to sell to local farmers and lumbermen. Anyone coming to the village left his team at Mr. Flagg's to be fed and cared for, while his own needs were provided for at the little hotel across the road.

In the shade of the north side of Mr. Flagg's barn, unemployed men of the village and farmers, in no hurry to get home after bringing their milk to the creamery, whiled away many a summer hour pitching horseshoes, but in colder weather the blacksmith shop and Uncle Elbert's store offered more comfortable hospitality. These things I know are true, for after his shouted greeting Mr. Flagg always gave us pennies which were straightway spent at the store for sticks of paraffin gum in striped wrappers with frilled and twisted ends.

Miss Locke's

THE FARMHOUSE INTO which Miss Locke led us was built by her father, Charles Russell Locke, about 1850 on the old Locke place known as Maple Grove. Miss Ellen, the sixth of seven children, told us she could remember when it was built. We followed her into the entry that opened from the side porch where she had greeted us, through the door at the right and into the sitting room. There we first smelled that smell that meant we had arrived. I don't know what made it, but earth cellar, wood smoke, and fir balsam were in it, and old house and new mown hay.

To our right as we stepped through the entry door was a sofa under the window looking onto the porch. In the corner at the head of the sofa an old secretary, half desk half bookcase, held the red-covered register with the names of all the boarders who came year after year. High up on top sat a stuffed owl with wide staring eyes. On a round, brown velvet-covered table between the two front windows were a large kerosene lamp, some books, and an album with photographs of Miss Locke's family. To our left stood a Franklin stove where open fires burned cheerily on cold August evenings. A door beyond the stove opened into the dining room, which extended across the whole back half of the main house. Next to the wall opposite the sofa was another table. On it were a box of double pictures and a stereoscope to look at them with. The two pictures were supposed to look like one, but I could never make them because my eyes didn't focus together. After I had my crossed eye operated on, the oculist had me look at a bird with one eye and a cage with the other and then try to put the bird in the cage, but I never could. Beside the table with the pictures was the door into the front hall. We went through it now, following Miss Locke.

I looked out the open front door, across the granite door stone, to the two-chaired swing, the road, the hay field, and Mt. Will beyond. The door to the bedroom opposite the sitting room was closed. Mother had had that room when Ellie was a baby, but now we all went up the carpeted stairs with the mahogany banister and newel post. I noticed that one of the white upright supports about two-thirds of the way upstairs was still missing and remembered how a year or two before Mother, always a good sport, had taken a dare that she couldn't get through the narrow space where the stake was missing. She went through feet first from the stairway and won the dare but had a large black and blue spot to pay for it.

Upstairs, I found that I was to have my old room on the northwest corner of the main house, over the dining room. Mother's room was opposite it on the southwest corner. Three of us girls were in my room, Pauline and Ellie with me this time. Helen and Phyllis would be in the ell bedroom.

As Miss Locke left us, I saw that the doors of the two front corner rooms were closed. I knew who was in them but would have to wait until supper time to see some of our special friends. I was almost afraid to go into my room lest something might be changed. But it was always the same. There were the two beds in the opposite corners, one double and one single, and the same bureau in the corner between the windows, with three big drawers, one for each of us. We always said the littlest one should have the bottom drawer, so Ellie got it. On the bureau, covered by a white linen scarf, were the kerosene lamp with its box of matches at one end, and at the other a nosegay of red and white sweet peas, a sign that Aunt Abbie had been there. She always put fresh flowers in the rooms of new arrivals. Between the single bed and the door of the hall was the same commode with the large white bowl and the pitcher full of cold water, the tooth brush mug and the soap dish, the clean towels on the rack at the side, the slop jar close by, and in the closet underneath the necessary chamber pot. There was no modern plumbing at Miss Locke's. Near the foot of the double bed was the door into the closet. The floor was covered with the same gray-brown carpet with red figures, and in front of the west window was the same little red rocking-chair.

The men brought up the trunks then and put one in Mother's room and one in ours, under the north window between the double bed and the bureau. After they had loosened the strap, I knelt upon the trunk and looked out of the window. Through the grove of maples I could see the outline of the wash house by the brook and farther up the road, beyond the willow picture-frame tree, could catch a glimpse of the Godwin place. The Godwins took boarders, too. Sometimes when Miss Locke's was very crowded, some of her boarders slept up there. At most Miss Locke could accommodate about forty, but as a rule we were between thirty and thirty-five. Nearer the house I could see the road that led up from the hay field to the back door of the barn. Out that window everything was the same. I hurried over to the west window by the little red rocking-chair and peered out through the adjustable screen. Up under the eaves were the same, or what seemed the same, huge old spiders. Along the outer side of the woodshed was the covered Ladies' Walk which led to the two large double privies. Morning glories were climbing up the criss-crossed lattice work which protected the walk. Beyond I could see the currant bushes by the brook and the steep hillside leading up to Bald Rock.

I knew I should be washing off the train soot before supper, but until Frank brought up the hot water, I had to look around again at the old familiar sights. Frank had come to live with Miss Locke when I was nine. He was about my age, one of five children whose mother and father had died of pneumonia within a week of each the winter before. Until he came Miss Locke had lived alone in the winter since her sister, Miss Phila, had died. Miss Phila was ten years older than Miss Ellen. She had lived in Illinois for some time, but after their parents' death she came home and with Miss Ellen carried on the family custom of taking summer boarders. Two of their brothers fought in the Civil War and both settled in Nebraska afterwards. A third brother died when he was a baby. Two sisters were married. Susan, three years older than Miss Ellen, married John Henry Douglass. I remember that the summer I was two or three their daughter, Henrietta, was a table girl at Miss Locke's. We have a picture of her ringing the big dinner bell on the farmhouse steps and of old Shep howling as he always did when the bell rang. The youngest sister, Elizabeth, married Charles F. Sargent of Lewiston.

In the early days when Miss Phila and Miss Ellen took boarders together, Miss Ellen did the outside work of the farm and took care of the animals. Miss Phila looked after the work in the house. From the time my family had known the place, however, Miss Ellen had managed everything herself. During the summer she had a man to do the barn work and drive the horses, with an extra man engaged for haying, one or two chambermaids, several table girls, and a cook. I remember best the tremendously stout but excellent cook, Gertrude Demeritt. She lived in a house opposite the mill yard near the post office. Every night at dusk her father came up in a buggy to drive her home. Then after her father died, she married Mr. Hobbs, who was Miss Locke's barn man during the last years. They both lived then in the house that had been Gertrude's home. I shall never forget Gertie's delicious soups, or crisp raised rolls for breakfast baked in gem pans, or lemon sponge pie, or caramel ice cream. After Frank came, besides helping with the barn chores and getting the cows, he used to carry around cans of hot water in the morning and before supper.

Still waiting for the hot water, I dashed across into Mother's room for a minute to look out her south window at the cottage, approached by a board walk from the driveway. I remembered that snakes sometimes lived under that walk. The cottage was a three story building with a wide porch across the front and one side. In the parlor were a Franklin stove, a piano, and several tables and chairs. All the rest of the building contained bedrooms. Now I could see people sitting on the porch all ready and waiting for one of the table girls to come out on the farmhouse porch and ring the big supper bell. Although Mother told me I'd better go now and tidy up, I couldn't resist one look out her west window. Below me was the back porch outside the kitchen, one end of which was glassed in and used by Miss Locke as her office. Beyond stretched the long row of sheds, containing the wood shed, the workshop where Frank did his "tinkering," the wagon shed, the milk room, the ice house in which ice cut the winter before was kept in sawdust and used for making the Thursday and Sunday ice cream, and finally, joining the last shed, the big red barn itself on a little rise.

There was Miss Locke now on the back porch with her black and white cat, Alfred. As she talked with someone I couldn't see, she caressed Alfred in his favorite fashion by picking him up and setting him down by his tail. That method had been used so much that the hair near the tip of his tail was worn off. Miss Locke always had time to caress Alfred or talk to anyone who wanted to see her. Her one concern was to help people have a good time. If they were happy and having fun, she didn't care what they did. The boarders who came, as we did, year after year she considered her family. My father liked to tell a story about Miss Locke. He had come unexpectedly one summer and alone, after the rest of us had gone home, and was given a room in the cottage. Very tired, he lay down for a nap before supper and slept until nearly ten o'clock. He was hungry then and thought he would go over to the farmhouse to see if he could find anything to eat. There in the kitchen was Miss Locke waiting for him with supper she had kept hot. "I knew you didn't come over for supper," she said, "and thought you'd be hungry before you went to bed."

Now Mother said I must go. But before I went back to my room, I had to take one quick look along the corridor of the ell. Its two windows looked over towards the cottage, and at the far end a stairway led down to the kitchen and out to the Ladies' Walk. From the corridor opened two bedrooms, one of which two of us girls sometimes had. I remember sleeping in it only once, the summer we girls gave up our big room to Mother's friend, Mrs. Cook. She had come unexpectedly and wasn't going to stay if she could have only the little front hall bedroom because she thought her husband might join her later. Miss Locke sometimes slept in one of the ell bedrooms, but if the house was full, she went up to the little room on the third floor under the eaves, which she called her hole. She never went to bed at night until she was sure all the lights were out. There were two other bedrooms in the attic and a closet in which boarders who came every year stored some of the things such as hammocks and tennis racquets that they didn't want to take away with them. The summer after Miss Locke died one of the boarders came to get some things he had stored there. Among his things Frank spied a tennis racquet with the initials P.N.C. on it. It belonged to my sister Phyllis and would have gone if Frank hadn't rescued it.

As I finally turned back to my room, knowing it was after six and I really must hurry now, Helen and Phyllis were coming out of their room in the ell. "You'll be late for supper," Helen said. "You haven't even washed the train dirt off your face yet. What have you been doing?" I ran on without answering her, but I knew what I had been doing. I had been reassuring myself that nothing at Miss Locke's had changed. Pauline and Ellie had gone down and not left much hot water for me. But with the room to myself I now lost no time. Quickly I washed my face and hands, brushed my hair, and tightened my hair ribbons. When the supper bell began to ring at half past six, I rushed downstairs, through the sitting room, and joined the rest of the family and the other boarders as they filed through the screen door into the dining room. Then I first realized that I was hungry.

Cedar River, Maine

WHEN THE SUN comes to Cedar River, it comes over the ridges to the east and it seems happy to be back for another day. When the sun sets, it tears itself to shreds in its disappointment. It casts colored glory across the tops of the trees. Then it retires and sulks its way around the rest of the world while it makes itself presentable for one more gift of its gleam to Cedar River.

Just before the light fades, the outlines of Deer Mountain become distinct, clean, and stern, a reminder that much rock must crumble before the earth is destroyed. This is a solace to the Cedar River people. They seldom look, they seldom observe, but they know that the mountain is there, and the mountain is a comfort. The shadows it casts are caves of retreat.

There is a solace also in the river flow. The river moves, yet the river stays. It is there, but it has passed. A man cannot step into the same river twice. The man changes and the river changes. Only change is constant. Change is eternal. Thus change differs from Cedar River, for Cedar River comes and goes. The years of its being are vague and its presence is uncertain.

Cedar River people have always been more undecided than Hamlet about whether to be or not to be. Their ancestors built them a town in a hidden land that was mostly gravel and river and ledges and ridges and hills. Sometimes the people grow weary of the need to force growth from seeds sown on a rock, and they retreat from reality. Thus they are not there when the census taker comes and their town torments the topographers.

But, usually, strangers who penetrate the ridge-clinging clouds are permitted to see what they are capable of seeing. Surprisingly, some strangers earn themselves a place in heaven by refusing to go back downriver and announce that they have discovered the origins of fantasy. They see, but they stay silent. They deserve the bliss of the blessed.

Other strangers, however, look at the froth instead of the ferment. They leave town quickly, fearful of being contaminated by the obvious stupidity, backwardness, and scorned simplicity. They never find Cedar River again, but they use the name of the village as a reference in some related travelogue, probably as the location of an adventure which is a big lie.

These people are more lied to than lying. The biggest lie of all is the lie that the surface of Cedar River tells such scorners. Because Cedar River, of course, has no simplicity. Simplicity is the one thing it never had. Simplicity cannot live with vagueness. Simplicity must be bounded.

And the boundaries of Cedar River are undefined. The woods intrude on the settlement and the settlement intrudes on the woods. Sometimes a man will go to his hayfield and find that the spruces have sprouted since the last cutting. Sometimes the deer will seek out a beech grove and find that someone has taken fifty or sixty thousand feet of logs and a winter's warmth, and the slash lies scattered.

Neither change is really a hardship. Hay gets increasingly unwanted as the tractors roar. There are other beeches and the beech trash will rot quickly, fast rot being a characteristic of beeches. Big bursting raspberries and tender hardwood sprouts will fill the cutover grove in a few years, feeding deer and bears and providing raspberry pies.

It may be the mingling of men and the wild things along the vague lines which separate the natural from the semi-controlled that has kept the Cedar River people from conforming to the patterned lives of the down river world.

Patterns are possible where a factory is a factory and an office is an office, hot in summer, cooler in winter, but an entity of sameness, in the same place, with the same contours.

But patterns become distorted where a different trail leads every season into a different woods and where even the purpose of the trail changes with the weather and the wind.

In the winter, the snow stretches on each side of the trampled route. In the spring, that route is forbidden because of the freshets and the swamps, but the diversion is among new flowers and the smell of growth. In the fall, there may be no trail at all, but only a wary walking and watching for fallen branches that will crack and warn the quarry.

In the winter the cold is a stimulant in the morning and a challenging enemy at night. In the summer the heat floats with the smell of sunbaked down timber, a separate smell for each species. The spring woods are friendly with fragrance of a headier kind. In the fall the sun grows more valuable and there is a sense of coming quietness.

So time has so many divisions that only two are important. There is daylight which permits certain activities. There is darkness which encourages others. Both are needful and both can be enjoyed. Years as years mean nothing. Years are relative. They are remembered only by events, and those events local.

Last Sunday was long ago and forty years ago was the day before yesterday. This confuses visitors because it confuses chronology. Cedar River doesn't care. By next week, Cedar River may have decided not to exist, but in a month it may change its mind.

Thus all that counts is what happened within the interest circle of the town. Dates are numbers to be written in a book and the book put away.

What matters is that Thomas Webster came home two years before Andy Parsons, stung by a trading defeat, took physical work with my uncle Tom, and got hemlock festered and died. That was the same year that Randy Gage hung himself, and it was just after that year that Uncle Oscar set his underwear on fire, and that was about six months or six weeks or six days after Zeke Benson tried to fly off the barn roof. Uncle Jake got the frogs in his stomach about two years later, because Doc Yates was the first one to tell about Susan going to church with the mice in her hat.

And all these things depended on each other and yet none of them had any relationship except the relationship of time and town, and neither time nor town had any real meaning or importance except in casual talk while the men whittled gouges out of the Post Office steps.

"Do you remember when Tom Rogers shot Brent Moore?"

"I was thinking about the Caruthers' windmill."

"When was that?"

"Seems as though it was the fall after the Square Eddy jam."

"It was before that. I'll tell you when it was. When was the fire in the hotel garage?"

"I don't know. They were logging at Burnt Creek—that's how I remember that."

"Well, then, it was the same summer we skidded Minnie."

"No, No, No, No."

Memories are not neat like an orderly classroom full of Mrs. Kelly's scholars. Memories are jumbled in a bureau drawer with a covering of folded handkerchiefs, placed just so, in order that a burglar looking for money will know that the housewife is tidy.

Impressions of a burglar are important.

Defiance of logic, yet with a logic that is local; realization that error is the usual result of effort and that results may be causeless or controlled by the unseen; scoffing at superstition that returns in the night, acceptance of moods; those are the characteristics of Cedar River, disorganized in its being, capricious in its existence, unconcerned wth its chances for glory.

Glory is winged and so are angels. Neither could land in the river grove. Yet both would be helped down off the mountain and given a room for the night and referred to in the same terms as a kind stranger who promised not to tell where he had been.

The room would have modern plumbing, the mark of Wilmer Hobber. Wilmer came to Cedar River twenty years ago, or maybe thirty years ago, or maybe ten years ago. He came the year after Cousin Susan married the short order cook who was married many times already. That was the same year that my cousin Paul ran across the field in hunting season with a pair of antlers tied to his head. Not one of the city hunters shot at Paul, and Paul collected seven bets in marbles, jack-knives, and fish hooks.

He also collected a few welt-raising wallops from Uncle Waldron, who tempted fate all the time but believed he was unique in the alacrity of his avoidance.

Later that same day, two sheep were sacrificed on the hillside and brought into town on a Detroit built altar, four hunters claiming them as Caribou and two insisting that they were musk oxen. The Canadian Club advertising agency did not welcome the heroes with cameras and a bolstering beverage, which was just as well because they had visited my uncle Oscar the evening before and had been bolstered to their bottoms.

One of the hunters had a hole in his hat.

The fine was one hundred dollars. That was a small sum compared to the price the glum group later paid Deak Trembley for the sheep. The sheep would have been startled had they been able to hear the recitation of their virtues and their pedigrees, being accustomed to being addressed by their owner as, "stupid, stubborn, cross-eyed, mongrel bastards."

Glory to the guns. Mighty is their range and varied are their targets and startling is the bzzt of their bullets past the ears of the loggers.

And glory to Wilmer Hobber, the prophet of plumbing, even though Wilmer vulgarized our language. People now speak casually of going to the toilet. In gentler times, folks used "Facilities."

Wilmer changed that. I'm glad he did.

I was downriver awhile back and a man spoke jeeringly of conservative notions, bred in a conservative economy. He spoke in favor of progress, which I consider mostly a problem. He said he didn't want to go back. He was in love with his washer, his drier, his con-

ditioner of air, his mixer and his muddler and his spongy synthetic
softness, wall to wall, immune to sinful stains except for the un-
avoidable piddling of his Pekingese.

"Years ago," he said, "people had iceboxes with big pans under
them and the pans had to be emptied or else the water ran out on the
floor. Think of the inconvenience of that. I didn't like my grandfather's farm. . . . I didn't like . . . I didn't like . . ."

I didn't like him. I suspected his grandfather's farm didn't like him,
either. I wondered if he had tried to find that farm lately. Farms have
a way of disappearing in the growing pines when there is no caretaker
left for whom they care.

But I sat quietly and I thought of the inconvenience of an icebox. I
sat quietly . . . quietly . . . for there was no urge in me to be singled
out for sarcasm. The inconvenience of an icebox . . . yes . . . inconvenience . . . yes.

The ice was heavy and the sawdust stuck. The lift was high and the
cakes were slippery and my front teeth went when the tongs slipped.
My father bought me a bridge, but the abutments wore out. My
partial plate flew to the timekeeper's lap, during my oratorical outburst
in a school debate. Mrs. Kelly clobbered me because she said that
Cranston would never have been given the decision if the bicuspids
hadn't bounced.

She said, "Had I wanted a comedian to defend the Volstead Act,
I would have picked Casimer and let him tell his story of Pat and
the apple pie."

But an icehouse was a lovely place to play, for young and old. It
was cool and dark and the sawdust was dry on top. The eight and
ten year olds could rest and hide in the acrid dimness at any time of day,
but in the evenings the sixteen year olds and their giggling girl friends
insisted on solitude, not being interested in the comments of the
young.

The source of the ice was a setting for romance. Even the icebox was better than the pundit's picture. We didn't have any pan to
empty. My father drilled a hole in the floor.

I couldn't tell that to the mocking modernist. He would have said,
"Why didn't your cellar fill up with water?" We didn't have a cellar.
I couldn't have said that either. He would have said, "With no cellar,
why didn't your plumbing freeze?"

Bless the logical. It exposes flaws. We didn't have any cellar and
our plumbing didn't freeze because we had no plumbing.

Bless Wilmer Hobber who came at some unknown time with a
truckload of fixtures, bought when the Cranston Commercial House

was torn down. There is a mark on time. There is a definiteness. The Commercial House was torn down twenty years after it was modernized and it was modernized just eighteen years before my cousin Paul bought the hardware store and started charging folks for things they hadn't bought. That should date Wilmer's coming to the satisfaction of any historian.

The Commercial House fixtures were well preserved. Wilmer brought us corner lavatories and hopper toilets and bathtubs on claw cast feet. Deak Trembley didn't want a bathroom but he bought a lavatory, anyway. He said it was just the thing for a horse trough in his box stall. It was perfect for four years until a new horse ate the stopper, which suddenly stopped the horse.

But most of the plumbing served better than that. It was at least an improvement, I suppose, over facilities.

Our facilities at home were at the back of the woodshed and the woodshed broke a forty acre stretch of field where the wind was unimpeded. Anyone who used the facilities brought in an armful of wood. Wood was the excuse. The need for wood justified the visit, removing the need to state the purpose.

But the wind blew hard across the field and Cedar River comment sometimes forgot the dainty in deference to jokes.

If the kitchen were full of people and a lightly built woman looked and said, "I think you need some more wood," and rose to go, some happy man in tune with nature would reply, "I beg your pardon, please, but that wind is blowing strong and if I were you, I'd pick up the wood FIRST."

Harsh was the humor, uncaring of convention. The earth seemed always close, and seems close still. The dust of the ground filters down into the tops of boots and the stains of the soil are often the forerunners of procreation. Nature marks her own. Even the stories concur.

And the stories breed belief. A man who lives in Cedar River is not easily startled by tales from the outside. He believes as he expects belief. Thus he is called gullible.

Cedar River believes stories about shrewd traders because Andy Parsons lived in Cedar River, and Andy could start down the road any old morning with a handful of turnip seed and end up in town with two crates of eggs and a spring lamb.

Uncle Oscar could arrive similarly laden, but Uncle Oscar wouldn't have been trading. Uncle Oscar would have been finding things where they weren't lost.

The story of the man who built a boat in the cellar would have seemed like idle tea-gossip to Cedar River, because Joe Caruthers once put a mail order manure spreader together in his living room and everyone in town made a suggestion about the next step. Joe's solution was the simplest one offered. He ran the wagon tongue out the window and hooked a skidding team to it and pulled the whole business right on through the side of the house, spreading lath, splinters, and plaster for fifty feet.

There was a fringe benefit. Joe got some lime in his garden.

Outsiders misunderstand. The hired comedian at the Ladies' Aid Benefit show told about a farmer who hung a tuning fork beside his cow a month before calving time and got a heifer that bawled in true "G."

Nobody laughed. Everybody believed it. After all, Jonas P. Hall played the violin to his kitten every night, and when the kitten turned into a cat and went courting, he had his pick of the fence felines because he could sit on the roof of the woodshed and work his way through the whole chorus of "Ramona."

Exaggeration must be a comparative. A town must be what its people are or what they would have been had they chosen to exist at the time when the observations were made. A town must be people and memories. That's what Cedar River is. That's what Lieutenant Jenks understood and what Lyman never would be capable of learning.

People, that's what Cedar River displays and shields, Gages and Caruthers, Jenkins, Reynolds, Halls—Fishbait Olson—Uncle Jake—men who wish and men who work and men who just don't give a damn—women, longing sometimes for romance, and sometimes shucking off the offered need.

Uncle Oscar's still, provider of too potent bliss, is gone. It went with drama stern enough to interest Hollywood except that Hollywood believes that nothing really worthy of its time takes place, or ever did, across a line just east of Kansas.

Andy Caruthers and I smashed the still with an axe. We knew that what we did was good and yet we lingered. We only put poor Uncle Oscar brewing batches in a crock, mild potions made of old potato skins and prunes and yeast and peaches. We didn't stop the message . . . the hint for health for all.

"If I was you, I'd just remember it's the bugs that brings diseases on. Don't never drink unless you're sure that what you're drinking will kill bugs."

That's Uncle Oscar speaking. He takes his own advice.

Cedar River doesn't worry. That may be the only thing a viewer needs to see. That may explain emergence and retreat.

The outside world fears war and lack of hygiene. The outside world fears psycho signs and sudden death.

Cedar River speaks of war, but war is vague.

"What the Hell? We had some wars before. We sent our men and most come back. We got a monument beside the river."

The quoted man is Jesse Hill. He went to war in nineteen seventeen. He now confuses war with American Legion Conventions at Atlantic City. He dreads the thought of both, but he went once and he would go again. He says Atlantic City is more deadly.

Hygiene is a word. Mrs. Kelly once was told by some Augusta dope to teach hygiene. She wouldn't do it. But Cedar River in a casual way can view its innards on a lighted screen, night after night, and not be worried by the terrible effects of not rubbing, rolling, or spraying. Cedar River doesn't give a hearty damn just how a statue smells or what a man should use to shave a peach.

And psycho-swash, the hell with that. Nobody in town ever got worried and paid a man a hundred dollars to find out that all his troubles came from childhood viewing of a fly caught in a spider web; a nasty, dirty fly when flying, but, when caught, a pitiable victim of an indecent ogre.

In Cedar River, kids on rainy days get bounties for the flies they swat inside the kitchen, spiders too. I don't know what the scale is now. It used to be a hundred for a cent, a hundred flies, that is. A spider brought a little more, but brought some hazards, too, for when a spider's smashed, it rains.

How dry are the fields?

Oh, Hell, it may not be the lack of worry. It may be because there's no routine. Every hour of every day is new. Maybe nothing happens more dramatic than the trees put on an hour's growth. Maybe Freddie Grouper falls through spring-shot ice because he tries to fish too close to breakup time.

If Freddie does—and Freddie DID—the word gets carried upstreet to the general store. No speed seems needed. People know that Freddie's going to cling or swim or else he's going to sink. It's up to Freddie for awhile. Freddie was the one who wanted pike or perch. The town needs time. There has to be a brief debate about whose ladder is the longest and the best to shove out on the ice so Freddie can catch hold. After a long winter in his woolies, it's just as well for Freddie to soak awhile. Otherwise he'll be obnoxious while he's drying out. He'll SMELL.

Hang on, Freddie, hang on, while the river washes away your sins of omission. You didn't spray or rub or roll. You smell like Freddie.

You smell like four months sewed tight, protected and pore clogged. Hang on, you smelly bastard.

That time, Freddie got out. The town saved him. They marched him down to the store and they peeled him and they rubbed him with old grain sacks and they gave him the dregs of a quart that Uncle Oscar had persuaded Clint Reynolds to buy for the sake of humanity, and to share for the sake of the nerves of the worriers about Freddie.

But more quarts were produced and after Freddie had gagged on his portion, and after the town had given him a few oral ideas about how stupid he was and how stupid his ancestors had been and how stupid his children would undoubtedly be, they all had a long drink in relief.

Then they all had another drink. They settled in and they drank for the rest of the day because their mittens were wet anyway and they had just saved a man from an icy grave and if that didn't deserve a drink, nothing ever did deserve a drink.

Freddie's rescue was only temporary. He drowned later. He drowned in the old quarry pit, looking for scrap iron that wasn't there. When he fell in the river he didn't drown, because folks on the bank could see him and hear him. In the quarry pit, he drowned because he was down there all alone.

One time he didn't, one time he did.

The town got drunk both times. Either result called for a drink. "Here's to Freddie."

Give him hell when you save him. List his virtues when you can't. Take a drink anyway, for effort made or unmade.

Either way, "Here's to Freddie."

I grew up with Freddie. I liked him. He was good in Geography. He was good in a fight. He had courage. He had too much courage. When I got pocketed by four Gages and one of them hit me in the back with a baseball bat, it was Freddie who jumped in and helped. We still took a beating, but it wasn't so lonesome.

Freddie was probably lonesome for a few seconds in that quarry pit, but thinking of that doesn't help a man sleep.

Silently, then, here's to Freddie.

And here's to the complexity that will always confute the shallow understanding of the man who muddles somehow through the haze, and stops his car, and stands on Mr. Turner's store steps, and drinks a charge of fizzy fluff and says, "God, what a graveyard. God, what a backwoods hole. I wonder what keeps them awake. I wonder if they hibernate in winter."

You hammerhead, they hibernate at will.

Symbolic smugness, stupid status-seeking snobbery, stands right where Jonas Hall once stopped a war with poetry.

Beside the stranger stands Agnes Slade. She doesn't hear him say, "Bunch of God Damned vegetables. A herd of cows has got more feelings."

She doesn't even see him. She hasn't seen much for a long, long time. She lives with Robbie Morton and Robbie Morton doesn't live in Cedar River any more. Robbie doesn't live anywhere. Robbie had a fault. He couldn't believe.

Robbie Morton knew but he didn't believe. That was Robbie's trouble. He knew. He knew as surely as he knew that the mountain core was rock, that the Square Eddy spring was sweet, that the night valley mist in August would evaporate with the sun.

He knew that he was the beloved of Agnes Slade. But he couldn't believe in the truth of this knowledge. He denied what he knew.

For Agnes Slade was the cause of the morning song of the birds. It was for Agnes Slade that they left their nests and sang. Only a fool thought differently.

It was for Agnes Slade that the moon glowed full and bright. Agnes Slade called the moon and the moon came up. It was for Agnes Slade that the little streams tried so hard to rush down the rocks to add their volume to the roar of the river in the gorges.

And Robbie Morton's solid realism denied the possibility that his dream of love was not a dream, but a fact; that Agnes Slade loved as she was loved; that she loved him. She had told him that she loved him. She had looked with love and acted with love. So he knew there was love. But he didn't believe.

A blither man would have accepted the proofs of his senses and accepted, consequently, the truth. A more casual man would not even have thought of doubting, would have enjoyed even the presence of pretense.

But Robbie's need was so great, his desire was so intense, his love was so complete, that acceptance of proof was impossible. His entire life had been a saga of disappointment. He had never quite been able to do what he wanted to do. When he succeeded, he succeeded only in part. He knew that he had nothing to offer Agnes Slade that could not be exceeded by some other man.

He saw Agnes three evenings a week. At each meeting he was lifted and exalted and elated and happy. Every touch was a message, every kiss was a pledge. When he left Agnes at her father's door, he was dreamy with a light headed glory. He knew he was loved.

About two hours later, he tossed in bed and he started to doubt.

By morning, his doubt was full. By noon, doubt was gone and disbelief had taken control. That was the sequence of Robbie's days.

The end was inevitable. Nobody can reassure forever, even one who understands. There came a night when Agnes said, "If you don't believe me—if you can't believe me—go away. All right. I don't mean what I say. All right. I'm lying to you. So go away. Don't come here anymore."

Robbie went away. By morning he was convinced that he had been right all along, that Agnes did not care, that he would be lonely forever.

He took a rifle and he put a bullet in his head. As he pulled the trigger, he took one more blow from fate. He realized that he was a fool. His knowledge of love became belief. But he was too late. He never even heard the roar or smelled the smoke in the quiet kitchen.

Agnes Slade never married. She lived for forty years alone. She lived with the memory of the fact that she had broken—that she had become too tired of a hopeless task to work toward hope.

But there had never been a chance in the world that she could do anything else. A man who is determined to succeed will not necessarily succeed. But a man who is determined to be defeated will almost always get his wish. Any man can destroy himself if he is bent on such destruction. And Robbie was.

Here's to the Cedar River simplicity that doesn't exist. Here's to Freddie Grouper. Here's to Agnes Slade. Here's to Robbie Morton. Here's to the complexity I found when I was very young.

It was a winter night and I was ten years old. My friend sat by the parlor window as the road grew dark. The great limbed oaks were outlined against the snow. In the summer, those oaks were friendly, but in the winter, their shadows shifted and their shapes changed.

My friend seemed one with the oaks. Her voice was a song but it brought shivers in reaching waves. She said nothing but still she spoke. She shared with me a moment that took no time.

Reality went up the road, outside the reach of the mood. Joe Hanrahan slogged along behind his big skidding team, the loosely looped trace chains clinking link on link as the unguided horses raised their heads every few steps, distrusting the night, looking for the bend by the big maple from which they would be able to see the stable with its hay and grain and warmth.

When they came opposite our house, one horse whinnied and the other lifted his head and whinnied, too. They shook their heads and telegraphed a message of unrest along the harness. They broke into a trot, snapping the slack out of the reins, bringing Joe into a shuffling run as he threw back his weight and tried to slow them to their broken pattern. But they were still trotting when we lost their sound.

"YOU did that," I said.

I think she laughed. Then the outside shadows blended into one shadowed whole and there was no light in the room at all. There was only a heavy greyness, which denied the sight of shapes and outlines, but accentuated the presence of my friend.

I walked across to her. I stood close enough to touch had there been anything to touch.

"Please go away," I said. "I was happy until you came."

She let her laughter rise, then, until I was sure there would be a clamoring for silence from the kitchen or from the rooms above.

She said, "Anybody can be happy. Unhappiness is the gift. The unhappy see what others do not see. Need and desire and demand, those are all gifts. Besides, I am nothing. In a minute I will be gone. But I will come back in the night. Because it is too late for you to turn away. You have started to look."

I snapped on the light, and the room, of course, was empty. I followed the filtered light path to the kitchen. My father stood by the stove. He had dropped something in the fire on top of the slow burning hardwood. I could see the flicker through the chinks in the top check draft. I snapped the switch and there was light in the kitchen, too.

My father turned. "Who were you talking to in there in the dark?" he asked.

"The devil, I think," I said.

"Tell me," he said.

I told him. He listened. He brought me a coffee cup and he filled it for me as he filled his own. That was new because coffee was forbidden even to my sister Liz who was two years older than I. But my father smiled.

"It's all right," he said. "A man needs a cup of coffee after he's been talking with the devil."

So I sipped as I finished my story. My father kept nodding.

"Bill," he said, "it's hard for you to believe but I was ten years old myself one time. I don't remember too well, but I think that's about the time my friend started to come to me. I couldn't drive her away and I'm glad. I never did all I wanted to do. I never did and I never will. But I'm glad she made me try."

"But I don't know how to try," I told him. "I don't know why the best things are the sad things, like when you get the first spring thaw you ought to be happy, but you're not happy for some reason. You feel all funny. You keep thinking you want to get someplace and there isn't any such place. Besides, I don't want to be unhappy all my life."

"All right," he said, "be stupid. Stupid people get what they reach for, so they're happy. They never know enough to miss the things they might have had."

"I don't want to be stupid. I want to be like Uncle Oscar and Uncle Waldron and Francis Gage, and do what I want to do, and be happy."

"I'm glad you know that Oscar and Waldron aren't stupid. But, Bill, don't ever think that Oscar is really happy. Oscar's too smart to be happy. He gave up but there was a reason. Waldron isn't happy, either. And when you put Francis Gage in the same class with Oscar, you're giving Francis a little break in the stupidity scale. That doesn't matter, though. The thing that matters is that you've started to look so it's too late for you to stop."

"She said that."

"Sure. She said it to me, maybe thirty-eight years ago."

"Did you want to be unhappy?"

"You're missing a point. Unhappiness isn't a constant. Someday you'll begin to see most of what she meant. She's you, you know. She's the beginning of real thinking. She wants you to dig under the surface."

"The surface is the most fun," I said.

"Yes," he said, "and it's a delusion, too."

That was that, and that was all. I can't go back any further than that, not into the deeper things. I can go back to memories of amusement. I can't go back to structure.

When I go back too far, I'm like the stranger on the steps, looking and not seeing.

But here's to the stranger and here's to my friend who kept me from following a course that would have led to him. Here's to Cedar River where what is, never was, and what was, still is not. Here's to a pleasant picture of turnip eating torpor and hilarious stupidity and sex and savagery.

Here's to the actions of many men, and the men's fathers, and, I hope, their sons.

Freddie Grouper had no sons. Here's to his sons unborn.

In what are we pledging the toast?

In the clear water of a spring that never flowed but stayed concealed in the subsoil of the forested hills.

Here's to my Maine, which is not on the granite coast where the cold sea is a reminder that the world is bleak and death is an actuality; where live the legends of the prudent sea captains and their cautious descendants.

Here's to the Maine of more frivolity and less adequate reasons for being; my Maine, which is in the river mists.

```
┌─────────────────────────────────────────────┐
│                                             │
│        CHARLES  W.  MORTON                  │
│           It Has Its Charms                 │
│                                             │
└─────────────────────────────────────────────┘
```

Solo in Wyoming

To REACH Pitchfork one took at Billings the branch-line train to the end of the railroad at Cody, and went from there by a light horse-drawn stage to Meeteetse, a little cow town some forty miles to the southeast, with a brick hotel—I believe it was the only brick-surfaced building for many miles around—the Weller House, where two and three guests to a room was the practice; a barber shop where a wood-burning stove heated water for the only bathtub in town available to the public (Bath: 50¢); a Chinese short-order restaurant which was the only really bad Chinese restaurant I have ever encountered; a large general store; a couple of saloons; and a livery stable. One of the saloons, operated by two brothers, Bob and Jack Fenton, was great fun, and I spent many of the final days of my stay in Wyoming playing solo there, from 9:30 in the morning to closing time toward midnight. Rickety board sidewalks and a few cow ponies sleeping at the hitching rails completed the Meeteetse scene.

Pitchfork was some twenty-five miles or more beyond Meeteetse, reached by what was called the Sunshine Stage, a light two-horse wagon which also carried the mail, fortunately for the passenger, for an excellent lunch was provided for the driver, by his contract with the Post Office Department, at a small ranch en route, and the passenger fared equally well at a cost of 50 cents. The Pitchfork brand, a design of three short prongs with a stubby handle, was famous all over the West, but Pitchfork itself, although shown on some maps, was no more than a ranchhouse and postal address, with a large barn and vast corrals of peeled logs. Nearby neighbors—in the Wyoming sense —were the Antlers Ranch at Sunshine and the Palette Ranch, one or the other of which was owned by the New York sportsman W. R. Coe. The brand of the Palette was an artist's palette.

Four ranches made up the Pitchfork complex: The Pitchfork, the Z-Bar-T, nine miles up the river from Pitchfork, another cattle outfit where the new house was going up and where I would be working; the

91, a horse ranch that was said to be doing a brisk business with the Army; and the TL, a sheep ranch that I never did get around to seeing. The scene as a whole was the broad, gently rolling brown bottom lands of the Graybull Valley, surrounded by rough and lofty snow-covered mountains. A pattern of haystacks, each protected by barbed wire, dotted the valley, and the main work of the cowboys from day to day was forking out hay to the Herefords, which were broken up into small groups and divided among many stacks, when the snow cover was too heavy for grazing. The weather was always spectacular, but even in early April the sun in the high altitudes was hot enough to keep the range fairly open, although the occasional blizzard might look like the end of the world. A dozen or more hands worked on the Z-T, some married and living with their families and others living in the bunkhouse, a rather too small room with six or seven beds and bunks, adjoining a dining room and kitchen.

There was no plumbing of any sort in the bunkhouse, but I believe the kitchen held a hot-water tank heated from a spacious coal or wood range. Soft coal was abundant and mined almost locally in that part of Wyoming. The washing water for the ranch hands was no more than a large bucket on top of the potbellied stove, with a dipper and a tin basin, and one emptied the basin out the door after using it. Just outside the bunkhouse an icy little brook called Rose Creek tumbled down the hill, and one could get fresh water from a pump outside. I preferred the pump to the tin basin, but it was a fast turn on a chilly morning. The outdoor privy for the hands was a commodious multipassenger unit in a shed off the barn. The house at the Pitchfork ranch was adobe or plaster and rather picturesque, but the Z-T bunkhouse was nondescript—a one-story clapboard building.

I set up in the bunkhouse the folding canvas cot that I had brought along, but a couple of nights there were enough. It was customary for the last man to turn in to cram the large potbellied stove that heated the place with all the wood it could hold and then to make sure that the windows and door were tightly closed. A half-hour later the stove was cherry red, the room temperature impossibly high, and the whole place echoing with thunderous snores. I shifted to a small wall tent of my own on a gentle slope outside, where I managed to keep dry and fairly warm in a tight lamb's wool sleeping bag and many layers of blankets.

The Z-T used various tractors, including a huge J. I. Case steamer, but I found myself on one of two small Cleveland caterpillars, of early design, in a tandem hitch pulling eighteen-foot double-disks, harrows, drills, and a manure spreader of discouraging voraciousness. It was

Ploughing on a bonanza farm, 1888.

shocking, after an hour of prying and heaving at the layers of the manure stack in loading the spreader, to find the whole cargo kicked off over the stern in what seemed hardly more than seconds. The old ranch hand in charge of our rig with whom I was working was named Wagner. Old Wag could outfork me by an embarrassing margin, and he could swear more impressively, as he did at the frequent break-downs of our caterpillars, than anyone else on the place—longer, harder, and with more real conviction so menacingly that one almost expected the misbegotten machine to heal itself and resume pulling. We used the caterpillars for all sorts of tasks, and my first job with them was as part of the tandem hitch when we went to work on a long, low log barn that was sagging heavily from one end toward the other. We hitched on to the ridgepole and pulled the structure into plumb, at which point log props were applied to the other end to keep it that way, and I don't believe this whole job took more than a half-hour.

One of the caterpillars was powered by a Buda engine, and this would quickly overheat and boil away its water every two or three circuits of the field. The other had a Wideley engine (although my spelling may not quite suffice), a much better power plant, but both tractors suffered from a ghastly need of frequent greasing, and both were prone to rupture their tracks and necessitate the most arduous repairs, on the spot and then and there. A lack of grease would cause the small idler wheels inside the track to freeze, which one discovered only after the track had ground away part of the wheel and produced a useless "flat" wheel. The other failing lay in the tendency of the heavy pins which connected the joints of track to work their way out and foul some part of the chassis. To make any repairs to the wheels it was necessary to dig a sizable hole, take out a pin from the track, and lower the ends of the track into the hole, thus getting direct access to the wheel. The ranch maintained a machine shop and plenty of spare parts for all the machinery, and a blacksmith whom I came to know very well, a tall, wiry Texan with faded blue eyes and thick, straw-colored hair and mustache, by the name of James Jefferson Knight. Along with the cook, an ex-Army mess sergeant in the Philip-pine war and the finest cook imaginable for such a crew as the ravenous hands of the Z-T, he was perhaps the toughest man on the place— sunny and amiable on the job but a rapid and morose souse once inside a Meeteetse saloon.

The incessant repairs and lugging water from the river with Old Wag in a ten-gallon milk can made a day's work with the tractors fairly heavy going. The cultivated acreage was four or five miles up the river from the bunkhouse, and our transport was a Model T, with the back seat removed and a platform at the rear where our gasoline and miscellaneous gear were carried. The route was cross-country, without any road, and almost any morning on the way up to our rig we would start up an antelope from the river; it would come flying up the slope, across our bows at perhaps 200 yards distance, and vanish over the hill in a matter of seconds, certainly the fastest animal at full throttle I have ever seen and seeming almost not to need to touch the ground.

When unencumbered by a tow, a small caterpillar was a furiously rough ride, veering and yawing at the slightest inattention on the part of the driver, for a touch on the steering wheel would brake it sharply on one track while leaving the other free, and in either hard-over position the machine could turn in its own length. Pulling a big load, it was much more stable, but as the driver of the rear tractor in the tandem I lived in a cloud of dust almost regardless of where the wind was coming from, getting the full output from the tractor ahead or from the machinery we were pulling behind. The massive white cloud formations, forever changing against the background of the blindingly blue mountain sky, were always worth watching as we roared along at a slow walking pace, with the unmuffled exhaust blasting away only a few feet from the driver's ear. Every so often a shadow would cross our course and looking up I could see an eagle, cruising the valley. I saw no other game on the Z-T, although the mountains were full of it. The Graybull was fished not at all except by the blacksmith, who would cut himself a willow rod, turn up a few "devil scratchers" from under the rocks along the bottom, and bring in a fine string of big trout after an hour or two of effort.

The high point of the day, socially, came for me after supper of an evening, when one of the foursome of solo players into which I had been admitted would look us over and remark with an air of jovial inspiration, "Deal the cards, you sons of bitches, and I'll frog without looking." This was, in bunkhouse parlance, the Invitation to the Waltz, a frog being the lowest bid in solo and not really a very hazardous offer. But it always got a game going in the bunkhouse and we played there almost every night. . . .

The Fenton brothers, a highly picturesque pair, were genial hosts to the two or three solo tables that were more or less constantly in use when we were in Meeteetse on an outing. The older Fenton was dressed as no one else in the vicinity was dressed, a cloth cap and a cardigan sweater setting him apart from all others. His brother had a long, ragged mustache, wore a shapeless and battered old felt hat,

a vest and never a coat, and kept a much-used towel tucked into his waistband. He was extremely polite to me, and whenever he served me a drink he would whip out the dirty towel and polish the glasses with it before setting them down on the bar. (A drink was two ounces of Yellowstone whisky accompanied by a small beer chaser.) Both Fentons wore neckband shirts, with a brass collar button and no collar. The biggest night at their place, or for that matter in Meeteetse while I was there, was when Dr. Dorrance, the multi-millionaire owner of Campbell's Soup Company, was passing through with a large pack outfit on a spring bear hunt and decreed that everything for everybody at both saloons for the afternoon and evening would be on him, a gala which must still keep his memory green.

Getting the twenty-five miles to Meeteetse from the Z-T was a problem. Anyone with a truck or a car would offer a ride, but there were long periods, often several days at a time when no one at all went over the tortuous road through the sagebrush and the countless prairie-dog villages. The only dependable method was to start walking and hope for a lift, but I walked it several times with never a sight of a ride. By about the halfway point the chattering and scurrying of the prairie dogs became a great irritant. The legend was that they could duck into their burrows too quickly even for a rifle shot, although I doubt this, but I never saw a dead one. They were not scavengers, but I was assured that no one but an "Injun" would eat one.

The blacksmith was usually my companion on a Meeteetse outing. Aside from his extraordinary skill at his forge, I remember him for his brown-paper Bull Durham cigarettes, which he twisted into a durable shape without licking the paper, and for his boast that he could tell time by consulting a two-foot carpenter's rule that he carried. I had many a chance to check him on this last, and I have no way of explaining his success. He would unfold the rule and bring down his thumb at some random point on it, meditate a moment, and then announce, within ten or fifteen minutes of exactness, the time of day. The figure where his thumb had come down had nothing that I could see to do with what he announced as the time. He was oddly mystical in his purported disclosure of his method, which went as follows and no further:

"Now there's twelve inches in a foot, ain't there?"

"Correct."

"And it's twelve hours around the clock?"

"Right."

"And there's twenty-four inches in two feet?"

"Right."

"And there's twenty-four hours in a day?"

"Yes."

"Well, there you are!"

The blacksmith's brown-paper cigarettes remind me that no one in Wyoming smoked "tailor-mades," which were regarded with suspicion no matter what brand and were usually called "pimp-sticks." Bull Durham was the universal smoke, with Duke's Mixture a poor second. I was the object of some curiosity by an old stockman in the Fentons' one day when I produced a package of "pimp-sticks" and lighted one. The old man looked at me with amazement and finally, unable to resist the opportunity, said to me, "Say—let me just try one of them things."

A few years later, on a long and enchanting motorcycle trip with my wife through France, we stopped at a pump outside a hotel in Chateaubriant. The porter was wearing a long apron of striped ticking and a visored cap and I took him for a Frenchman. But he noticed a Bull Durham tag hanging from my breast pocket and disclosed himself as an American from California. He had gone AWOL at the end of World War I and been stranded in his porter's job ever since. He asked me if I would give him the half-empty sack of Bull, but I dug into the locker and produced a couple of full sacks for him which had a profound emotional effect on him. "I save up for a ticket home," he said, "but just as I get almost enough to buy it, I blow it all on getting drunk. But I'm gonna start saving again right now." He looked over his shoulder and lowered his voice. "These frogs," he said, "are mean when you have to work for them."

The walk to Meeteetse was such a nuisance that I decided to buy a horse, and the foreman of the Pitchfork, a pleasant and much respected man named Ott Casady, said he had just the right animal, an eight-year old sorrel mare who had been running free on the range for the past year. The mare, I learned, would be brought in with a hundred or more other horses at the week-end, she would be mine for $40. and he would lend me a saddle and bridle while I tried her out. Her arrival at the corral of the Pitchfork one noon was a part of a magnificent demonstration of professionalism by Casady and his men. Casady was the only man on the place who wore anything fancy in the way of chaps. His were gray leather, with a decorative motif in silver studs, emphasizing the three-pronged fork of the Pitchfork brand. I do not know where he got them, but the catalogues of the Miles City Saddle Company were the favorite reading matter in the bunkhouse of the Z-T, and one could find warrant in them for spending into the thousands on an equestrian outfit. Most of the style of the cowboys and hands was functional and without ornament. Casady, in his handsome chaps and riding a powerful big horse that carried his bulk like a feather, was an impressive sight.

A truck gave me a lift to Pitchfork. Casady and two or three of his hands were taking their ease on the top rail of the corral fence. Several branding irons were keeping hot in a small wood fire. There were many colts in the herd, he said, who had spent their first year without ever seeing a man, and he thought they would all be coming along any minute now. He pointed across the flat where, two or three miles distant, one could see dust. "There they are," he said.

The dust, approaching at an amazing pace, disclosed a great mass of horses, running hard, guided and urged on by three or four riders, waving their hats and heading the whole thundering, breathless advance into the wide fan-shaped fencing that would funnel it into a lane leading to the corral. The horses were scarcely slowed by the lane, and the first arrivals burst into the big enclosure on the dead run, keeping at it in a counter-clockwise circling that was soon slowed by their sheer numbers. To me it was a scene of wild confusion, but Casady and his men could identify an astonishingly large number of the horses, some by name, others by their previous ownership or for some distinctive habit or accomplishment. They all identified the sorrel mare readily enough, and one of the hands, at what seemed to me the risk of his life, took his coiled rope and dropped down into the milling mass. His throw was so effortless that he seemed to move no more than his wrist, but his twitch on the rope brought the mare down, tripped by his noose on a foreleg, and he had a bridle on her in a jiffy. She was slick and very frisky, and I rode her back to the Z-T with much self-esteem. I unsaddled her in the barn, led her to a pasture, and turned her loose. This was a mistake. It was like stalking a wild animal on foot to get her into a corner and put a bridle on her the next time out.

I will not dwell on the trials I endured from this horse. She was mean and never mean the same way twice. She would tolerate two automobiles and bolt from the third, the same with mailboxes or even a stone beside the road. At times she would stop and eye a telephone pole with such trembling, ears-cocked, ears-back panic that even I began to think the pole was doing something to scare her; if not at that moment, perhaps it had on some previous occasion. At that instant, after seeming to compose herself, she would bolt again. She very nearly threw me when the sleeve of my slicker, neatly tied on behind me, came adrift and touched her flank to which her reaction was one of bucking and sunfishing. If I left her at a hitching rack, she would lean back and pull until she broke the reins. It was suicidal to light a cigarette while riding her in the dark. My worst moment with her came when we put up suddenly from the road just in front of us an eagle or a hawk which had been enjoying a dust bath. She went through her entire repertoire.

Casady obligingly took her off my hands. He decided that she was locoed, suffering from nervous instability caused by eating locoweed. In season, the weed produces an attractive little flower and one of a cowboy's duties is to keep the stock from grazing on it, for it affects cattle as well as horses.

There were many odd characters at the Z-T: a Swiss choreboy who lavished all his spare time and money on an ill-matched team and a buggy of which he was very proud, in the manner of a large property owner; an old Swede, Andy, perhaps eighty years old, who kept all his belongings—including a kerosene table lamp and china shade—in a tin truck with a curved top and who could take a spading fork and prepare the ground for a huge kitchen garden in one long day of non-stop work; Doc, the self-styled veterinarian, forever fending off ribaldries about the mortality and strange symptoms his treatments were causing among the cattle; a cowboy known only as Big Red, soft-voiced, polite, and by far the biggest man in the whole country-side; a remarkably disheveled man named Brown, who lived with his two or three children in a sheep wagon, in which they would come in for supplies at long intervals from his job of keeping the barbed-wire fences in repair; John Sayles, the foreman, who could have stepped comfortably into a role in *High Noon* or *Shane*, who knew the scores

of verses of "The Chisholm Trail" and many other marvelous ranch songs. The most amusing man in this assortment was a teamster whose name I have lost who arrived one spring evening as we were all sitting on the steps of the bunkhouse after supper. He was riding a large, dispirited horse and followed by a white pack mule carrying his bedroll and effects. He dismounted, opened the gate to the yard, and found himself defied by the mule, which balked and refused to be led or dragged or booted through the gate. No greetings had been exchanged, but finally a voice from the steps broke the silence.

"That's a fine big horse you're got there, friend," said the voice. "Whyn't you put a rope on the critter and haul him in?"

The stranger continued struggling with the mule, which relaxed suddenly and came ambling into the yard. "I woulda'a" the stranger called back to the group on the steps, "but the tree of that old saddle's a mite weak."

The next morning at breakfast, while the men were already tucking away their gargantuan portions of wheatcakes, potatoes, and ham and bacon from the ranch's smokehouse, the cook was standing in his kitchen doorway when the stranger appeared. "Hello," remarked the cook to no one in particular, "Here's the mule man again!"

Such a start could have blighted the affairs of some men, but the mule man was no novice at settling in and he was enough of a prima donna to take such a crack as almost a compliment, much as Henry Ford might have indulged those who joked about his Tin Lizzie. He was so full of talk and tall stories of his adventures that he quickly made himself at home. He was, incidentally, the only man I met in Wyoming who still wore a revolver at all times, a .38 double-action Smith & Wesson, from which most of the bluing had long been worn away, and he was fond of exhibiting an almost illegible permit to carry the gun issued in some small town in Montana many years earlier: a certificate, if you please, of his respectability and status in the community.

The mule man was a tireless solo player and the first, after supper each evening, to take the big plug-tobacco tin with the basket-like handles and sort out a deck from the mixture of greasy cards it contained. I do not remember that anyone ever put a new deck into circulation at the Z-T, and since such a player as the mule man smoked a cob pipe and chewed tobacco as he played, the cards all showed the effects of much fingering over months and years. His stories were bizarre; one was a description of a mysterious pestilence which littered the banks of some river in the Northwest with millions, said he, of dead salmon. "And sir," the story concluded, with the mule man assuming the air of one who could not expect such untraveled folk as ourselves to believe him, "there warn't a dog nor a coy-o-tee for miles around as had a hair on his body for eatin' 'em!"

By far the most spectacular man on the Z-T was the cook, Red Carlin, a powerful looking figure of middle height, a brick-red complexion, sparse ginger hair, bloodshot eyes, and a saturnine view of all authority. Like his small bedroom and the kitchen, his attire was always immaculate: a chef's white hat, a white shirt and trousers and several layers of aprons, and white sneakers as spotlessly clean as everything else he wore. He would replace immediately any garment that became the least bit stained. His pies were of absolutely classic delicacy, and I believe he would have been welcomed as a great cook anywhere in the world. He was very kind to me and invited me into the kitchen for coffee and a bit of pie or cake whenever I was in the vicinity between meals, which was all too rarely.

Red disappeared for a day or two on drinking sprees in Meeteetse every few weeks, but he was too good a cook to be fired for such lapses. His ultimate departure came when he brought back to the ranch from one of these outings a stocky little chap who looked not unlike Red himself, an unemployed teamster whom he introduced to us as Shorty Towle. Alcohol was forbidden on the ranch, but Red and Shorty, as a non-working guest, continued to hit it up in great style, and after a few days it was decreed by the proprietors that Shorty would have to go.

Red's response to this order, which came while he was turning a great outlay of steaks on his grill for our noon dinner, was to leave the whole meal to go up in smoke, telephone to Meeteetse for an automobile to pick him up, pack his suitcase and, in his unfamiliar "store clothes" sit on the steps with Shorty awaiting their ride to town. His successor, who arrived a few days later, after an interval of what seemed to us semi-starvation, was hopelessly incompetent and as dirty as Red had been scrupulous. It was August, and I had been there almost five months. I decided to go home.

In Meeteetse I found that Red was lodged somewhere nearby and spending most of his time in the poker game, based in a log cabin on the edge of the village, a public-private sort of game where almost anyone was welcome to sit in. The game was straight draw poker or five-card stud, table stakes and everything in cash, and it worried me to find Red so heavily involved in it when I dropped in at the cabin one night. Pots of a couple of hundred dollars were commonplace. It was quite beyond my resources, and I was superstitious enough—and still am in gambling matters—to be worried too lest my presence somehow affect Red's luck adversely, for he seemed to be losing considerable money on fairly good cards. I slipped out without attracting his attention and decided to restrict myself to the small time solo game at the Fentons'.

The final week of my sojourn in Meeteetse brought me a casual meeting with Shorty Towle one day at the Fentons'. He had gone to work hauling coal and supplies to an oil-drilling rig some fifteen miles back into the hills, and he invited me to throw in with him in the sheep wagon in which he was camped on the bank of Wood River, a couple of miles south of town. It gave my whole stay in Wyoming a marvelously pleasant wind-up.

The routine was simple enough but Shorty's four-horse hitch—young, aggressive, and unpredictable animals that he called affectionately "my ponies"—made our daily travels exciting enough. At the end of each afternoon Shorty took on a ton or so of soft coal in his heavy freight wagon by pulling up under the hopper of a Meeteetse dealer, only two or three minutes and no work being needed for this process.

He next picked up the day's supplies at the general store and a pint of whisky at the Fentons' for himself, and we were back at his camp by twilight. The horses were corraled at a bend in the stream, where they could drink at will, a vertical cliff forming about half of the enclosure and a crude fence of logs and wire the rest. They were fed hay and grain, and it was unsafe to get near the rear of any one of them, for they would kick eagerly at anything or nothing. Harnessing them of a morning was an exercise in delicate slow motion, as if we were handling unstable explosives.

Shorty's standard of housekeeping in the sheep wagon was as severe as Red's in his kitchen. Everything was scrubbed and in perfect order. He was a good cook and we lived very well, largely by his practice of helping himself to any part of the oil driller's supplies that he fancied. The drillers were highly paid, only the best of everything would suffice for them, and we prospered accordingly. Shorty's best specialty was a baking powder bread which, cooked in a frying pan on top of the stove, came out as a single, light, skillet-sized biscuit. "Sheepman's loaf," Shorty said it was called, and it went very well with eggs and ham and bacon. The wagon contained an astonishing number of cupboards and drawers and a double bunk, crosswise, at its front end.

As a last act before putting out the lantern and turning in of an evening, Shorty put the pint of whisky to his lips and let the equivalent of three or four big drinks trickle down his gullet in the fashion of a Spaniard getting under a jet from a wineskin; he was the only man I ever saw who could take on whisky like that, without swallowing. In the morning, on getting out of his blankets and before firing up the stove, he tipped up the bottle again for most of what remained. The liquor seemed to affect him not at all, beyond bringing from him a sigh of satisfaction.

Our route to the oil derrick was altogether cross-country, with no roads at all but the faint track made here and there by the wagon itself on previous trips. The freight wagons had brakes of a sort, an iron shoe that could be made to press against the broad metal rims of the back wheels, activated by a cross-member terminating on one end in a socket into which a wooden pole was driven. From the upper end of the pole a stout rope went to the driver's seat, sometimes to a pedal, more often to a cleat, hanging loosely and ready for him to haul on by hand; the longer the pole, the greater the leverage and pressure on the brakes. Cross-country driving with a relatively light load like ours for four horses is easy enough on the level or uphill, but some of the dry gulches we crossed were so steep that much braking was needed to keep the wagon from over-running the horses. At one slope in particular it was all Shorty could do to hold them back from bolting. One of his "ponies" had dropped dead here some weeks earlier, he explained, and he had dragged the carcass down the gulch a few rods where its bones were already beginning to whiten. "They get a whiff of it along about here," he said, "and they don't like it a-tall."

The biggest freight wagon I saw in the West was the beer wagon, which came over the road from Cody to Meeteetse every month or so, a high-sided mountain wagon, piled to the sky with cases of beer from a Billings brewery; it had huge wheels, a lofty brake-pole, and a broad seat where the driver and one or two companions, beer bottles in hand, enjoyed the pleasures of a trip that must have taken at least two full days at a slow walking pace. One could imagine the wagon lurching and creaking over the stones of the river crossings, its ten or a dozen horses scrambling for a footing, and all Meeteetse turned out for its approach. With such an audience the driver became the stylist: it seemed almost without attention on his part, save for a ceremonial crack of the whip, that he turned the long hitch around and brought the wagon to a triumphant stop, the traces settling into the dust, at precisely the door of the Fentons' saloon.

I never learned how the drill came out, but a lot of wildcatting in the vicinity paid off in later years. The rig that Shorty was supplying was a study in loneliness, with no sign of other human existence to be seen in any direction. The drill and its steam engine were clanking and chuffing in all vigor when we got there, but it looked to me like a very long shot; the little pile of coal that we augmented so slightly seemed a trifling resource for powering so ambitious a venture. The silence when the drilling stopped for the dinner hour was overwhelming.

Dinner with the dozen or more drillers was superb. The men lived in a well-kept bunkhouse and took their meals in the cookhouse, presided over by a middle-aged woman and her beautiful daughter, perhaps twenty, and it was plain both were treated as the absolute authorities, having the unquestionable last word over everyone else on the premises. Their cooking alone could have warranted such a status; their dinners might have come from the kitchen of a rich Iowa farm at threshing time; but they were remarkable personalities into the bargain: warmhearted, gay, zealous, and amiably in complete control of their work and their environment. The hospitality of the whole establishment to such outsiders as Shorty and myself was a tonic to be felt all the way back to Meeteetse as our empty wagon rattled over the hummocks of Buffalo grass. I can only hope that both women went on to marry wildcatters who struck it rich.

My worries about Red Carlin's poker-playing were needless, I found a year later, when I went through Cody with a friend from Indiana, at the beginning of a pack trip into the Shoshone Mountains. We dropped in at the Cody Café for breakfast, and there was Red, the proprietor, once again in his white aprons, giving me a comradely greeting. He had just about cleaned out the Meeteetse poker players, I learned, and he bought the café with part of his winnings.

Two years after that, in the second year of our marriage, my wife and I were in Cody on our way to the wilds. It was her first experience of Wyoming, and I was eager to have her see Red Carlin, whose saga I had told her, so we began the day, after stepping out of a stuffy Pullman into the chill of the early morning, at the Cody Café.

Red was not there. I asked the waitress about him. She was one of those types who seem always to have one hand at her hip and the other patting her back hair, and she looked at me superciliously. "Ain't you heard?" she asked.

"No, not at all. Heard what?"

"He ain't here any more. He's dead."

Her manner was so portentous that I could not help asking how it had happened. She seemed, also, to be disapproving of me already as a friend of Red's.

"He married one of the waitresses, and he killed her with a butcher knife," the waitress said. "And he hung himself in the jail at Fort Collins." I did not learn what had brought Red to Fort Collins, and I may be mistaken about the location, but that is what I thought the waitress said. At any rate, Red was dead by his own hand, and the customers of the Cody Café were the poorer for his passing.

The outlet of the Niagara River with Lake Ontario in the distance, 1853.

3
Going Back to the Soil

THE NOSTALGIC SELECTIONS in the preceding section of this book described a way of life that has disappeared from our country and will never return. A good many of us, nevertheless, have sought to recapture it somehow by giving up city living, which for one reason and another was becoming too much for us, and resettling in the country of our boyhood. It seems appropriate, therefore, to include in my anthology a few reports from literary persons who have tried this memorable experiment. I suppose I should apologize for including a chapter from a book I wrote in 1942, but it is undeniably pertinent.

July

July 13. Being weary today at my desk, so that the strength and joy had gone out of me, I went into my garden, and there in the morning sunshine, among the apple trees, I began opening my hives to look for queen cells, to see what must be done to increase the storage of honey. For a time I was dull and slow, wholly intent upon the processes of my labor wherein much depends upon an exact knowledge of the law of the hive. Presently I was conscious of a bird singing in the apple tree just over my head. It was the "easy—so easy—so easy" of one of our most cheerful neighbors, the song sparrow.

"So easy indeed," said I. "It is precisely the advice I need—on a fine morning like this, in summer."

"So easy—so easy—so easy," responded my friend.

"Indeed so," said I. "So easy to be happy on a day like this. Such warm sunshine, such cool shadows I think I never knew before. Such odors: such sounds!"

"So easy—easy—easy," agreed the little bird.

It was then I began to think of the evils of the world, so long weighing heavily upon my spirit—wars, strikes, poverty, hunger, greed, cruelty. It may be, I thought, that men will have to be turned back to the soil for a thousand years or so to exorcise them. It may be that the remedy, as in ancient times, lies here upon the open land.

For I thought, as I knelt there by my hives, of the absolute veracity of these natural processes. Here one comes to know the immutable logic of cause and effect. One cannot fool a hive of bees! There is no gambling short cut to honey: no getting by with clever words. Reward rests exactly upon effort, effort exactly upon knowledge. Man is constantly forgetting this law, becoming impatient of this order, despising the slow processes of creation and growth, seeking by silly force, or sillier duplicity, to satisfy his greed by short cuts. We who kneel by our hives know well that it cannot be done. We know that the attempt to do it results in what we see abroad in the world today: hunger, poverty, unemployment, hatred, bitter depression and dismay. It cannot be done!

July 21. Now is the heyday of summer: everything voluptuously in growth. It is the full, warm, robust middle age of the year, with good health and thriving normal life. The earth, ripe with products as well as promise, smiles now with full contentment. The corn in my field is even with my shoulder, the rowen alfalfa, freshly green, has come eagerly to the second blossoming. All the cut meadows, in spite of dry weather, are again greening; the potatoes, not yet blighted, carpet their broad acres, and the onions and tobacco, the chief commercial crops of our valley, are at their best. They will indeed grow larger, but will never again look so well. The early peaches in my orchard—the Mayflower—hang loaded with red-ripening fruit, never so abundant as this year. The raspberries are past, or nearly past, but the blackberries are coming on, though the fruit, maturing in dry weather, is of poorer quality than usual. The early apples—the Yellow Transparent—are full-grown, nearly ready to use, but the later apples, especially the Spies, are backward. All the hives are filling with honey: I shall soon be taking off some of the supers. In the garden we have zinnias and calendulas and hollyhocks at their best, and great red and white roses. Surely, a good, abundant, smiling time of the year!

Here I live. After wandering, this valley is my home, this very hillside, these green acres. I want no other. This is my progress, the succession of the seasons; this my reward, the product of the earth. Here may I think and love and work. Here have I lived and here I would die, for of all places under the sun I know of none that contents me better.

July 27. Rain in the night, all night long. It has been hot and dry, a week or more of burning sunshine, parched meadows and withering corn. The earth of fields and garden has grown powdery dry and at cultivation lifted a smoke of dust. The hills were hazy, and the leaves of the trees looked parched and sick. The ripening fruit has been coming pinched and seedy and sour.

But last night came the rain, all night long. I awakened in the dark with the cool sweet breath of it upon my face. I lay there, still and happy, and listened to the rain come down. There was not a breath of wind, not one gusty shower. It was as though nature had drawn a long sigh and, repenting her hot anger of past days, had begun to weep softly, copiously, to assuage the fever of the burning earth.

I heard the rain tapping on the roof, whispering among the leaves of the ash tree next my window, drumming in the downspouts. I could smell the fragrance—the unforgettable fragrance—of new rain upon parched verdure and thirsty dust. It came straight down and filled all the night with comfort and releasement.

How pleasantly, then, my thoughts went out to the suffering fields, sharing the gratitude of the grass, pausing at the edge of the corn to listen to the sibilant leaves cupped to the blessing of the sky. I stopped by the withering blackberry rows and thought of the blessed moisture soaking into that ashy soil, and the roots, deep hidden, reaching out like thirsty children to the welcome bosom of mother earth.

From time to time the downpour slackened, and then I heard the dripping among the trees and from the eaves of the house, exactly like hushed voices telling one another sleepily of their joy. I tried to catch what it was they were saying, but never a word could I make out, but knew that it was all in verse that they spoke in their sleep: the poetry of the rain. Presently I could hear a renewal of the rappings and tappings, as though the earth, still unsatisfied, was telegraphing the heavens for more—and then, presently, a new largess of the rain.

It seemed to me that all these days past I too have been withering with the dry earth, parched for want of the rain of heaven, and I too am eased and relieved: my thirst quenched in a new serenity. I slept again, but lightly, conscious all through the night of the voices of the rain.

At dawn I was up and out to see gray clouds hovering low in the sky. It seemed as if all nature, trees and grass and vines and flowers, was literally lifting up its head in praise of God. Some of the birds, deep hidden among the trees, were chirping their joy and some, especially the robins, were abroad upon the field and lawn, heads up and tails down, eagerly hopping about.

So I went down into it and was glad to feel the rain on my face and in my hair. I, too, like the wilting verdure, drew myself erect. I saw how greedily the curled leaves of the apple trees were holding this nectar of the gods, and each separate long needle of the red pines kept a pearllike drop at its point, so that the whole tree glistened with a kind of radiance; and the tall-grown asparagus had put on filmy necklaces of jewels to welcome the dawn. How good this day: how fine the rain: how happy am I. We that thirst have had our fill.

The Pleasures of Lake Champlain

W E STOOD AND LOOKED at Lake Champlain, that long jewel between
the mountains, so big and blue and familiar and appealing. We
had grown hungry for it again. Our own lake at home seemed small,
and it seemed we did nothing on our farm but work, work. So we
had put our old canoe on the old Buick, thrown our tent and gear
into the back seat, arranged to farm out the children with Esther Kent
at her place for a week, and here we were, actually at the water's edge.
It sounds easy, but it had taken three weeks of careful planning, including three days of the usual fence fixing so that our cows and heifer
would not get out of the pasture or into the garden. Just as we get
hungry for the ocean, we get hungry for Lake Champlain sometimes—
to travel on it and soak in it and take risks on it; and to sleep beside it
with the sound of ripples in our ears, and to see the thunderstorms walk
over it in walls of purple froth, and watch mist rise from the coves in
the mornings.

I'm always sorry more people don't understand the joy of knocking
about in small boats. Not that I'm any authority on the subject—
having navigated mostly in old dories, battered canoes, sprits'l skiffs,
and, best of all, an ancient twenty-three-foot keel day-sailer bought
second hand from a couple of Swedish carpenters in Bridgeport, Connecticut. You have to have something that will float, of course. But
the main joy is leaving the land—shoving out on your own. And I
often think it is the coves, shores, beaches, blue water, towns far away,
the sunlight and the tinkle at the bow—they are what you're after.
And they are as good and enchanting in a twelve-foot skiff as in a
fifty-footer, and much less expensive. This is one thing people who raise
their eyebrows at "yachting" do not realize: if you cannot have it in
an expensive way, you can have it in a cheap way. The water is still
the water.

The boat is a means to an end. Like a heavy coat in a blizzard, she
makes life possible there. And she is art of a lissome, functional kind,

refined by centuries of the most searching experience. No wonder people are forever likening them to women. It is no use saying what a boat is. A boat is fun and a boat is joy if you think so, but if you have a tendency to seasickness a boat is a pure and simple curse. Francis Herreshoff, writing "The Common Sense of Yacht Design," is mixed up in art all the time, the balance, the weight, the strength vs. lightness, the speed vs. stability, the beauty vs. stoves and bunks and self-bailing cockpits. Every boat is a mass of mutually exclusive desirabilities, a mass of compromises.

Which brings us at last to our boat, our canoe, one of the greatest compromises in the history of water traffic. We bought her on the Lake Champlain shore for thirty dollars from an old man whose boathouse was falling down. It was a big old house built in the side of a rock cliff, but the builders had never got their claws into the rock, and now the whole thing was oozing over the edge. Formerly he had made a business of renting canoes and repairing them when the renters returned them to him with holes in them. This led to some remarkable development of his carpentry talents, but not much else. "How old is she?" we asked him of the only craft that still had nice lines and was not swaybacked.

"As to that I can't say," he replied. "I bought 'er from a couple of young fellows who were going away to the war in 1916."

Even at that time World War I was quite a long way back. But we had to buy her because we had to get out on the lake that very afternoon. And we've still got her, patched and repatched, veteran of many a stormy voyage.

On this our latest trip we put the canoe in at Ferry Bay, stowed our weathered gray tent aboard, our grub box and axe and blankets, two folding army cots (we were being very luxurious this time), sail and leeboards, and paddled off. The sun was shining and the water was so clear you could see bottom in fifteen feet. We felt so good we were scared we would die of joy.

We always feel uncivilized, going down the lake. We have our food, our beds, our means of locomotion. We are on our own, for covering distance, for the risk of drowning, for poking round the points. It does not matter that there are white cottages with porches, and occasionally people in other boats way off. They do not exist for us except as a slight menace. Sometimes we get out the grub box and the Primus stove and boil up a pot of tea, drifting in the middle of the lake, the paddles laid down, our heads back on the gunnels or load, our feet hanging over. If we want to slip into the lake for a dip, we can crawl aboard again over the ends quite safely, one at a time, for we have

Lake Champlain, 1878.

practiced, and when the big canoe is loaded she is quite steady. We come ashore on some long white stone beach like the one below the narrows where an abandoned lighthouse sits on a cliff. We come into a secret cove of white sand and fir trees, the shore of a great estate stretching two-and-a-half miles along the shore—posted, of course, with NO TRESPASSING signs that say $200 fine—and there we camp all night in the starlight and paddle off in the morning when the mist is rising from the bays. We go ashore in a little harbor at the foot of a giant mountain on the New York side where there used to be a small colonial iron mine; silence broods by the ruins of a rock-and-timbered dock.

Years ago the steamboats plied Lake Champlain. On the little old four-car ferry that runs (sometimes) between Ferry Bay, Charlotte, Vermont, and Essex, New York, we met an old man once who told us he worked aboard a steamer that went down the lake three times a week, touching at Ticonderoga, Crown Point, Port Henry, Westport, Thompson's Point, Essex, Shelburne, Burlington, Port Kent, in and out to all the little harbors on the New York and Vermont sides, picking up potatoes, apples in barrels, horses for sale, farmers in wagons, letting off and taking on drummers at the small country landings. The steamer even served dinners aboard, in a glassed-in dining saloon. Apples went by freight steamer from the level clay orchards of Addison and Ferrisburg, Vermont, across to the railroad at Plattsburg, New York, and there was much barge traffic from Montreal through the lake to the Hudson and New York. It was a water thoroughfare, a busy place. Once Burlington, Vermont, was the biggest lumber port in the U.S.A., with docks where the barges from Canada brought in the raw planks and baulks for finishing. A few slum children fish from the rotting remnants of those wharves, and that is about all that remains of the busy waterfront. The great water thoroughfare has become a modern desert, incredibly beautiful, lonely, and less civilized than it was sixty years ago. We think it one of the most beautiful sheets of water in the world, and always imagine that if it spread its blueness and sunshine between twin mountain ranges of Europe, it would be very famous. Along the western lake side run the Adirondacks, some very high, like White Face, Marcy, and the jumbled peaks around Placid. Down the eastern or Vermont shore, all the way from the Canadian border to far below the lake's southern tip run the Green Mountains, blue and old and humpy against the sky, fifteen or twenty miles back across the lake plain from the shore. Drifting in a boat, you see the peaks change silhouette—Jay, Mansfield, Camel's Hump—and think of times you've been way up there in the mountains and seen the lake and islands and its huge bays spread like a map. Not so very far back in geologic time this area lay beneath the sea. From the clay of the Champlain valley plains—best farm lands in Vermont—people have dug up old whale bones, people who, perhaps, will never see the ocean. Somehow it is not like other lakes, enclosed, a dead end, a pool. This one joins with the sea at both ends; touches all the world while it lies smiling between the green fields and the mountains. It's the old water highway and the old warpath of nations, and even to me it is a spirit lifter and a path. Most people have such focal points in their lives, I suppose.

So many things have happened along this lake, it would take a book to list them—and some books have, in the dullest possible manner. Ethan Allen died on a hay load, driving over the ice from South Hero Island to Burlington. He just quietly passed away, and the horses jogged on along the bushed ice road track till some chance meeting revealed the fact that they had no driver. In wintertime you should see the shanty villages of tiny houses on runners, clustered on the ice, their stove pipes all belching smoke, and an old Ford belonging to a fish buyer jogging along the village ice-street. Off Burlington there are sometimes clusters of as many as ninety shanties, with far out, off the points, five or six belonging to the restless ones who claim the smelt are bigger out there and bite better. At Port Henry on the New York side are villages of miners and their children too, and their wives, who spend half the winter lugging stuff out to their ice communities—rugs, boards, boxes, barrels. It is pleasant to know that the piles of ashes, fish guts, rusty buckets, broken carton shanties, wrecked sleds and odds and ends will all disappear from these ice communities in the spring thaws.

Sometimes when the lake is slick with smooth ice, in the earlier winter before the deep snows, you see the iceboats winging, seventy miles an hour, their runners crooning, and the muffled, bundled, fur-clad crews literally congealing no matter how they dress. With a skate sail out from Burlington you can make it to the lighthouse on Juniper Island in less than twenty minutes—if you can get around the big crack that lies open even in cold weather off the dog-leg shoal.

Once with a high school principal when the ice was slick I went fishing up toward North Hero. We had borrowed a collapsible plywood shanty that folded flat, with hinged corners and a hinged top that you laid on the walls and fastened down with screen door hooks. All this and his son's Flexible Flyer were loaded on the car, together with stove, coal, kindling and the rest of the necessary gear. When we got to the shore of the fishing bay, we loaded our junk on the sled and set out over the ice a mile or so to a very special fishing ground he knew. A fierce wind was blowing when we commenced unfolding our collapsible rig. The wind caught the plywood, the coal bag began to slide away, the sled started moving, and all certainties vanished. We finally got the walls of the shanty up and the odd corners hooked. I was inside this floorless pen and Dan outside, when the wind com-menced to carry us off. The ice was slippery, there was nothing to hold onto, Dan couldn't stop us either, and so we sailed along—me yelling bloody murder. He was scraping away with the ice chisel, trying to get a grip somewhere with its blade. But the wind kept blowing and we kept bowling merrily along, revolving slightly, like a slow top. I was getting good and sick of it by the time he handed in the ice chisel. With that I was able to dig into the ice under the sill and pry us to a stop. Then he ran and got an axe and we quickly chopped a hole and froze her down before she should run away with us again.

Winter and summer, it is always something. In the blinding sun-shine days of late winter cars ramble here and there all over the lake ice, and the tolls at the two big bridges fall off markedly.

Sieur de Champlain, it is said, you know, here lost a continent for the French. By assisting a band of friendly Indians and firing upon a party of Iroquois, the French lost the Five Nations, the British won the French and Indian War, and France lost America. Sounds a little too neat to be true. But I often wonder where along the lake, at what cove or beach, on what point, under which cliff it was that Champlain introduced the Indians to firearms and the unpleasant excitement of bullets coming at you.

Nobody knows all the battles and famous trips this lake has seen. Indians on the Deerfield Raid paddled this lake, and up the Winooski, up the Mad River, into the Connecticut and down to Massachusetts. Rogers' Rangers on their famous dash to extinguish the red terror on the St. Francis left Crown Point and followed the lake to the swampy banks of Missisquoi Bay.

Ten miles or so out from Burlington are the Four Brothers, the Vanderbilt Islands that nobody seems to know, where seagulls are so thick they drive visitors away. Maybe they know the Vanderbilts and tolerate them.

The relative of a certain Burlington shopkeeper lives aboard an evil old motor barge that crawls the lake. And with the sharp and darksome relative is an equally sharp and darksome wife. They fish, they gather driftwood. They sell stuff second hand—a boat they found adrift, but the painter rope was cut with a sharp knife; a mattress that was drifting, but it shows no mark of water; a bed they found, but where? Many a lakeside cottage has missed a lamp, a few blankets, some chairs and hammocks. The bargeman and his wife know where they went, for the bargeman and his wife are the last of a long line of lake pirates. Though he comes ashore and works sometimes in winter, the bargeman gets restless in the early spring. After the ice goes out, before the summer visitors come, he takes to his roving life on the lake again, collecting old brass, rugs, baby carriages, occasionally an outboard motor, maybe.

Somebody else who roamed the great lake was Mary E. Wilkins Freeman, who wrote that great story, "The Revolt of Mother." She and her husband, who was a Middlebury professor, had an Oldtown sponson canoe with a little bronze centerboard built in amid-ships. In this they sailed and paddled the lake for a week or two each summer, loving it very much. But now they are both dead and their canoe lies rotting in the hayloft of a Panton barn.

Sometimes you see the cruising folk ashore from yachts wandering around in Burlington, brown and free-looking in sun glasses and slacks. I know a man who tied up at Chiotts' dock, looked below and saw a timber jutting out four feet below his keel. "We can't lie here," he said, taking in his warps. "Why not," said his wife, "have you forgotten there is no tide?" "Gee, so I had," he said, and made fast again.

And so we go cruising down the lake and past an island or two I'd like to buy. In place of Indians, the summer boy and girl camp canoes dart here and there, miles from land, though a thunderstorm hovers.

And it isn't the history or the people past or present. It's the lake itself. In storms the waves dash in on the gray old boulders and wash the points of long red rock and gurgle and spout in the cliff caverns. What we like is sand beaches and miles of stones; the hidden harbors and cliffs of deep black depths beside bent-strata rocks that arch and twist into red somersaults; the miles of blue, with a sun that makes you squint, and a fair breeze that bends the mast; the hayfields by the water, and the cows and apple trees; daylight sinking orange behind the Adirondacks; or dawn coming pink from behind the Green Mountain peaks; the tent in a cove where wavelets tinkle all night; stars, cool swims, hot noons; white squalls and glassy calms; always the beauty and danger. All you can do is feel it tingling down your arms and into your mouth and eyes and nostrils like drops of crystal and radishes and salt.

What we like is the bigness and beauty. What we like is the drops falling from the paddles as we swing together in a kind of effortless dance. We have paddled together, Kay and I, so many hundreds of miles, here and in Labrador, that we push along in unison without trying to. But if our stroke happens now and then to fall apart and get separated and independent, that does not matter; we do not believe in making a fetish of things. Kay in the bow, the load in the middle, and I in the stern—so we jog along mile after mile. If a fair breeze comes, we put up the sail and shift the load so we can loll amidships on cushions. We usually cream along within a quarter mile of the crooked shore, so that if we should capsize in a squall, it wouldn't matter very much. I feel that such caution is somewhat reprehensible, but on lazy days it is more fun not to worry.

Features of shore, trees, points, rocks there were that reminded us of our earliest days in the old Coonrod house. As we approached the gray rock ledges, excitement gripped us and that enchanting "recollection in tranquillity" that sometimes shines out like a lighthouse. We landed on the old gray rocks, and went up the huge natural steps past the blackberry canes. Here was the same stillness and content we had known in the long afternoons when we first sat there with our baby. We had to run up through the pig lot and the woods to the old black house. It was just the same, nobody living in it, and had the same black, blank air of staring blindly across the lake at the Adirondacks. It was only a little, and for a short time, with lights in the windows and smoke coming out the chimney and a woodpile in the dooryard, that we had been able to dent that black staring blindness, and now it had returned. It was sad but not too formidable, since we knew how quickly a family could knock that black, blind pose into a cocked hat. We stood on the hill and looked down at the lake and thought of the winters and the ice. We used to love the lake very much in winter too, a great plain of dazzling whiteness in the sun. There would be prisms and reflectors of rough ice standing up like daytime lanterns here and there miles away, sometimes in clusters, sometimes alone; and as the sun walked, the lights went out and others caught ablaze.

Standing above the lake, we remembered so many things. We had a police dog named Mike, with upright ears and the liveliest face, who loved to pull a sled. We had a little homemade sled for Kim to ride in, with a babycarriage handle, and Mike would pull it all day long, the only trouble being that as you walked behind, Mike almost pulled your arms out. Now and then of a sunny day when the winter wind wasn't too steely we'd bundle Kim up in furs and blankets in the little sled, hitch Mike, and set off for Bolland Manvers' fish shanty—a little dot a mile or two offshore. He would always be so happy to see us. Once coming back ashore at dusk a bad wind blew up, ten or twenty below and really fierce as it swept that great expanse. We pulled the furs close over the baby till only the tip of his nose stuck out, and he went to sleep while we trotted along behind Mike as fast as we could leg it. Kay was sure the baby would freeze, and she kept running along-side and taking off her mitten to feel whether he was still breathing.

I'll never forget how I loved the winter storms on that lake, running through them alone and not worrying, and feeling free. It was mostly in February that the great white oceans of roaring flakes came down in solid weight onto the miles of icy plain, blotting, erasing, isolating it. Usually that was a blessed time to be home, when the drift literally plugged and suffocated nostrils and the cold searched out every button-hole. But every once in a while after long battles with the manuscripts, the silly words, the interminable paper, it was the great pleasure of life to run the frozen lake in storms. The great ice boomed and the wind sang, and its wildness and untouchable-ness and strength and savagery and beauty were something I must know and be close to. It is all very close, somehow, to that chase of the unknown, fleet-footed, capricious, dangerous, wild and knowable female by the unappeasable male; only, this was some wilderness Diana the Huntress that no one has ever seen. In the snow, far from shore, half lost except for the wind's direction to go by, I knew that way off there was Westport, in New York State, snug and smug, with lights shining in the modern age. And right side by side with it was the ageless, timeless lake, brutal and beautiful as a jungle, as wild here in the snowstorm as it used to be before Sieur de Champlain ever "discovered" it. And this would go on, always, in the middle of the lake, this wildness, this beauty, un-spoiled, unchanging, demanding self-sufficiency of humans or death, in the summer blue and the winter white.

The same sensation has come to me, rocking four or five miles off the town of Burlington and seeing the great cascades of tin cans and broken bottles winking along the steep backside that the city presents to the water—rocking far off and thinking how good it is to be alone, or with one other. And the breeze blows cool and the ripples sparkle and the mountains change their shades from green to blue to mauve. And here it is again, the wild and the civilized side by side, and we in the middle, picking and choosing a little of each.

At evening we came ashore on a rocky island, small, with patches of grass and a few trees in the middle. There were sharp ledges just a few feet offshore and we had to wade in and carry the canoe up. A curious current was setting against the island, which seemed in-explicable until we examined the mainland shore and saw that we were directly off the mouth of the Lamoille River. In a niche of rock we built our fire, made tea in the old black kettle, browned some toast, heated up a can of beans, with a bunch of celery and some sweet chocolate to go along with our meal. There was a nice flat place to set the cots, and because the night was clear and the stars were coming out we didn't bother with the tent.

The airplane beacons far off on Snake Mountain and Mount Philo began to sweep the sky. Now that the lake was quiet and dark, the island seemed very remote. A motorboat with red and green sidelights jogged past toward Westport, faint music coming from its radio. It was a day.

The Most Difficult Step

No one can really tell anyone else how to make a living at anything. Success in any line of human endeavor certainly depends in the first place upon the conception of success in the mind of the individual. In the second place it depends upon his personal make-up; his health, his helpmeet, his talents, his zeal, his wisdom, and a hundred other attributes too numerous to mention. I choose to add another factor which I am sure cannot be ignored—and that is chance, or fate, or what you will.

Of these three factors, the most important one, as far as living in the country is concerned, is the individual's conception of success. If successful living means the accumulation of a sizeable pile of worldly possessions, then let him who holds this conception of success think no further of making his living in the country. It is true that in the past great wealth has been accumulated from the land, and that even today certain agricultural operations have resulted in fortunes to the operators. All of life or living in the country does not necessarily consist of farming, but farming as such, which has been practiced or undertaken, wherein the sole object has been the accumulation of a fortune, has inevitably resulted in either impoverishment of the land or the failure of the undertaking. In fact, it generally results in both.

Anyone who seriously contemplates living in the country must make his most critical decision at the very outset, and upon this decision rests the fate of his new venture in living. He must decide as to whether or not he is willing to revise drastically his whole scale of values. This sounds easy, but it is not. It is, in fact, one of the most difficult things that the human spirit can achieve. Involved are habits of behavior and thought, and convictions which are based upon our current philosophies of social science and education.

The ramifications of this accepted standard of values are woven into the very fabric of our national ideology. The present and persistent flow of population away from farms and from country living has been one result of the acceptance of these values.

Our modern emphasis on the importance of material things, our insistence that the very conditions of life are dependent upon modern improvements, is another manifestation of this. I quote from page 1166 of the 1940 Year Book of the Department of Agriculture.

"The farmer today demands a standard of living in keeping with the contribution he makes to the national economy. He sees no reason why he should not enjoy most of those conveniences found in our cities and towns as a matter of course. But to obtain all these things takes money, far more money than farmers forty years ago dreamed of having. Automobiles, tractors, radios, bathtubs, washing machines, refrigerators, etc. must be bought."

All of these things are embodied in our national philosophy, a philosophy which might well be termed "Sentimental Materialism." To question this philosophy, to doubt the soundness of these values requires a great deal of courage indeed, yet he who contemplates living in the country must raise these questions and must have this courage.

To make a living in the country naturally means to live there, and to live there means to have a home there. Now the living and the home are the important things. The home is the place toward which each member of the family turns when he is away. It is the focus of his life. It is the place where all the people and the things dear to him are assembled. Father or mother, son or daughter, home is a part of him. He has given some of himself to it, both physically and spiritually, and by the same token he is a part of it. Home is the place that the young man dreams of as he accepts the responsibilities of manhood, and likewise it must be his dream who would make a living in the country. To be warm and dry, to be adequately clothed, to have healthful food, these are necessary; but the goal must be a home and a way of life, not a way to make a living.

As a matter of fact, the best place to make a living is not in the country, nor has it been since the days of the pioneers. Steadily for the past century the sons and daughters of Vermont have left the Green Mountains of their native state to seek their fortunes in the cities and in far places. The gray and broken homesteads, the tangled overgrown meadows of the abandoned farms are mute evidence of their leaving.

The glamor of the city, with its high-speed life and its specialized occupations has been a magnet which in times of prosperity has never failed to attract farm people. In times of depression, on the other hand, the trend is in the opposite direction, away from the cities and back to the farms. This relationship between the movement to and from the farms, and prosperity and depression, is highly significant. When there is promise of gold everyone reaches for it greedily. When there is misery many seek the haven and the sanctuary of the farm. Here is historical evidence of a condition which should give the casual yearner for life in the country pause to think. If his conception of success is measured in terms of money, let him figure out why these others left the farms, and further, why some of them returned; then he can decide as to how badly he wants to try to make a living in the country. If, on the other hand, he can agree with Thoreau that modern improvements are improved means to unimproved ends, if he is willing to accept a lower standard of living, if he has the skill and guts to become a jack-of-all-trades, if he is willing to take on more and harder physical work, if he is convinced that he can build his own way of life, then he can be sure that he will be immune to the forces which affect the flow of the country migration. If he is sure of these things, if he is convinced that true well-being is not dependent upon material things alone, then he is ready to take the first steps toward living in the country. But let him study the matter further.

While the material rewards of living in the country cannot be expected to be great, he who has the spirit and the vision can build a life more rewarding socially and culturally than he ever dreamed of. A life more full than he has ever before experienced, a life not possible of achievement under city conditions of living. The fundamental and basic structure of country life must be built by him who lives the life. Almost nothing is ready-made for him. The weather and the soil are his concern. The processes of nature are his stock in trade. Neither packaged food nor entertainment, nor social intercourse nor culture, lie so convenient to his use as they do in the city. There is no movie around the corner, there is no restaurant or delicatessen down the street; nor is there a theater or bowling alley or concert hall within easy reach. The countryman must for the most part process his own food. If he is to have music other than that of the radio, he must make it himself. If he is to have the drama he must be ready to take his part in the amateur theatricals of his community. His recreation, if taken at all, will be taken simply and directly from the material at hand, from the woods and waters, the fields and streams. And what is perhaps more significant, he must read and think and study, if he is to have any ideas.

It is true that the social and cultural life of many who live in the country, if existing at all, is a meager thing indeed. In fact, the professional social worker who finds himself ensconced in that special part of our great bureaucracy which occupies itself with rural living conditions, is concerned exclusively with just that meagerness or lack. The bureaucrat's idea is somehow to transplant the cheap distractions of the city to the countryside, and thereby make country living bearable. To him life in an unimproved house back on a dirt road, buffeted by bitter winds and drifted deep with snow in winter, isolated and quiet at all times, would be unbearable. So he would somehow transplant the so-called advantages of the city to the country, and thus make country life acceptable. Attitudes and convictions such as these are the result of wrong thinking, and they are the outgrowth of a false set of values. If these values which are current in our Hollywood type of civilization are to be applied to the country life, the case is a hopeless one. City ways will never come to the country, and he who chooses to live in the country while eking out a livelihood will find that the returns are slim and the existence intolerable if his hopes are builded upon such convictions. If his hopes for an adequate reward for his labors are based upon economic and technical conceptions and profit motives, if his hopes for a pleasant and happy life are dependent upon cheap movie excitements and roadhouse diversions, then my sincerest advice is to stay away from the country.

We are being told all the time that work is a curse, and as he devotes less and less of his time to labor, the happier man's lot will become. We are led to believe the millennium will be at hand when at last man will achieve a life of total leisure, all work being performed by automatic machines. If this seems to be a reasonable and desirable hope, then stay away from the country. The poet Gibran says through the lips of his "Prophet": "And if you work only with distaste, it is better that you should leave your work and sit at the gate of the temple and take alms of those who work with joy." Unless you can agree in essence with the spirit of the above, then it would seem that any hope of building a full and spiritually satisfying life in the country is out of the question.

Farthest Field to the North

COLD FRIDAY IS the name of a field on this farm. On the old survey map, and in the older deeds, a number of our fields bear odd names, given them at forgotten moments in the past by men whose own names nobody any longer remembers. Thus, a field called Legonier lies on the south and east slopes of the middle ridge. Hit-Or-Miss is the outermost strip along the country road. High Germany sweeps up to the crest of our highest ridge. Cold Friday is the farthest field of this farm to the north. Cold Friday looks to the north in more ways than one.

It is a flat-top, as we say hereabouts by way of contrast to the commoner round-tops. One of them, Little Round Top, on the Gettysburg battlefield a few miles to the west, lifted itself, in three days during barley harvest, 1863, permanently into the horizon of history. From that "high water mark" (though it was traced in blood) certain energies of this Republic receded, though they did not end. Certain other energies were violently liberated, though they were not necessarily the energies that those who fought or died there supposed they were fighting for, or could even imagine. For in those dusty grain fields, woods, and orchards, a way was cleared for the United States to become something without its like in history: a technological colossus; and that fact, for good or ill, was to be decisive for all mankind. The sounds of that decision in the making must have carried clearly to Cold Friday. This was, of course, a battle of the first great modern, mechanized war; and the vast triangle of its action extended from Chambersburg (in the Pennsylvania mountains to the west) to Wrightsville (on the Susquehanna) to Pikesville (on the outskirts of Baltimore). The defeated past and the looming future, in the shape of detachments of thirsty, battle-frantic men, swept down the Littlestown Road, not three miles from Cold Friday, skirmishing fiercely in every quiet village where roads crossed. . . . Cold Friday is part of an historical landscape.

Weathering has left a platform of earth—some ten or twelve un-level acres—hoisted above and apart from the other fields. For Cold Friday is thrust from the rock-oak ridge behind it, like an outwork. Most fields invite the world; Cold Friday confronts it. Its slope to the south looks directly down on the roof of the Creek Farm house. Below its steeper face to the north, the Big Pipe Creek forces the shallow rapids that check its fall to the Monocacy, the Potomac, and the Ocean. Cold Friday, therefore, is the kind of height on which, in the past, men have sometimes built their ultimate defenses, calling them, variously, strongholds, citadels, acropolises, burgs, or kremlins, but meaning always the site of a last stand.

Here, in my turn, I meant to sink my ultimate defenses, when I reached Cold Friday, somewhat late in life, stumbling out of the revolution of the twentieth century. Here I determined to root the lives of my children—to live here and die here in this particular earth—which was for them, in the routine language of deeds, "and their heirs and assigns, to have and to hold in fee simple forever." I meant to root them in this way in their nation. For I hold that a nation is first of all the soil on which it lives, for which it is willing to die—a soil bonded to those who lived on it by that blood of which a man usually loses a few drops in working any field like Cold Friday. I was also fully conscious of another resolve: to end the wanderings of my house which for generations has been in flight westward—as Huguenot fugitives from France to Ireland, as soldiers from Holland to Britain, as revolutionists fleeing from Ireland and Scotland to America. On this earth, I was determined, our line would remain or end. Thus, for me, Cold Friday stands also for all the fields a man must cross to reach it.

I did not take such thought to Cold Friday when I first went there. First, I put it in corn. After the corn came alfalfa. But when the alfalfa wore thin, and grass began to run it out, I left the field in rough pasture, to cattle for three seasons of the year, or to the furtive life that drifts over it—the deer and the hunter, the random trespasser. For Cold Friday is a defiant field. Two of its free sides are too steep for modern farm machines to climb. The third is denied by a spring-head that wells from the base of the hill and has settled in a wet spot that gains a little every year on the firm ground, and which I am content enough to see gain. It is my little sacrifice to the energies of nature, to all that is chthonian in it before which anyone who lives directly against the earth and under the seasons hourly stands. Machines can reach Cold Friday only by way of a narrow, twisting trace through those rock-oak woods behind. It is not worth the effort, or half a hay-load knocked from the wagon by overhanging branches, with the labor of stacking to be done again for nothing. So I surrendered Cold Friday to itself. For long periods, I never went there. There was no reason to go. Cold Friday lies too far from the barns where people work and the houses where they live.

Then, in 1952, it became impossible for me to go anywhere. My life became chiefly a necessity to outlive a series of crises of health or to convalesce between them. During the first long convalescence, I lay in the room of this house which is closest to the sheep barn. Waking before daybreak on snowy nights, I could sometimes hear the thin, wiry cry that means that a lamb has been born and has probably got itself in some corner where the ewe cannot find it. (Ewes seem perversely to choose the coldest nights to lamb, and few lambs are so helpless at birth that they cannot get away and freeze.) I was powerless to go find the lamb, to rub it dry or restore it to its senselessly blatting mother. I could only lie and listen. At such times, I was surprised at how often the image of Cold Friday came to my mind. I could see the field clearly, in my mind's eye, under its unbroken cap of snow and the down swoop of the west or north winds. This distinct image, recurring so often, puzzled me. One night, there came with it the opening line of "Prometheus Bound": Power (to his companion, Force, and to their prisoner, Prometheus): "We have come to the last path of the world, in the Scythian country, in the untrodden solitude." I was first amused —the Scythian country; that is Russia. But then it seemed to me that some deeper logic of meaning had long been at work and had taken form in the image of the field before the meaning had risen to consciousness. The last path of the world—that was Cold Friday.

When I could move about again alone, I did not go at once to Cold Friday, though the thought was often in mind. The mind resists going, even on a junket, to the last path of the world. It resists the more, the more it suspects that such a phrase mirrors a reality. Reality can be a temptation, and the mind resists the temptation of facing the full reality, the ordeal of particularizing what, in part, it foreknows. But when I could get back to Cold Friday, I went again and again, simply to sit alone in the jeep, or stand, to look off from the field. . . .

A Time for Summary

THE KATYDIDS HAVE rasped their last calls of the season, the frogs have hibernated in the mud, the whippoorwills have gone South, and if man would only abide by the season we could settle down to a few weeks of peace and quiet. November brings that pause between Summer and Winter when a man should be able to listen to his own thoughts and call a truce in the noisy war with his environment.

Up here in the hill country, this area of small but venerable farms, we are catching our breath after tending to such fundamental matters as getting the hay into the mow, filling the silos and stowing the garden's yield in the freezer and the root cellar. The country fair is over. The political campaign has almost run its course. Tomorrow we shall go to the polls and, with luck, the dust will settle and the uproar die down before the first snow flies.

I was up on the mountainside the other afternoon taking a census of the partridges which, the terse local way, we simply call "birds." I knew the birds had a good season, a big hatch and a profitable Summer. As a countryman, I saw the signs weeks ago. But I was surprised at the number of birds I flushed from the briar patches and the clumps of wild barberry where they were feeding. Some rocketed from the brush almost at my feet with a startling roar, and some winged away in swift silence. A partridge can either scare the wits out of you or be as quiet as a shadow. There was a time, long ago, when they were so tame you could knock one over with a short stick. Now they are wary. You need a shotgun and sharp reflexes to get a brace of birds. Partridges learned about man quite a few generations back. Having learned, they survive.

When I had satisfied myself about the birds, I sat down on a rock where I could look through an opening among the trees and see the distant hills and the clean horizon. Sitting there in the sunlight and the silence, I thought how the world reveals itself in its true dimensions in the Autumn, how a man's vision is invited to reach and his understanding to expand. That thought invited parallels, including the notion that a man on his way to the polls in early November could, if he would, look around and see the world in its basic contours, and the notion that neither men nor issues can hide in the leafless woods. But these notions were conceits and no doubt superficial, apt as they seemed at the moment. I dismissed them and came back to the trees, the far hills, and the scattering of small farms I could identify from where I sat. They represented something vital, something about mankind and man's tenure on the earth. They embodied traditions and a way of life that, up till now, have been a basic pattern in America.

I had to draw that reservation, that "up till now," because in the back of my mind was the report, made not long ago, by an advisory committee surveying national economic factors. That report examined the infinitely complex farm problem and recommended that the government solve it by wiping out more than two and a half million small farms and moving a whole generation of farm boys off the land and into industry. It was obviously based on statistics and, like most statistical thinking, it ignored many factors that invariably slip through the statistical net, particularly when people are involved. It was another example of the notion that bigness and organization can solve anything and that human problems can be solved by pushing people around. But since we are more and more at the mercy of the statistical thinkers and their machines, that report was like an icy wind blowing out of a dismally regimented tomorrow.

For a few moments, there on the mountainside, my thoughts leaped from human wisdom to human folly, from dreams to failures, from hopes to despairs. Then I felt the sun on my back and smelled the day and let my senses and sensibility tell me that this was good, this was satisfying and reassuring, just to be here on the mountainside in the November afternoon. The year was in order, the rhythms of time and growth and change just as they had been for eons, and I was there to see and know and participate as far as man can ever really participate in such matters. Then I came back to the house to do the evening chores and close out another day in my small segment of time, my own life.

Now, indoors at my desk a few days later, I have the uneasy feeling that I am writing a kind of memoir although I am chronicling events of this moment, this Autumn of the year in the mid-60s of the twentieth century, A. D. I feel somewhat as I felt the other day when we were making repairs to my old barn and I found a strange implement in a pile of rubbish in a far corner of the loft. It was the handle of a flail, and it must have been left there long before I came here. It was a reminder of a time when the farmer who lived here made at least some of his own tools by hand. The hickory haft was fitted with a maple swivel, whittled and steamed to shape long ago. I had never used a flail. Nor had the neighbor who was helping me, though he has been a farmer all his life. But somehow, just holding that flail handle and examining its workmanship, both of us participated in the past, in the long tradition of the land. We were, however tenuously, a part of human history.

When I examine the simplicities of this present Autumn, here close to the land, I wonder if I, too, am shaping a flail handle. Perhaps a few years hence, only a few years the way time now races, someone will find these words in a rubbish heap and wonder at them and what they stand for. When I write about trees and birds and the view from a hilltop, I wonder if they are important in the face of the elections, and foreign aid, and taxes, and missiles and satellites. Then I know that arguments end, men die, and nations rise and fall, but that so long as there is an earth and a procession of the seasons there will be trees and birds and vistas from hilltops. And, unless we are all incredibly stupid and recklessly wicked, there will be men here to see these things in Autumn and to feel, if never wholly to understand, what they signify. There will even, I am sure, be men living on the land, planting and reaping and abiding by the land's own ordinances.

So if this should be another flail handle, let it be straight and true to the best of my ability. Let it represent the now and the here that I know.

*   *   *

Any Autumn is the sum of its preceding Spring and Summer. We had a late Spring, but a moist one, followed by a dry, cool Summer. It was what we call "a bug year," insect pests in the garden and voracious inchworms in the woods. Hay was short but haying weather was ideal. Corn was slow but persistent and made a good ensilage crop. Gardens weren't up to par, but the insects ate as many weeds as vegetables. Things balanced out, as they usually do if you give them time.

Up in the woods the worms stripped many trees, and short-term prophets said the woods were doomed unless we aerial-sprayed. Hating all poisons, we put our faith in time and natural controls, remembering similar devastations that failed to kill the trees in ten-year cycles in the past. Only two agencies that I know of have ever been able to strip those hills of their woodland—the ice that came down from the north 10,000 or 12,000 years ago and scoured the land to its very skeleton, and man who came here a mere 300 years ago with his axe, his saw, and his torch. So we refused to let them spray, and the worms ate leaves, stripped quite a few trees. But by August the worms were gone and the woods were green again with a second leafing. I lost no more than half a dozen trees, none of them important trees at that, on the whole mountainside.

September brought an early frost. But we expected it and brought in the garden harvest. When frost came, we were grateful, since no man should be slave to a garden after ripe tomatoes begin to pall on his palate. We cleaned up the garden and called it another job done, another Summer completed, and we had time to watch the color come, first to the woodbine and the sumac, then to the birches and the ash trees, finally to the maples and the oaks. We had time to pick wild grapes and make jelly from them, and to see the milkweed pods begin to burst and glisten the wind with silk, and to marvel at the harvest moon.

Autumn came well before the equinox, and a few days after the equinox the drouth was broken by a long, slow rain that, despite the objections of the meteorologists, we always call the equinoctial storm. We had depended on that storm to come and renew the wells and springs, and when it came we said again that things even out, weather included. As though to demonstrate this, after that storm we had a spell of Indian Summer weather, a series of days when it was good just to be alive.

It wasn't a good year, statistically. But on the land you learn to think in longer terms than one season or one year. Next year probably will be better. But you know that there are bad years as well as good ones, just as there are bad days. You know that even the good years don't come for free, and that in any year you will pay for the long, hot Summer days in the currency of January's short, cold days and February's miserable ones. You know, too, that nobody, not even the United States Senate when it can muster a quorum, can legislate a rain when the corn crop needs it. You learn that nobody, not even the Supreme Court by unanimous vote, can forbid a woodchuck to raid a garden.

Even in a hurrying, impatient world that yearns for quick, easy solutions, the man on the land has patience driven into him by the trees and the grass and every growing thing around him. Long ago it was said, "To every thing there is a season, and a time to every purpose under heaven." Every day of his life, the countryman has that truth impressed upon him. Try as he may, he cannot much alter the seasons or change the sequence of natural purposes. All he can do is attempt to understand these things and work with them. That inevitably tempers the arrogance that has led the human race into so many disasters.

Autumn is a time for summaries, even more so than the end of the calendar year for those who live where the natural world sums up its seasons soon after leaf-fall. The plant summarizes growth in a seed that is pregnant with tomorrow. The tree summarizes another circuit of the sun in a closed circle of fiber that adds to the strength with which it will face the Winter's storms. The insect totals its brief individual life in a cluster of dormant eggs or a cocoon or a hibernating pregnant queen. All of them are implicit with a future, a tomorrow.

Perhaps the summary I have been trying to draw up here has a touch of all these things. To be even approximately complete it should include scarlet leaves and ripened nuts and barking foxes and cloud-high geese honking in the moonlight as they V their way southward with the season. It should be savored with the scent of wood smoke from an open fire and the tang of the pickling kettle in a farm kitchen. It should have the color of moon-size pumpkins and ripe apples and bittersweet berries. Somewhere in it should be the glint of starlight on a moonless night and the glitter of frost at dawn.

And there must be a quiet voice somewhere saying, as a man said to me only a few days ago, "Man and boy, I have lived on this land seventy years, and my father and my grandfather lived here before me. I've sweated and I've froze, I've worked and I've rested, and I've gone hungry a time or two. But never very hungry and never very long. And every Fall I look back and know it's been a good life. What more can a man ask?"

*   *   *

I often wonder about that question. What more can a man ask? Seeking answers, I always come back to the land as I come back now, thinking of that report which would move so many more people away from the land.

Life on the land never was wholly a life of ease, and it still isn't, though in terms of hard work and financial reward it is better today than ever before in history. But a good many of those who have left the land—and this has been true a long, long time—went in search of comfort and leisure and what we call better opportunities. The social philosophers have said over and over that if man could only escape the long hours of exhausting physical labor and the limiting isolation of farm and village life, he would emerge into the sunlight of a utopia where everyone would be happy, everyone would participate in culture, and the individual would discover identity and flower as a person.

So they left the land, asking ease and leisure. They helped change the pattern of life. In business and industry, they now work forty hours or less a week. Machines do most of the back-breaking work—and at the same time reduce the number of jobs available. But those who work with the machines have more ease and leisure than their grandfathers ever dreamed of, and their standard of living exceeds that of any other people on earth.

But utopia still eludes us.

Mass employment has tended to reduce workers to the functional status of a social insect, and conditions of mass living exert pressures of conformity that only the most rugged can resist. The norm is idealized, the average cherished, and even our education emphasizes adjustment to the ideas and the customs of the group. Leisure has become a problem and boredom is endemic. Young novelists and playwrights, writing as they must from their own experience, hold up a mirror of confusion and pointless search and a confused and rootless audience applauds them.

Searching for a better life, we have created a new and different but not wholly better world. We have eased the burden of labor by abdicating to the machine, which is both mindless and heartless. Analyzing and synthesizing, we have created an incalculable store of materials and things. Factually, we have accumulated vast libraries of technical information about the physical elements of our world. We have in some measure eased the pressures of physical poverty. We have somewhat prolonged life and eased the pain of living.

But a life based on facts and things still leaves largely unanswered the question, "What more can a man ask?" For we have eased want but not destroyed the wanting. We have learned facts, but ultimate causes and reasons still elude us. We have created machines that can answer our questions when we know how to phrase them, but we still haven't learned how to ask the machines why, and where, and what for. In creating this new world, this seedbed for utopia, we have lost and are still losing something vital to us as sentient, living individuals.

So I come back to the land and life upon it. And to specify I must become personal, speak out of my own knowledge.

These things I know:

Fundamentally, man is a minor creature on the face of the earth. I am bigger than a fox but smaller than a cow, and though my life span is longer than that of either fox or cow I, even as they, shall die and disappear in the end. As a species, I am vastly outnumbered everywhere I turn, by the mice, by the grasshoppers, by the birds, even by the frogs and the fish. Yet if I choose I can make the land do my bidding, up to a point and only if I cooperate with the land's own demands. Even without planting a seed or a root I can live off the land, after a fashion. If I cooperate with the soil and the seasons I can produce from the land enough sustenance for perhaps a dozen families. But the choice is mine, to subsist on the land or to produce from it.

If I choose, the land will provide me with shelter, a home. I can live in a cave among the rocks, in a hole in the ground, or in a habitation made of stones or mud or timbers. When I would warm myself, the land provides fuel. When I am thirsty, the land provides water that I can pollute or keep clean, according to my habits—and the habits of my neighbors upstream, of course. For clothing, the land offers fibers and wool and skins that I and my own kind can make into cloth and leather. I have the skills, or can learn them if I am patient, to use what the land offers.

Whether I subsist on the land or prosper here, I will eventually vanish and be forgotten. My footsteps will mark a path across the land, proof of my presence here; but ten minutes after I am gone the grass will grow again where I walked and the rain will smooth the sand where I knelt to plant or to drink. My own kind may remember me for a little while, bless my few acts of kindness, curse my unthinking cruelties, repeat a few of my words; but the fox and the hawk, the maple tree and the briar, will have no recollection of my ever having lived. The moonlight and the rising of the sun will not be altered one iota by my having lived or died.

But while I live I will know sunrise and moonlight, Summer and Winter, growth and harvest. I will watch flowing water and falling snow, and growing grass and nesting birds. I will know beginnings as well as endings, and I will marvel at the progression from egg to worm to butterfly and to egg again, the endless cycle. I will have the chance to participate, to dream, to wonder, and to hope. Not for a better tomorrow any more than for a good today. I will have seen one day after another no two precisely alike any more than two snowflakes, though of the same fundamental pattern, are precisely alike.

While I live I will ask questions. And seek answers in myself, in the world around me, in the skies above. And I shall learn anew each day that answers are sometimes less important than the questioning. I shall continue to believe that facts are not answers, but only the tools with which to fashion more questions. Having experienced fallibility, I shall remain skeptical of omniscience.

Knowing something about the universe as well as the world around me, I resist the temptation to equate change with chaos, proliferation with confusion. Knowing trees, I understand the meaning of patience.

Knowing grass, I can appreciate persistence. Knowing skills, I am impatient with mere competence and cherish excellence. Young, I had visions. Old, I shall demand the right to dream.

Thus I come to my own answer to the old man's question.

One more item:

To live with the land is to know, beyond doubt or argument, that change is inevitable. Not even the rocks or the mountains endure forever, so why should one way of life be immutable? My quarrel is not with change but with false prophets. Perhaps the statistical thinkers are right. I doubt it, but if they are, let this be a footnote to their cold, impersonal charts and columns of figures, this report from one man in a rural valley that welcomes another November, another beat in the eternal rhythm that throbs both in the stars and in my own mortal heart.

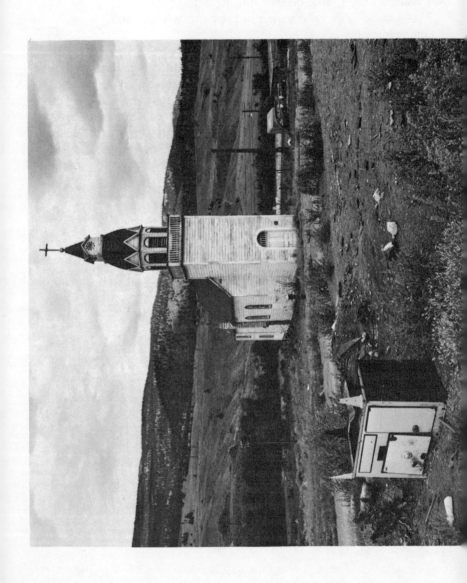

4

The Price of Progress

THERE IS NO ESCAPE from the fact that man's impact on nature has been unremittingly bad. Every iota of evidence, in every field, verifies this conclusion. Most startling of all, evil has resulted even in those instances wherein motives were of the purest. Greed and lust for power may be expected to leave behind them a trail strewn with destruction and ugliness, but it distresses us to discover that the hand of homo sapiens blights even when it is extended in the most benevolent mood. It seems that the way to get along with nature best is to disturb as little as possible, to conform rather than attempt to change. But in modern times we have rejected any such relationship.

Now, as far as this anthology is concerned, the reader meets for the first time with controversial material. In the present section, the writers treat of the changes that have taken place, most of which have met, at least initially, with wide public approval, for have they not all been brought about under the banner of progress? But the writers of these articles emphatically disapprove. Their samplings represent but a tiny part of the serious and compelling writings that document the present course of our society, but they raise all sorts of questions as to the wisdom of that course.

I wish I could have included more than just the first chapter of the late Rachel Carson's The Silent Spring; I would have liked to include it all. Surely it is one of the seminal works of our time, and though it was greeted with howls of anguish and scornful vituperation from certain influential publications (Time Magazine, particularly), the passage of time has supplied vindication for all of Miss Carson's grim pronouncements.

The Poisoned Hills

ALL THAT MORNING, in the April sunshine, our road had carried us through mountain forests, green and lush. Then, like a pleasant dream sliding into a nightmare, the country swiftly changed.

The forest thinned away. The trees grew smaller, became stunted, disappeared altogether. Bushes shrank and vanished. Grasses died away. Blighted land replaced the forest. All around us dead hills, red, raw, ribbed by erosion, stood stark in the sunshine. Hardly two miles from dense woodland we were in the midst of a moonscape on earth. Ahead of us the road led through a land of desolation, through a man-made desert, through a hundred square miles of poisoned earth.

We were in the southeast corner of Tennessee, in the Ducktown Desert of the Copper Basin. Chattanooga lay 70 miles to the west behind us, Gatlinburg and the Great Smoky Mountains more than a hundred miles to the north and east along the Tennessee–North Carolina line. Like Nickajack Cave, which lies at the junction point of three states, the Ducktown Desert occupies a position where three states—Tennessee, Georgia, and North Carolina—join. The boundaries of the three commonwealths meet near an old church on a desolate elevation which bears the ironical name of Pleasant Hill.

All the hills were pleasant here less than a hundred years ago. What had happened? What had left these slopes around us sterile and lifeless? What had produced this desert in the midst of a green landscape? We pulled in for gasoline at a filling station perched like an oasis on a barren hilltop. Our questions were an old story for the proprietor. Ten thousand times a year he had heard them. Bewildered tourists had interrogated him so often that he had had a pamphlet printed in self-defense. From it and from other sources we learned the history of this tragic area. It is a classic tale of land abuse. It is also, in its way, a murder story. For it deals, literally, with the murder of a countryside.

Until about 1840, Cherokee Indians occupied the land. Hardwood forests clothed the hills and shaded brooks meandered toward the

Ocoee River. Then General Winfield Scott, carrying out orders, rounded up the Indians and herded them west. White settlers moved in. Not far from the village of Ducktown copper was unearthed, and a scramble of fortune hunters began. The village boomed. It was at one time more prominent than either Knoxville or Chattanooga. It had a newspaper, the Ducktown *Eagle*, before the Civil War. During the war copper from Ducktown played an important part in keeping Confederate armies in the field.

At first ore was hoisted to the surface with a hand-operated windlass. The bellows of the smelting furnaces were powered by old-fashioned water wheels. And the refined metal was packed on mules 70 miles to the railroad at Dalton, Georgia. By 1853, however, gangs of laborers had cut a road through the Ocoee Gorge to the west and for decades thereafter ironshod wheels of heavy wagons rolled behind straining horses to carry copper 40 miles to the railroad at Cleveland, Tennessee. We had followed this same route, now U.S. Highway 64, that morning as we passed through the Cherokee National Forest.

In the early days of copper mining, it was a custom to roast the ore under large log fires before placing it in the furnace. This eliminated the sulphur. As the Ducktown area developed, the demand for wood mounted. One company alone consumed 20,000 cords of wood and 500,000 bushels of charcoal annually. Convict labor was pressed into service to chop wood. Axes rang all day long. The forests receded in an expanding circle. At the same time the flaming piles of wood, sending up their showers of sparks night and day, ignited the surrounding grass and bushes. Behind the receding forests, in times of dry weather, almost daily fires ran across the open spaces. Over and over again, year after year, flames swept the earth bare of vegetation. Always it came back. But always it was consumed again.

Even worse than ax or fire, however, was a third enemy of the vegetation. This was the clouds of sulphur-dioxide gas that rose from the roasting piles and hung in a noxious pall over the hills of the Copper Basin. It attacked the grass and plants and bushes that remained. It damaged the breathing pores of the leaves. Evergreen needles became brown. Leaves on deciduous trees turned white, red, red-brown, or yellow. Growth rings in the trunks of the dying trees became thinner with each succeeding year.

Different kinds of vegetation respond in different ways to the poison of this gas. Blue violets, for example, when enveloped in sulphur dioxide, lose their blue and turn green. Larch trees are highly susceptible to the fumes in spring but more resistant in fall. Hemlocks, white pines, and sycamores are easily killed by the gas; red maples, white oaks, and black gums are more resistant to it. On still days, when there is fog

View of the White Mountains, New Hampshire

or high humidity, the damage is greatest. Vegetation on hillsides facing
the roast yards and smelters of the Copper Basin was first affected by
the fumes.

In addition to attacking the growing plants, the sulphur dioxide
entered the soil, either directly by absorption or indirectly by atmo-
spheric precipitation or through absorption by vegetation. This tended
to increase the acidity of the soil.

By the end of the roast-yard era, that is, about the turn of the
century, all the trees were gone from the region and all the lower
forms of vegetation were going. The hardy sedge grass, which had with-
stood the attack longest, was giving way before the endless burnings.
The protecting skin of the earth, vegetation, was being sloughed away.
Patches of bare soil expanded. Those twin instruments of erosion—the
chisel of the rain and the hammer of the wind—did the rest. The
climatic extremes and the heavy Appalachian rainfall of the region
speeded the destruction. Swiftly the fertile topsoil slipped away down
Potato Creek, down Bushy Creek; millions of tons of it washed away
as silt down the Ocoee and the Tennessee, down the Ohio and the
Mississippi. Left behind, like a red flayed carcass, were the raw hills
of sterile undersoil.

They rose around us as far as we could see. They formed a nightmare
region, symbolic of all the erosion-ridden fields, all the dust bowls man
has created on this continent. Only a few minutes before, we had
stopped by a mountain spring amid woods to listen to a hooded warbler
sing high in a yellow birch. Small birds had been everywhere. The
forest edge along the roadside had swarmed with them. There life was
at an exuberant peak. Here it seemed almost entirely absent. We heard
the faraway jingling song of a field sparrow on one of the patches of
sod that still clung to an eroding hillside. We saw three English
sparrows picking on the bare ground before a clapboard house that
huddled disconsolate on a treeless plain, its roof tinted pink by dust
from the desert hills. But in all that accursed red land we saw only one
wild songbird among the million then migrating north.

It was drinking from a small streamlet of clear water that flowed
down the groove of a deep gully. Even there, where water was plentiful,
the sterile soil supported hardly a single plant. Beside the rill, bending
down, then lifting its head high as it drank, was a white-throated
sparrow. Its crown was brilliantly streaked, its throat patch snowy,
the yellow before its eye vivid in the intense sunlight. In this bleak
setting this migrant, pausing on its journey to damp, mossy, shaded
northern woods, looked incomparably beautiful.

Near the edge of the desert, where the patches of sedge grass were
larger, half a dozen cows wandered about, feeding as best they could

on the sparse pasturage of these shrinking islands in a sea of erosion. A few meadowlarks, I was told, still return to nest on these patches that hang like pieces of sloughing skin to the hillsides. During the time nestlings are being fed the larks fly from patch to patch, as though among the islands of an archipelago, in their search for insects.

But insects, like other forms of life, are scarce in the Ducktown Desert. We saw a few small blue butterflies, azures of spring, drifting along the roadside. And once, when we stopped on a hilltop to view the dead landscape around us, we discovered minute red ants swarming over the red soil. They were racing wildly, bumping into one another, milling about a small caterpillar a few inches from the anthill. Here was a great prize in this austere land. Never have I seen ants of a similar size running with greater speed. The untempered glare of the sun beat down upon them. Its heat shifted them into high gear.

I laid down a thermometer beside the anthill. Its mercury slid swiftly upward until it touched the 115-degree mark. What would a midsummer reading be? Without the balance wheel of vegetation, the bare hills of the Copper Basin heat up rapidly under the sun and cool off just as rapidly with the coming of night. Between midafternoon and night on a September day the thermometer may fall as much as 35 degrees. The greatest daily range of temperature known is found in parts of the Sahara Desert, where the mercury often plunges 110 degrees, and sometimes as much as 130 degrees, between midafternoon and night.

In other ways the disappearance of vegetation has modified the local climate in these badlands of the South. During summer months, for example, the heat is usually greater at the eastern edge than at the western edge of the area. The prevailing winds are from the northwest. They flow across the vast griddle of bare ground and are heated as they go. Moisture in this red soil also evaporates at an abnormally rapid rate. When scientists of the U.S. Forest Service made tests they found that the speed of evaporation on the naked hills was five times as great as in the neighboring forest.

As we drove past the great smelter of the Tennessee Copper Company, at Copperhill, in the heart of the Ducktown Desert we looked up and saw lofty stacks discharging their fumes high in the air above us. After years of litigation, the U.S. Supreme Court, about 1907, ruled that the copper companies of the area were responsible for controlling the sulphur dioxide that had previously been liberated into the air. In consequence, special equipment was installed to recover sulphuric acid from the smelter smoke. The result is that today the Copper Basin is the largest producer of sulphuric acid east of the Mississippi. To aid in dispersing what fumes remain in the smoke away from the immediate neighborhood, higher smokestacks were built. One of the stacks that towered above us was 400 feet high.

Can the Ducktown Desert ever come back? Can this moonscape ever be made fertile again? Extensive researches were carried on in the area before World War II by the TVA and the Tennessee Copper Company. The Tennessee Valley Authority was concerned because erosion among the naked hills threatened a rapid silting up of some of its dams. Under the direction of the Civilian Conservation Corps hundreds of thousands of trees were planted. Check dams, formed of brush and hogwire, were set up in gullies. Hilltops were mulched to retain moisture and prevent runoff. From Africa, Japan, the Mediterranean countries, plants were brought to Tennessee and tested as cover for the poisoned hills.

In nearly a hundred different plots, scattered over the area, the scientists tried out plants with strange names and remote origins— kudzu, Sudan grass, trailing lespedeza, Italian rye grass, crown vetch, Bermuda grass, bird's-foot deervetch, Bahia grass of the Pensacola strain. And one by one they crossed them off the list. A single plant, *Eragrostis curvula*, or weeping lovegrass, a native of South Africa, proved useful in the completely denuded areas. Among the innumerable trees tested, black locust showed itself most effective in the gullies and pitch pine on the exposed hillsides.

Before World War II virtually brought to a halt efforts at reforestation, more than 2,400,000 trees were set out. We looked around us. A few small clumps of pines huddled together amid the waste. These were the trees that had survived, an almost negligible number. The vast majority had succumbed to the insurmountable conditions of life in this desert produced by man. So far man has failed to undo the damage he has done. The problem of the poisoned hills—a classic instance of forest and soil destruction—remains unsolved. Unless more effective aid is forthcoming from man, the desert has only the long hope of nature's slow repair.

We drove on through this land no spring could awaken. Here no showers could stimulate probing roots and rising stems. Here no sun could contribute to the production of chlorophyll. The hills were stricken and the land lay dead. But, as we drove on, grasslands reappeared. Small trees, at first widely scattered, grew more numerous. They gained in size. Then we were in woodland once more, the desert left behind. All the lushness of spring surrounded us as we climbed on winding roads through mountain country to the east. But in our mind's eye, all the way and during days that followed, we saw the bare ribs of the earth, that strange, dead, red earth which spreads away over the tragic hills of the Ducktown Desert.

Fro-Joy

I HAVE OFTEN WONDERED whether it is just a lot of sentimental rot—
this idea that people had more fun in a horse-drawn society. The
automobile has won out in fair competition, but it has much to answer
for, it seems to me, quite aside from its reputation as a killer. It has
taken us apart and and put us together again, and changed the backdrop. A generation ago this town had a thriving steamboat service.
There was something doing here. There were fish factories and there
was a dollar to be made. Today the motor roads to the north of us
carry the freight; the steamboat has been laid off, the wharf is in
ruins, the factories are gone, and the population has dwindled. High
school boys, with a diploma under their arms, must either look to the
clam flats for a living or to the world beyond the horizon. High school
girls go up to the cities, and learn shorthand—a briefer way to express
what might well be said briefer anyway.

Today this town hasn't even a doctor. It doesn't have to have a
doctor. If you chop off your toe with an ax you get into somebody's car
and he drives you ten miles to the next town where there is a doctor.
For movies you drive twenty-five miles. For a railroad junction, fifty.
For a mixed drink, twenty-five. For a veterinary, twenty-five. For a
football game, fifty, or one hundred, or two hundred, depending on
where your allegiance lies. For a bush scythe, ten. For a trotting race or
a bingo game, ten. Everything in life is somewhere else, and you get
there in a car.

This has certainly done things to our culture. If we are not satisfied
with the merchandise which we find in the general store we drive till
we find something that does satisfy us. This is tough on the local
storekeeper, who has his troubles anyway. Sliced bread arrives in town
going sixty miles an hour in a bakery truck which is the gravest menace
to every child on the road. Bread, in my town, is the staff of death.
Ice cream arrives going fifty, and there is a little nameplate tacked
to the door of the cab, giving the driver's name and explaining that

he is pledged to safety and courtesy and has driven 209,587 miles without an accident—(eight times round the world carrying Fro-Joy in an unfrojoyous decade).

Very few housewives bake their own bread. They fry doughnuts a couple of times a week, but there is almost no bread-making. One of our greatest extravagances is homemade bread, which we buy for twenty-five cents a loaf from a lady ten miles away and which often means a special journey to town—twenty miles round trip. It is wonderful bread and worth the effort probably. The whole car smells of it on the way home. But it is a strange way for us to live. I have half a notion to learn to make bread myself: I imagine it's no harder than mixing a good Martini, and I might come to enjoy the work.

The automobile is at the bottom of every plot. In the next town to ours the grade schools have recently been consolidated. The motor car was responsible. One large school building in the center of town now serves the whole community—which covers many square miles. The children ride to school in busses, some of them a distance of four or fives miles. The small one-room schoolhouses are abandoned, and education marches on. The advantages of the consolidated school, I am told, are many. The scholars have a fireproof building and a basketball court with an electric scoreboard. They hang their things in cloakrooms which are ventilated with a flue which has a rotary windwheel carrying the smell of warm clothing up into the sky, instead of out into the classroom. They come in contact with a larger group and come under the influence of more teachers, some of whom are specialists in their subject. There is even a color scheme: the building is yellow and the busses are yellow. I think there can be no doubt that education, in its academic sense, is improved by the centralization of scholars.

Whether the improvement is general nobody knows. Certainly there is something lost. One thing that is lost is the mere business of walking to school, which is something in itself. In my community scholars still get round on the hoof. They pass our house at seven in the morning, clicking along in a ground-eating stride. Some of them make a four-mile trip to school—eight miles in all. And if there is a basketball game that night they will turn right round after supper and do the whole course over again without batting an eyelash. Sometimes a passing motorist gives them a ride, but they never ask for it and never expect it. There is no such thing as hitch-hiking in this town, no thumb is ever raised in entreaty. In all the time I've been driving these roads I've never been asked for a ride, which is almost unbelievable considering the distances that must be covered, often in zero weather or in storm. Walking is natural for these children, just as motoring is for most others. As for me, although I am motorized to a degree, I enjoy living among pedestrians who have an instinctive and habitual realization that there is more to a journey than the mere fact of arrival. If the consolidated school served by busses destroys that in our children I don't know that we are ahead of the game after all.

Walden

IT WAS June and everywhere June was publishing her immemorial stanza; in the lilacs, in the syringa, in the freshly edged paths and the sweetness of moist beloved gardens, and the little wire wickets that preserve the tulips' front. Farmers were already moving the fruits of their toil into their yards, arranging the rhubarb, the asparagus, the strictly fresh eggs on the painted stands under the little shed roofs with the patent shingles. And though it was almost a hundred years since you had taken your ax and started cutting out your home on Walden Pond, I was interested to observe that the philosophical spirit was still alive in Massachusetts: in the center of a vacant lot some boys were assembling the framework of the rude shelter, their whole mind and skill concentrated in the rather inauspicious helter-skeleton of studs and rafters. They too were escaping from town, to live naturally, in a rich blend of savagery and philosophy.

That evening, after supper at the inn, I strolled out into the twilight to dream my shapeless transcendental dreams and see that the car was locked up for the night (first open the right front door, then reach over, straining, and pull up the handles of the left rear and the left front till you hear the click, then the handle of the right rear, then shut the right front but open it again, remembering that the key is still in the ignition switch, remove the key, shut the right front again with a bang, push the tiny keyhole cover to one side, insert key, turn, and withdraw). It is what we all do, Henry. It is called locking the car. It is said to confuse thieves and keep them from making off with the laprobe. Four doors to lock behind one robe. The driver himself never uses a laprobe, the free movement of his legs being vital to the operation of the vehicle; so that when he locks the car it is a pure and unselfish act. I have in my life gained very little essential heat from laprobes, yet I have ever been at pains to lock them up.

The evening was full of sounds, some of which would have stirred your memory. The robins still love the elms of New England villages at sundown. There is enough of the thrush in them to make song inevitable at the end of day, and enough of the tramp to make them hang round the dwellings of men. A robin, like many another American, dearly loves a white house with green blinds. Concord is still full of them.

Your fellow-townsmen were stirring abroad—not many afoot, most of them in their cars; and the sound which they made in Concord at evening was a rustling and a whispering. The sound lacks steadfastness and is wholly unlike that of a train. A train, as you know who lived so near the Fitchburg line, whistles once or twice sadly and is gone, trailing a memory in smoke, soothing to ear and mind. Automobiles, skirting a village green, are like flies that have gained the inner ear— they buzz, cease, pause, start, shift, stop, halt, brake, and the whole effect is a nervous polytone curiously disturbing.

As I wandered along, the toc toc of ping pong balls drifted from an attic window. In front of the Reuben Brown house a Buick was drawn up. At the wheel, motionless, his hat upon his head, a man sat, listening to Amos and Andy on the radio (it is a drama of many scenes and without an end). The deep voice of Andrew Brown, emerging from the car, although it originated more than two hundred miles away, was unstrained by distance. When you used to sit on the shore of your pond on Sunday morning, listening to the church bells of Acton and Concord, you were aware of the excellent filter of the intervening atmosphere. Science has attended to that, and sound now maintains its intensity without regard for distance. Properly sponsored, it goes on forever.

A fire engine, out for a trial spin, roared past Emerson's house, hot with readiness for public duty. Over the barn roofs the martins dipped and chittered. A swarthy daughter of an asparagus grower, in culottes, shirt, and bandanna, pedalled past on her bicycle. It was indeed a delicious evening, and I returned to the inn (I believe it was your house once) to rock with the old ladies on the concrete veranda.

Next morning early I started afoot for Walden, out Main Street and down Thoreau, past the depot and the Minuteman Chevrolet Company. The morning was fresh, and in a bean field along the way I flushed an argiculturalist, quietly studying his beans. Thoreau Street soon joined Number 126, an artery of the State. We number our highways nowadays, our speed being so great we can remember little of their quality or character and are lucky to remember their number. (Men have an indistinct notion that if they keep up this activity long enough all will at length ride somewhere, in next to no time.) Your pond is on 126.

I knew I must be nearing your woodland retreat when the Golden Pheasant lunchroom came into view—Sealtest ice cream, toasted sandwiches, hot frankfurters, waffles, tonics, and lunches. Were I the proprietor, I should add rice, Indian meal, and molasses—just for old time's sake. The Pheasant, incidentally, is for sale: a chance for some nature lover who wishes to set himself up beside a pond in the Concord atmosphere and live deliberately, fronting only the essential facts of life on Number 126. Beyond the Pheasant was a place called Walden

Breezes, an oasis whose porch pillars were made of old green shutters sawed into lengths. On the porch was a distorting mirror, to give the traveler a comical image of himself, who had miraculously learned to gaze in an ordinary glass without smiling. Behind the Breezes, in a sun-parched clearing, dwelt your philosophical descendants in their trailers, each trailer the size of your hut, but all grouped together for the sake of congeniality. Trailer people leave the city, as you did, to discover solitude and in any weather, at any hour of the day or night, to improve the nick of time; but they soon collect in villages and get bogged deeper in the mud than ever. The camp behind Walden Breezes was just rousing itself to the morning. The ground was packed hard under the heel, and the sun came through the clearing to bake the soil and enlarge the wry smell of cramped housekeeping. Cushman's bakery truck had stopped to deliver an early basket of rolls. A camp dog, seeing me in the road, barked petulantly. A man emerged from one of the trailers and set forth with a bucket to draw water from some forest tap.

Leaving the highway I turned off into the woods toward the pond, which was apparent through the foliage. The floor of the forest was strewn with dried oak leaves and *Transcripts*. From beneath the flattened popcorn wrapper (*granum explosum*) peeped the frail violet. I followed a footpath and descended to the water's edge. The pond lay clear and blue in the morning light, as you have seen it so many times. In the shallows a man's waterlogged shirt undulated gently. A few flies came out to greet me and convoy me to your cove, past the No Bathing signs on which the fellows and the girls had scrawled their names. I felt strangely excited suddenly to be snooping around your premises, tiptoeing along watchfully, as though not to tread by mistake upon the intervening century. Before I got to the cove I heard something which seemed to me quite wonderful: I heard your frog, a full, clear *troonk*, guiding me, still hoarse and solemn, bridging the years as the robins had bridged them in the sweetness of the village evening. But he soon quit, and I came on a couple of young boys throwing stones at him.

Your front yard is marked by a bronze tablet set in a stone. Four small granite posts, a few feet away, show where the house was. On top of the tablet was a pair of faded blue bathing trunks with a white stripe. Back of it is a pile of stones, a sort of cairn, left by your visitors as a tribute I suppose. It is a rather ugly little heap of stones, Henry. In fact the hillside itself seems faded, browbeaten; a few tall skinny pines, bare of lower limbs, a smattering of young maples in suitable green, some birches and oaks, and a number of trees felled by the last big wind. It was from the bole of one of these fallen pines, torn

Walden Pond, 1969.

up by the roots, that I extracted the stone which I added to the cairn—
a sentimental act in which I was interrupted by a small terrier from a
nearby picnic group, who confronted me and wanted to know about
the stone.

I sat down for a while on one of the posts of your house to listen
to the bluebottles and the dragonflies. The invaded glade sprawled
shabby and mean at my feet, but the flies were tuned to the old vibration. There were the remains of a fire in your ruins, but I doubt that
it was yours; also two beer bottles trodden into the soil and become
part of earth. A young oak had taken root in your house, and two or
three ferns, unrolling like the ticklers at a banquet. The only other
furnishings were a DuBarry pattern sheet, a page torn from a picture
magazine, and some crusts in wax paper.

Before I quit I walked clear round the pond and found the place
where you used to sit on the northeast side to get the sun in the fall,
and the beach where you got sand for scrubbing your floor. On the
eastern side of the pond, where the highway borders it, the State has
built dressing rooms for swimmers, a float with diving towers, drinking
fountains of porcelain, and rowboats for hire. The pond is in fact a
State Preserve, and carries a twenty-dollar fine for picking wild flowers,
a decree signed in all solemnity by your fellow-citizens Walter C.
Wardwell, Erson B. Barlow, and Nathaniel I. Bowditch. There was a
smell of creosote where they had been building a wide wooden stairway
to the road and the parking area. Swimmers and boaters were arriving:
bodies plunged vigorously into the water and emerged wet and beautiful in the bright air. As I left, a boatload of town boys were splashing
about in mid-pond, kidding and fooling, the young fellows singing at
the tops of their lungs in a wild chorus:

> Amer-ica, Amer-ica, God shed his grace on thee,
> And crown thy good with brotherhood
> From sea to shi-ning sea!

I walked back to town along the railroad, following your custom.
The rails were expanding noisily in the hot sun, and on the slope of the
roadbed the wild grape and the blackberry sent up their creepers to
the track.

The expense of my brief sojourn in Concord was:

Canvas shoes	$1.95	
Baseball bat	.25 }	gifts to take back
Left-handed fielder's glove	1.25 }	to a boy
Hotel and meals	4.25	
In all	$7.70	

As you see, this amount was almost what you spent for food for eight months. I cannot defend the shoes or the expenditure for shelter and food; they reveal a meanness and grossness in my nature which you would find contemptible. The baseball equipment, however, is the kind of impediment with which you were never on even terms. You must remember that the house where you practiced the sort of economy which I respect was haunted only by mice and squirrels. You never had to cope with a short-stop.

Earthly Paradise

El Centro, California

I FIRST HEARD OF Imperial Valley in one of those cheery truck line
cafes to be met with nearly anywhere between two widely separated
towns at the most solitary points along the western highways. These
are places where the drivers of the gigantic express motor lorries climb
down from their high seats behind the steering-wheel after hours of
travel: for a gulp of hot coffee, a steak sandwich and above all a chat
with colleagues coming from the opposite direction.

I have seldom seen these "highway jockeys" in agreement about
anything. Friendly strife is their element. Their nerves are constantly
strained. In the loud rumble of the motors they are often unable to
speak a word for hours, and must even swallow their curses at clumsy
drivers. This is pleasing to their employers.

All the dammed-up communication and irritation can pour itself out
when they stop for a quarter or half an hour at Rosie's Cafe, the
Truck Driver's Home or Steak Heaven. It is all the more astonishing
when these quarrelsome men for once agree. This was the case when
the talk turned upon Imperial Valley. One of the drivers told how he
had recently been paid a special premium for a shipment of tomatoes
he had brought in record time from the Valley to San Francisco, and
from all sides other stories were immediately forthcoming about this
strip of land, to which adjectives such as "fantastic" and "incredible"
were applied.

This song of praise left a comparison in my ear. One of the drivers
had spoken of a man-made paradise. And I promised myself a visit to
this earthly Garden of Eden.

I heard again of the legendary California valley when a colleague
in New York served me with fresh strawberries in the middle of
February. "They're not deep-frozen," he explained, "they've come by
air from my wife's brother in El Centro. Just as we in Manhattan sell

our morning paper the night before, so the harvests in Imperial Valley are predated. In December my brother-in-law harvests his spring vegetables and in the late spring he sends us mainly autumn grapes."

Generally such legends deflate more and more, the nearer one comes to their place of origin. But with Imperial Valley it was different. In Los Angeles, less than a day's distance from this region at the southern tip of California, the tales of wonder were more luxuriant than they had been farther east. "Down there you'll find the California they imagine in other countries," an orange farmer told me. "That's the most fertile bit of land in the whole world. Do you know, I've seen grapes from the Valley as big as—practically as big as tangerines!"

When I finally asked at the Greyhound station on Sixth Street, Los Angeles, for a bus ticket to Brawley in Imperial Valley, someone behind me said: "Careful, son, that's the place where the farmers have to jump aside as soon as they plant a seed. Otherwise the thing comes up and hits them on the leg."

Like many a wonderland that stirs a people's imagination, Imperial Valley lies deep in the heart of a desert; it is, in fact, former desert transformed through a sublime human effort into an isle of plenty. I travelled from Los Angeles to El Centro at the end of December. Even at this time of year summer began as soon as we entered the desert. In Palm Springs, the resort of the Hollywood film colony, founded and made famous by clever real-estate agents, the Christmas guests were sitting in shorts and white frocks along the palm-fringed boulevard, and around the blue-green swimming pool people were acquiring their holiday tan. Only four months later it would be unbearably hot in the day-time, endurable only in air-conditioned houses. At a little wayside station in the midst of the rocky wasteland, I saw lizard-like reptiles sunning themselves at noon. Dry heat radiated back from dusty crags at the side of the road. But ahead of us in the middle of the highway rolled a couple of dewy fresh lettuces, dropped from a truck on the way from Imperial Valley. The great oasis could not be far off.

A hundred years ago this stretch of land was a terror to all who wished to cross it. It stood in the way of emigrants, like the Sahara. "When we travelled through this desolate region full of dry hot sand it was sown with discarded remains the emigrants had left behind, like the road of a retreating army," wrote Dr. Oliver Wozencroft in a travel diary published in 1849. "We found along our path dead or dying animals, guns, pistols, supply packets and other things that had made up the luggage of the unfortunates."

But in addition to such impressions of hopeless despair the doctor brought samples of earth out of the wilderness whose analysis convinced him that this arid land could be made fertile through irrigation. Remains of oysters and mussel shells showed that this basin, lying below sea level, had been covered in antiquity by the waters of the Pacific Ocean. The mighty Colorado River, flowing through the valley, had gradually dragged down on its back from the mountains so much earth and slime that it had heaped up a dam at its mouth and condemned the barred-off arm of the sea to slow desiccation.

It took fifty years for the California doctor's idea to be put into practice. At the beginning of our century the Colorado desert was still as desolate and frightful as when Wozencroft had described it.

But in June of 1900 the first canals were dug according to the plan of the Australian engineer Rockwood. Four years later the river rebelled, stepped out of its bed and used the new canals as gates for an invasion. From 1904 to 1907 the stream, in constantly renewed attacks, repeated the attempt to reconquer its valley. Stronger and higher dams were built, more fit to withstand the flood catastrophes. Finally, in the years 1928 to 1936 the powerful Hoover Dam high in the mountains, which with its gigantic cement walls placed itself daringly in the way of the Colorado, stopped it, and by its turbines guided it and was enabled to switch it on at will by means of locks.

Since then Imperial Valley has not needed to fear inundation. An extended system of canals, tributaries and enclosed brooklets has been dug to convey the river water into the former desert. Controllers at switchboards regulate the ups and downs of the locks, the water level in the trenches and side trenches. They can send the desired quantity of water into each "irrigation rectangle" of the four thousand five hundred square miles. "At home we must pray for rain," say the Mexican casual labourers who work in the Valley; "here they have only to phone 'central' and the water streams in!"

Imperial Valley makes a startling impression from the air. The view from the plane of that vast green garden set in the pale brightness of the sand dunes and interlaced with broad and narrow strips of water is a thing of splendour: a vision of abundance wrested from nature. The only elevations on these flat acres are high, geometrically-arranged rectangular heaps of carrots, pyramids of onions, motley hillocks of grapefruit, cucumbers and avocados.

I was unprepared for being invited on a little flight, as naturally as elsewhere one is invited for a drive. But the big farmers and members of co-operative societies are flying enthusiasts. They have their fields sprayed from the air with chemicals against pests and diseases, send part of their crops by air freight in the winter months to the markets in the big American cities, and not infrequently fit up landing places on their own properties. There are landowners who fly from sixty to a hundred and twenty miles every morning to their farms in the hot Valley or to the provision exchanges in El Centro, and back early in the afternoon to their homes on the Pacific, to Hollywood or to the mountains above San Bernardino.

More numerous are the owners who have practically ceased to concern themselves with their tracts of land and go for weeks or months without seeing them. They have handed over the management of their properties to a co-operative which, with its machine equipment, scientifically schooled agricultural engineers, their packing house and own sales organization, can farm more dollars out of the earth than would be possible for the single owner.

So the farmer becomes a sort of shareholder who has his dividends paid to him yearly by the co-operative, lives in town, and in some cases practices a different calling there. He is a salesman of agricultural machinery, a vegetable broker, a real estate speculator. Sometimes he opens a furnishing business or super-market in the immediate vicinity of his fields, where his manager and workers buy their provisions.

This does not seem too unlike paradise until one gets a closer view. Only the minority of the absentee owners have left their estates voluntarily. The others have been forced to it by the increasing mechanization and bureaucratization of agriculture. They would not have had a chance in a lone fight against this development forced upon the Valley by agricultural big business. A few stubborn individualists who tried to hold out soon went bankrupt. They could not compete with organized mass production.

The absence of frost and of weather fluctuations has made possible a systematic cultivation and exploitation of the soil modelled on industry. In Los Angeles, Imperial Valley has been described to me as a big natural hothouse. The more closely acquainted I became with this extraordinary bit of land the more I had the impression of having come upon an immense factory under the open sky. Here the man-devised laws of rationalization and intensification take precedence over the old laws of nature. Thus the same fruits and vegetables could often be harvested three or four times in the course of a single year. The work was organized as on a large conveyor belt.

"From seed to dinner table in one month," asserted a "salad manufacturer's" slogan I read in El Centro. I could well understand that if the situation on the produce market justified such an effort the limits set by darkness would be ignored. Several firms have purchased searchlights from surplus army stocks, and let their people work the whole night through, to have their produce ready before the season begins.

Of the seventy thousand residents now earning a living in the wonderland where a generation ago only the beasts of the desert dwelt, nine-tenths are workers and employees. The lowest stratum is composed of seasonal labourers, legal or illegal immigrants from nearby Mexico. They are employed where the new agricultural machines cannot as yet work more cheaply than manual labour, and are paid according to a fixed tariff. Socially a class above the Mexicans are the American farm workers. They must be skilled mechanics in the first place, and each year learn to operate and service an increasing variety of machines. Many of them know less about agriculture than a town worker who tends a little garden on Saturdays and Sundays. But they do know in detail the complicated mechanism of the onion-picking machine, tomato-shaker, hay-binder and larger family of tractors. "I hate the smell of manure and love the smell of oil," one of these motor fans said to me as he fitted a turnip-gathering appliance on to his mechanical plough.

Technical agricultural knowledge is expected only of the experts set above the casual labourers and field mechanics; these are not themselves farmers, though occasionally they are farmers' sons. They have graduated from agricultural colleges, and their academic status places them on an approximate level with the engineers employed in industry. They determine the course of production on a scientific basis and are interested in increasing the output of the soil and the efficiency of the workers. The stop-watch, tape-measure, and motion study long successfully adopted in factories are being introduced by these men into agriculture.

The packing-houses have made particular strides in rationalization. Through the whole length of such a building run brooks containing cleaning and colouring chemicals, into whose current carrots with earth stuck to them are poured from a mechanically tilted truck, to emerge at the other end clean and several shades stronger in colour. At once the binding machines seize them and transport them in symmetrical bundles round a revolving table, along a conveyor belt to the clippers which trim off superfluous green. Then they roll to the packers who throw a layer of carrots and a layer of dry ice into passing crates. The last station is a robot which nails the cases and shoves them into the waiting lorry. The lettuces take even less time, since they need not be bundled. The tempo has been so speeded up that a single packing-house can now prepare as many lettuces for shipment as all twenty were able to do in the days of handwork.

The only bottle-neck in the ever broader and swifter stream of production is slow and tedious Nature. To spur her to a faster pace is the task of the Valley's experimental station in Meloland near Brawley. "One of our problems was the tomato crop," said the young University of California research worker who received me. "Tomatoes ripen irregularly. On the same cane you get a fruit whose red skin is nearly bursting, another still green and a third that has just begun to turn pink. So long as this continues to be the case the bushes must be hand-plucked at a variety of times. Now we have developed mechanical tomato-pickers which will shorten the harvesting process. But in order to make use of them we had first to produce a shrub whose fruits would ripen as nearly as possible at the same time. Besides, the tomatoes had to loosen themselves from the bushes earlier than they used to so that the machine would not have to shake the plant too hard. And the skin had to be more resistant so as to remain undamaged by the fall into the mechanical picker's basket. Now with the help of other institutes working on similar lines we have evolved such a tomato. If Nature doesn't co-operate with our new time-saving machines we must and can compel her to."

The Meloland experimental station is a comparatively small outpost of the "green revolution" being carried from the laboratories into American agriculture. Behind it stand larger laboratories of natural biology in which, among other things, the process of plant growth through radioactive tracing material is being explored with unprecedented thoroughness, thousands of cross-breedings are being attempted, and entirely new species of plants produced by direct intervention in the genes of the seed.

These few white bungalows, these small experimental plots and humble-looking hotbeds in south-west California are mission houses of the conviction that the work of nature, down to the tiniest plant cell, may be observed, altered and improved upon. If in Meloland species of grass are invented which can resist great heat, if an unwithering flax is produced, a melon that will grow just big enough to fit the housewife's standard refrigerator, and dates or almonds of the exact size required by the chocolate factories, these are practical local applications of an endeavour going much deeper into the life principles of nature.

The "green revolution" in America no longer meets with opposition. The last generation of farmers mistrusted the ideas of the advocates of scientific methods. But the new generation, particularly the agrarian experts, the "fertility engineers," are differently disposed. "It used to take decades to get the farmers to change their methods," remarked the young research worker at Meloland. "Today they're as eager for our latest laboratory results as manufacturers for new inventions and patents."

That is particularly true in Imperial Valley, where the time-honoured ways of land cultivation had never taken serious root. New methods are constantly tried for turning the paradise into a super-paradise. The great oasis grows farther and farther into the desert, the output is greater and greater. But there is a large but. A shadow hangs over the entire region, a thing they do not care to mention in El Centro, Holt-ville, Brawley and Indio. It is the ancient and all-too-living theme of a threatening flood, a deluge in the not-remote distance.

"A man-made paradise? I'd sooner call it a fool's paradise," said the queer old local editor who lives in a small town on the border of Imperial Valley; "but I can't write about it. People don't want to hear the truth. The landowners and estate agents bring pressure to bear be-cause they're afraid the value of their property might go down. People try to ignore or belittle a serious danger that threatens thousands of people and millions in money. It's good to be able to talk about it for once."

It seems that man, in harnessing the Colorado, prepared the way for a more powerful enemy with more ancient rights in the great basin of Imperial Valley: the Pacific Ocean, which now, aided by the short-sightedness of the dam builders and irrigation technicians, threatens to return to its old bed.

In millennia of labour the great river erected at its mouth in the Gulf of California a natural dyke of considerable length and breadth in front of the basin which was later to become Imperial Valley. Each year the incoming tides of the ocean swallowed up a part of this dam but the river, dragging daily about five hundred tons of sand, earth and slime on its journey through the Rocky Mountains and seven western states, would always repair the damage.

When in the thirties of the present century the river had the yoke of the great new dam laid upon it, it was forced to leave nearly all these natural building materials behind in the mountains. They now began to fill the artificial Lake Mead, behind the Hoover Dam. Thus they were absent from where they were most needed: several hundred miles to the south, to fight the greedy waves of the Pacific.

With astonishing speed the ocean availed itself of the situation arising from the disturbed balance of power. In 1940, only five years after the opening of the Hoover Dam, the tip of the Gulf of California had pressed forward fifteen miles into the land. Ten years later the whole former bank, an area of many square miles, was flooded by a lagoon, the Salada, daily increasing in size.

Far more dangerous than this slow influx of salt water is the attack of the tidal waves upon the foundations of the large alluvial land barrier. Twice a day, as I had occasion to see for myself, the surf tears great pieces of land from the shore and pulls them back into the depths of the gulf. Thus the height of the natural dyke, which never exceeded thirty feet, has decreased in eighteen months by nearly half. The disappearance of the natural wall between Imperial Valley and the Pacific Ocean is a matter of time.

If this development is not arrested the man-made paradise, its twenty-five settlements, its rich acres, its streets and open spaces are bound to be overwhelmed by a flood of catastrophic proportions.

But strangely enough the prospect of such an occurrence seems to trouble neither Congress nor the few informed inhabitants of Imperial Valley. Although serious authorities have issued warnings in articles appearing in the New York press, lame denials have been the only response. Probably the interest and pressure would be greater if the battlefront lay in American territory. The fact that the dyke formed by the Colorado River, which protects America's most fertile soil, is on Mexican terrain in a region not easily accessible favours indifference to the threat of deluge. "If there is indeed a danger for Imperial Valley," say responsible voices at Washington, "it is the reverse of that. We consider a drought far more likely than a deluge." The root of this fear is to be sought in the structure of the Colorado Dam. It has been calculated that Lake Mead, behind the Hoover Dam, will eventually silt up with sediment from the river and a gradual stoppage of the water conduits become inevitable.

It was once believed that this would happen within a hundred years. More precise measurements have made possible a more optimistic outlook. Apparently it will take at least two hundred and seventy-five years for the blockage of the dam to become dangerous. Imperial Valley must count on a diminution of the water supply which made possible its rise from desert sand to garden oasis. "But who wants to think as far ahead as that?" asked a government official with whom I talked about the matter. "Let future generations find the answer."

"So you think 'After us the deluge'?" I enquired.

"Or the drought," he laughed. "But don't worry. By that time we'll find a solution. There are always new answers to new questions."

Thus he testified firmly to his belief in the duration of the earthly paradise.

The Greatest Threat to Life
on Earth

INSECTS RUN A disassembly line of extraordinary scope, with a cost to man that is astronomical. From all the food we grow, they take at least a tenth. As "nature's lumbermen" they destroy more timber every year than all the forest fires and fungus rots. And ever since the turn of the century, when Ronald Ross earned a Nobel Prize by discovering that mosquitoes carry malaria, the list of diseases transmitted by insects has grown steadily. It now includes many maladies of man, of other animals, and of most kinds of crop plants.

Little by little we accumulate new pests. "One World" for man affords new combinations of food, insects, and disease which make trouble for the human race. We introduce foreign insects to local vegetation and foreign vegetation to native insects. The European corn-borer meant nothing in a maize-lacking Europe. The striped Colorado beetle had no significance until "Irish" potatoes were planted within its reach.

Insects and fungi do so much damage to man's health, crops, and possessions that control of them is essential. Yet his remedies may be worse than the ills they are intended to cure.

Use of chemical treatments against insects began by accident in France. The wine-makers of Bordeaux were bothered by boys who entered the vineyards and stole the luscious grapes as soon as the red color showed clear and dark. To deceive the boys, the growers concocted a gelatinous mixture of copper sulphate, lime, and water, and sprayed it on foliage and fruit alike. Not only did the material conceal the ripeness of the fruit and discourage theft; it also repelled leafhoppers and diminished losses from fungus diseases. Soon the rest of the world heard of the discovery and began using "Bordeaux mixture."

At first most of man's remedies were simple. To kill the young of potato beetles, he adopted the dye called Paris green, a compound of arsenic trioxide and copper acetate. He discovered the value of lime-sulphur sprays for caterpillars, such as those of apple-destroying codling moths. Lime-sulphur was replaced after about a dozen years by a superior poison, lead arsenate, invented in 1892 to save America's shade trees from the immigrant European gypsy moth. Oil poured on ponds killed mosquito wrigglers until 1931, when Paris green was found to do a better job. Most of these materials were cheaper, although less effective, than the "botanicals"—plant extracts such as nicotine from tobacco leaves, pyrethrum from certain daisies, and rotenone from the roots of Far Eastern and South American plants related to clover.

Nicotine is one of the most dangerous poisons known, yet it has no value as an insecticide until it is concentrated and purified. Tobacco leaves are just as susceptible to insect attack as any other foliage, and, to protect them, tobacco-growers began spraying with lead arsenate. Both lead and arsenic are highly toxic to man, but tobacco-consumers were not safeguarded from these substances in tobacco smoke because in 1906 tobacco had been declassified as a drug. It is not a food either, and therefore not covered by the Pure Food and Drug Act.

Arsenical insecticides entered the tobacco leaves upon which they were sprayed. Also, accumulating in the soil of tobacco fields, they were taken in through the roots and spread through the plant, adding still more to the arsenic content of the harvestable leaves. From 1932 to 1951 the arsenic per cigarette increased from 12.6 micrograms to 42—more than three hundred per cent. At the same time, cigarette consumption in the United States rose threefold. Thus, nine times as much arsenic was distributed in cigarettes, vaporized, and inhaled in cigarette smoke at the end of this period as at its beginning. By contrast, cigarettes of Turkish or Macedonian tobacco still have an arsenic content of only .81 micrograms; arsenical insecticides are scarcely used in these areas.

According to Nobel Prize winner Dr. Otto Warburg, the human race has special reason to be concerned about inhaling arsenicals, whether in tobacco smoke, in the fumes from burning coal, petroleum oils, and natural gas, or in the dust from wear of synthetic-rubber tires, road tars, and similar products. Arsenic compounds interfere with the respiration of living cells and can cause cancer. In the same years that arsenicals turned up increasingly in cigarette smoke, arsenic compounds in fumes and dust grew more common, and lung cancer increased two hundred per cent in women and six hundred per cent in men, with cigarette-smokers showing a rise in lung cancer of as much as nine thousand per cent. How much of this is due to tars formed through incomplete combustion of tobacco is unknown. Most tobacco companies are striving to reduce the tar, although arsenic continues to be a hazard. One new cigarette on the market in 1959 was advertised in recognition of this fact: "No tobacco tars, No nicotine and, more important, No arsenic!" The brand (Vanguard) contained no tobacco either. The poisons used on tobacco fields have turned on man.

Lead arsenate and Paris green find less use today, although they were not replaced because of their danger to the human race. They simply ceased to be effective enough against some insects. After lead arsenate had been used for less than thirty-five years, apple-growers in Colorado suddenly realized that the codling moths had got ahead of them. The caterpillars survived ten or twelve sprayings a year, whereas in 1900 two annual sprayings had given good control. These insects had become resistant to the poison, and also to an assortment of others. Some orchardists found themselves unable to raise marketable fruit, and gave up their businesses. In Washington, Virginia, and other states the same resistance to poisons was encountered. Insects were changing.

Even the most potent chemicals grew less effective. In California the citrus-growers had kept their trees free of scale insects by placing canvas tents over the trees and fumigating the insects with hydrocyanic acid— another of the most dangerous poisons known. By 1930 the scale insects grew resistant to the cyanide gas; as few as three per cent died of a standard treatment instead of the former ninety-odd per cent.

Chemists set to work synthesizing insecticides and in 1942 came out with dichloro-diphenyl-trichloro-ethane, now familiar as DDT. It was cheap and amazingly effective, seemingly tailored to the chemical nature of an insect's body. If a fly stood on a thin film of the poison, enough penetrated through its feet to be promptly fatal. The insecticide could be sprayed on walls, dusted on crops, or used to destroy mosquito wrigglers in ponds.

DDT became available just in time for use in World War II. Fleas and lice—companions of soldiers and displaced persons who have little chance to change clothing and keep sanitary—ceased to be a problem. Civilian and military personnel could be kept free of these insects merely by blowing DDT dust into openings of their clothing. Experts on military medicine sighed with relief, for they dreaded fleas and lice. Fleas could bring a recurrence of bubonic plague, the "Black Death" of the Middle Ages. Lice transmit typhus fever, "Red Death," the scourge credited with causing Napoleon's retreat from Moscow, among other pseudo-military defeats. Lice also carry trench fever and relapsing fever.

DDT could be sprayed from aircraft over whole islands in the South Pacific, wiping out all mosquitoes and ending any concern over malaria, dengue, filariasis, and other tropical diseases. Similar techniques applied to forested areas in the United States and Canada were expected to eliminate the gypsy moth and other foes of lumbermen. DDT killed the bark beetles that carry Dutch elm disease from tree to tree; surely this would save New England's American elms. Orchardists tried DDT as a coating over growing apples, anticipating that at last they would be free of codling-moth caterpillars.

Codling moths succumbed to DDT. So did enemies of the two-spotted mites, and these diminutive sap-sucking relatives of spiders became important pests for the first time. They seem immune to the poison, for their feet and bodies differ chemically from those of insects and do not pick up DDT. Mites began destroying foliage wholesale, weakening trees so much that they produced poor crops of apples.

Then DDT-resistant houseflies appeared in Italy (1947), California (1948), Illinois (1949), and elsewhere. In the laboratory, scientists studied them and found that they had really changed. They tolerated not only DDT but other chemicals as well, and mixtures of many among the previously effective insecticides. Over a seven-month period the successive generations raised in captivity increased their immunity from three-fold to two-thousand-fold. Apparently the flies would soon be able to denature any poison as fast as it entered the body. Chemical weapons were losing their value.

Today the old types of mosquitoes are being replaced by new ones immune to DDT. They are spreading from Italy, India, Florida, and California. DDT-resistant lice were encountered in Korea. Despite all our new insecticides, the codling moth, the two-spotted mite, the gypsy moth, the scale insect, and the Colorado potato beetle are still with us.

There is nothing miraculous about the way insects stepped up their ability to break down poisonous molecules and render them harmless. Human organs, notably the liver, do this all the time. Insects merely took advantage of their prolific reproduction and short life span, enormously speeding up the process of evolution by which each species adjusts to new conditions. Since 1900, when the study of inheritance really got started, man has had two generations in which to develop further. In the same period, fruit flies have gone through as many generations as mankind since 57,770 B.C.!

Every time any animal reproduces by sexual means, new combinations of parental characteristics come together. In addition, a small fraction of one per cent among the off-spring show entirely new features through a hereditary trick called mutation. If mutation produces an insect that has greater ability to destroy poisonous molecules than its fellows, this one has a wonderful advantage. It, and others like it, are the ones that survive to reproduce and pass on the new ability.

Man's chemical warfare on insects provides just the kind of tests for which these creatures are especially fitted. Poisons are routine hazards to animals that have adjusted and survived for three hundred million years. By contrast, no fly-swatter ever turned an insect able to escape at ten miles an hour into a jet-propelled body capable of twenty. Man needs to use more ingenuity in developing "conventional" weapons.

Real progress is possible through more insect-proof methods of agriculture and storage. Man can beat termites by building with metal or plastics or ceramic materials. Synthetic fibers have already gone a long way toward eliminating clothes moths. The incinerator and garbage-grinder leave little an insect can use.

We are prone to overlook our natural allies among insects and insect-eating birds and bats. It was only in 1959, after aerial spraying of Maine balsam-fir forests proved unsuccessful in controlling the devastating woolly aphid, that entomologists began releasing the West German beetle *Laricobius erichsonii* in areas of high infestation. *Laricobius* was ready for the job; it used its wings and legs to reach sites on the trunks of balsam trees where the aphids (plant lice) sit, mouth parts pumping sap. DDT sprays from above had come nowhere near them.

Beetles, especially ladybeetles and their young, consume vast numbers of plant lice. Ground beetles thrive on caterpillars, including those of pests in gardens and fields. Birds reduce insect numbers spectacularly. The mosquito population drops when swallows and bats are active. Nuthatches and downy woodpeckers account for between eighty and ninety per cent of the overwintering apple worms in New Hampshire; disease and exposure to cold kill an average of just over two per cent each; parasites and man's poisons stand between the surviving few and damage to the fruit. Living agents of biological control, unlike chemical compounds, can change gradually and automatically along an evolutionary course that keeps up with harmful pests.

Other technological weapons of modern man affect both foe and friend. Every nuclear explosion increases the world's radioactivity. And it is known that radiations, whether from X rays or fall-out, increase the mutation rate. This speeds up the evolutionary process in which insects already outdo man. A nuclear attack and its all-out retaliatory action might end civilization, wiping out man as well as most of the vertebrate animals on land. Some insects—ants and the slow-growing young of the seventeen-year cicada, for instance—would have their own bomb shelters. And if the attack came in winter, the hibernating insects and the cave bats might survive, to emerge into a strange springtime after the fall-out radiations had decreased naturally, perhaps to a tolerable level. When the dust had settled, no doubt insects would be on the wing again, survivors of a still more violent poison of man's devising.

Repeated failures with chemical warfare should have shown us that no poison can ever be a panacea. Yet in the United States alone, more than six hundred different kinds of injurious insects cause annual losses exceeding four billion dollars. Agriculturalists and foresters are unwilling to accept this as inevitable, or to rely on biological control.

In many parts of the world, DDT in concentrations that can be spread economically is no longer effective for house-flies, mosquitoes, cockroaches, bedbugs, fleas, lice, or such caterpillars as those of codling moths. Other and more potent insecticides are used, usually with preference for those which are chemically stable—retaining their poisonous qualities for months or years. During 1957 a total of 65,000 tons of chlorinated hydrocarbons (such as DDT, dieldrin, and heptachlor), 22,500 tons of copper sulphate, 17,500 tons of arsenicals, and 2,000 tons of organic phosphate insecticides (such as parathion) were used to protect agricultural and forest lands, to abate the nuisance of biting insects, to control disease-carrying insects, and to safeguard stored foods. The materials, labor, and equipment cost billions of dollars. Usually the poison was judged entirely upon its effectiveness in killing specific insects in the field, without regard for other animals affected.

Chlorinated hydrocarbons, including DDT, are stable enough to be cumulative. Although spraying at the rate of two pounds to the acre may have no immediate effect upon birds, the poison builds up year after year if repeated. Birds are poisoned by three or more pounds to the acre. In one area of Patuxent National Wildlife Refuge, nesting birds decreased by twenty-six per cent after four successive annual treatments at the rate of two pounds to the acre. In another, the five commonest kinds were sixty-five per cent fewer than before the insecticide was used, with insect-eating warblers and wrens reduced by eighty per cent.

So many birds, particularly nestlings, died within a few weeks after Princeton, New Jersey, applied DDT to save its elms from Dutch elm disease that foresters recommended a new course in future: spray in early spring before the arrival of migrating birds, and then not again until the middle of July, when young birds would be large enough to tolerate the poison. This routine was followed in 1957 in and around the campus of Michigan State University. The university's robin population, long a joy to students and faculty alike because it averaged one

Sydney, Nova Scotia.

breeding pair for each of the 185 acres in the campus, was about ready to migrate south when the DDT mists were applied to the elms at the standard concentration of six per cent. No birds were affected—at that time. But when the robins returned in the spring of 1958, they began dying on all sides. No nest on the campus proved successful, and the only robins seen there after midsummer were three adults and one young of the year, presumably visitors from elsewhere.

Three milligrams of DDT will kill an adult robin. The birds got this lethal dose by eating earthworms, always a favorite food on the campus. The earthworms had fed on fallen elm leaves, which were coated with DDT. The worms concentrated the poison in their bodies until a robin needed to eat fewer than a hundred to be doomed. Yet the elm treatment at Lansing, Michigan, had followed the current recommendations to the letter. Elsewhere, efforts to control the elm disease have left as much as 196 pounds of DDT to the acre in the top three inches of soil!

To learn how far DDT can be passed along, one group of scientists took alfalfa that had been sprayed with the insecticide, fed it to cows, milked the cows and churned the cream, fed butter from the cream to rats, then killed the rats and tested for DDT in the body fat. The poison was recovered there in substantial amounts, its toxic properties intact.

Officers of the U.S. Fish and Wildlife Service saw such destruction of fish and fiddler crabs—important foods of marsh birds—in the swamps of Delaware from aerial spraying with DDT that they tried to block all spraying of marshlands with even one pound to the acre during a three-million-acre campaign against gypsy moths in an arc from Long Island through northern New Jersey, eastern Pennsylvania, and central New York. DDT has been seen to be especially deadly to young fish in nursery shallows and ponds because they eat insects and crustaceans loaded with the poison.

In recent years protests from many quarters have followed the announcement of each new plan to apply insecticides on a wide scale. A case taken before a federal judge in Brooklyn, New York, in 1958 was decided in favor of the defendant, upholding the right of state and federal governments to order the spraying of DDT aerially for control of insects without permission of landowners affected. Although the defense won the case, spraying was postponed or curtailed in many New England states out of respect for the sentiments of the public.

America's outstanding authority on birds, Dr. Robert Cushman Murphy of the American Museum of Natural History, has exerted his influence toward stopping the wide use of poisons on plants and soil.

The National Audubon Society and many other conservation groups have lobbied vigorously against poisoning programs, regarding them as "the greatest threat to life on earth." Under this concerted action, even the terms applied to the poisons have changed. Formerly the insecticides, fungicides, and herbicides were grouped into the more comprehensive category "pesticides." Now a new term has appeared: biocides—"killers of living things." It was used in the accounts describing the hasty withdrawal from the market and frantic testing of cranberries before Thanksgiving of 1959, following the discovery that some growers had misused a weed-killer on the bogs and tainted the fruit.

Biocides were encountered again later in the same year when several shipments of chickens were condemned and destroyed because they were found to contain traces of a dangerous chemical. These actions were in keeping with the 1958 ruling of the United States Supreme Court that the word "harmless" in the Food, Drug and Cosmetic Act of 1938 means "absolutely harmless," and that foods to which poisons have been added are "not to be used at all." Curiously, the Food and Drug Act applies to fruits, vegetables, and fish, but meat comes under the jurisdiction of the U.S. Department of Agriculture, which has less strict rules.

Public alarm over biocides worries the chemical-producers. They fear that research costs will be prohibitive if it becomes necessary to spend several million dollars and a period of perhaps five years in testing each new product before it can be marketed. Fish-canners are also distressed. They realize that salmon, our foremost food fish, moves from the oceans to fresh water to reproduce and depends upon early development in streams. The flesh and bones can be contaminated by radioactive wastes dumped in the ocean, or by DDT and other biocides draining into the streams from the land.

Saving a spruce forest from budworm can mean ruining a salmon crop in another way. Fisheries scientists have demonstrated recently that improvements in the nourishment of young salmon in their freshwater stages correspond to larger size at the time of migration to the sea. Larger size goes with greater vigor and ability to compete in the oceans, and with better harvests when the mature fish return to the rivers to reproduce. On the other hand, when biocides from aerial spraying of forest-covered watersheds drain into salmon streams, they kill the aquatic insects on which the young fish depend. This leads to undersized, malnourished smolts going to sea, fewer survivors, and a decreased catch by the fishing industry.

Conservationists have correctly pointed to the willingness of legislatures to vote millions of dollars for application of biocides, but virtually no money for research on the broad effects of these programs. One major conflict concerned the stinging ant *Solenopsis saevissima*, which became established about 1918 at the port city of Mobile, Alabama. Although it is known as the "fire ant" from the intense burning sensation it produces on human skin, the quarter-inch insect affected so few Alabamians that little attempt was made to eradicate it. Some farmers complained that fire ants built fort-like mounds a foot high and nearly three feet in diameter, each a cement-hard hazard to agricultural equipment. If a mound is disturbed, the ants swarm out and make manual labor nearby decidedly painful. Owners of land with heavy infestations sometimes found it easier to abandon the land than to get laborers to work on it. Nor are these effects of fire ants new. In 1863 the famous explorer Henry Walter Bates told in his book *The Naturalist on the Amazons* of whole villages deserted as soon as fire ants moved in.

Entomologists are still uncertain whether the dark-reddish fire ants of Mobile mutated during the 1930's, or whether a second invasion from South America struck the same city. Suddenly the original ants were supplemented by a smaller, paler type, a far more aggressive race that even attacked and destroyed colonies of the dark form. In South America the dark kind is found in northern and central Argentina and southern Uruguay. Probably it reached the United States aboard a ship from Buenos Aires or Montevideo. The light-colored race occurs more widely in South America: in the Guianas, far up the Amazon and elsewhere in Brazil, in Bolivia, Paraguay, Uruguay, and Argentina.

Whatever the source of the paler fire ants, they posed far more problems. Although they built smaller mounds, they spread rapidly out of Mobile. By 1940 they reached Mississippi to the west and Florida to the east. In 1953 entomologists found them in Louisiana. By 1957 they were in Texas, Arkansas, Georgia, and had progressed northward in Alabama almost to the Tennessee boundary. Oklahoma and both Carolinas reported fire ants in 1958, Virginia in 1959. At first it was hoped that frost would kill them each winter. But the ants merely burrowed more deeply, staying below frozen soil.

In South America, fire ants subsist chiefly on seeds, insects such as caterpillars, and the "honeydew" they gather from living plant lice. In the United States they supplement this diet occasionally by destroying seedlings of corn and other important crops, and devour helpless young birds in the nest. Quail chicks scamper around too actively to be bothered by ants. Yet these insects reach them too, by swarming into eggs as soon as the little bird inside pips a hole for escape. Fire ants attack newborn lambs, pigs, and calves, sometimes with fatal results. And they rout field laborers harvesting cotton, corn, potatoes, peanuts, and strawberries.

Alabama began a co-operative program to control fire ants in 1937, seven years after the first official report of damage by this insect. By 1950 the entomologists had found no insecticide giving better than 90-per-cent control. Treatment was still experimental, applied locally from equipment on the ground. Only Alabamians felt much concern over the fire ant. The 1952 *Yearbook of Agriculture*, devoted entirely to insects, mentions fire ants only in connection with their attacks on quail nests.

The explosive spread of light-race fire ants in the 1950's brought these insects into painful contact with far more people, and demands reached the U.S. Department of Agriculture for emergency measures. For three successive years Congress allocated $2,400,000—$7,200,000 in all—for an eradication program extending from Texas to Florida. Between thirty-one and forty-seven thousand square miles of infested and susceptible land were to be treated by aerial spraying with dieldrin and heptachlor at the rate of two pounds to the acre. These two chlorinated hydrocarbons are fifteen times more powerful than DDT, and remain in the soil at dangerous concentrations for three to ten years.

The U.S. Fish and Wildlife Service protested immediately. Sports fishermen sent lobbies to Washington and to state legislatures. Nevertheless, the Florida lawmakers approved a bill to pay $500,000 for their share in the program. The governor vetoed the bill, recalling a State Board of Health report showing that a single pound of dieldrin to the acre of marshland destroyed the entire fish population of more than thirty species. The legislature overrode the veto, despite the further information that a pound to the acre killed virtually all larger animals in treated water except a few snails and other shellfish.

Sports fishermen pointed out that their hobby alone led to expenditures close to two billion dollars annually, a quarter of this spent in the threatened area. They deplored any more that would "risk destroying priceless fish and other wildlife in at least five states." Everyone agreed that when poisons are broadcast from aircraft, some areas are missed entirely, leaving islands from which a pest can re-infest adjacent land. Other areas accidentally receive double doses, although the first treatment is calculated to apply the highest concentration to get the best kill consistent with safety. Yet all this work involves chemicals whose long-term effects on man and domestic animals, let alone on wildlife in general, have not been determined.

Conservation departments in Alabama, Georgia, Louisiana, and Texas hurriedly published descriptions of the outcome after treating the first 6,250 square miles in 1958. In less than two days after the granules of insecticide hit the ground, "alarming numbers of dead insects, many of them important in insect control or as bird food," were killed in Georgia and Texas. As promptly, naturalists found appalling numbers of songbirds and game birds lying dead in fields and streets, woods and marshes. Quail in Alabama and Texas were decimated or wiped out. Ornithologists could count only between three and eight per cent of the number of kinds of other birds seen previously.

More than a hundred head of cattle near Climax, Georgia, died suddenly after being sprayed with dieldrin from airplanes. Brood sows lost their litters. Rabbits were hard hit or exterminated, and fox cubs were found dead in their dens; the two insecticides were recovered from the flesh of these animals. Squirrels, nutrias, cotton rats, white-footed mice, raccoons, opossums, and armadillos died in large numbers.

In Louisiana the earthworm population suffered an eighty-per-cent destruction, and anglers complained that their carefully prepared worm beds were wiped out completely. Water animals proved even more susceptible: fishes, crustaceans, even snails were devastated within two or three days after the aerial poisoning of marshes, ponds, and streams. Survivors were still dying seven weeks after the spraying ended. Fire ants, however, remained in many places.

The fire-ant eradication program, which did not eradicate the fire ant, is the largest attempt so far to use a new weapon before testing it and insuring the specificity of its application. Perhaps, as an exhibit, it will help prevent any future action of the same kind, no matter how acute the local panic.

To many people it is incredible that the program was tried at all. No mention of any serious loss from fire ants in any southern state appears in the *Cooperative Economic Insect Report for 1957*, published by the U.S. Department of Agriculture. The *1957 Yearbook of Agriculture*, devoted to the subject of soil use, lists the fire ant only among twenty-two injurious insects for which dieldrin has proved effective. Early in 1959 the federal government scaled down its recommendation on dieldrin from two pounds to the acre to one and a quarter pounds, with no explanation of how the higher figure had been set in the first place. In Alabama, where the fire-ant problem began, the state Ways and Means Committee held hearings to learn what damage the ants had actually caused; its considered judgment, passed along to the legislature in 1959, was that the fire ant posed no threat to agriculture or livestock production; Alabama declined to participate in the federal-state-farmer program during the next biennium. At the same time, proponents of ant control by biocides in Georgia admitted that the fire ant is primarily a "nuisance."

America's beloved "eagle man," Charles Broley, who banded more eagles than anyone else on earth, attributed the rapid decline of our national bird largely to sterility from feeding on fish and mice containing biocides. Laboratory confirmation can scarcely be attempted in the case of such a large bird, but something similar has been found about quail and pheasants. If breeding quail are fed DDT-tainted grain, more than eighty-seven per cent of their chicks die within the first three months—even if they receive no additional DDT. Pheasants that receive even lower amounts of DDT throughout their growing period produce few eggs, although the fertility and hatchability and chick survival seem unimpaired. Effects of this kind, and the loss of normal supplies of insects as food, are believed to explain the drastically smaller populations of bluebirds, warblers, wrens, swallows, nighthawks, and whippoorwills seen today.

Probably mass applications of biocides should be avoided except in dire emergency, or be restricted to areas where man has altered the natural community of plants and animals for raising one particular crop to the complete exclusion of all else. Poisons for injurious insects are somewhat like antibiotics for human diseases. They tempt the practitioner to use them for quick results even before a firm diagnosis has been made. As with antibiotics, the side effects from insecticides can be disastrous. Moreover, a penicillin-resistant strain of *Streptococcus* seems a parallel to a DDT-resistant race of houseflies. Both have mutated in response to poisons applied routinely.

In the field of medicine, the need for aseptic precautions has never lessened because antibiotics were available. In the field of economic biology, a return to the old methods has been found valuable too. Water management is now seen to be preferable to the use of insecticides on mosquito breeding areas. It is better to build a dike and flood a marsh, allowing fish to control mosquito wrigglers, than to cut ditches and attempt complete drainage. Permanent ponds inhabited by fish produce few mosquitoes. Instead, they yield more fish, ducks, muskrats, and a high water table in adjacent soils. By working to restore balance in the web of life, man is using nature's weapons. He may not receive the hoped-for hundred-per-cent yield on his crops, but his future can be more secure.

To Survive on Earth

As a biologist, I have reached this conclusion: we have come to a turning point in the human habitation of the earth. The environment is a complex, subtly balanced system, and it is this integrated whole which receives the impact of all the separate insults inflicted by pollutants. Never before in the history of this planet has its thin life-supporting surface been subjected to such diverse, novel, and potent agents. I believe that the cumulative effects of these pollutants, their interactions and amplification, can be fatal to the complex fabric of the biosphere. And, because man is, after all, a dependent part of this system, I believe that continued pollution of the earth, if unchecked, will eventually destroy the fitness of this planet as a place for human life. . . .

Nuclear war would, I believe, inevitably destroy the economic, social, and political structure of the combatant nations; it would reduce their populations, industry and agriculture to chaotic remnants, incapable of supporting an organized effort for recovery. I believe that world-wide radioactive contamination, epidemics, ecological disasters, and possibly climatic changes would so gravely affect the stability of the biosphere as to threaten human survival everywhere on the earth.

If we are to survive, we need to become aware of the damaging effects of technological innovations, determine their economic and social costs, balance these against the expected benefits, make the facts broadly available to the public, and take the action needed to achieve an acceptable balance of benefits and hazards. Obviously, all this should be done *before* we become massively committed to a new technology. One of our most urgent needs is to establish within the scientific community some means of estimating and reporting on the expected benefits and hazards of proposed environmental interventions *in advance*. Such advance consideration could have averted many of our present difficulties with detergents, insecticides, and radioactive contaminants.

It could have warned us of the tragic futility of attempting to defend the nation's security by a means that can only lead to the nation's destruction.

We have not yet learned this lesson. Despite our earlier experience with nondegradable detergents, the degradable detergents which replaced them were massively marketed, by joint action of the industry in 1965, without any pilot study of their ecological effects. The phosphates which even the new detergents introduce into surface waters may force their eventual withdrawal. The United States, Great Britain, and France are already committed to costly programs for supersonic transport planes but have thus far failed to produce a comprehensive evaluation of the hazards from sonic boom, from cosmic radioactivity, and from the physiological effects of rapid transport from one time zone to another. The security of every nation in the world remains tied to nuclear armaments, and we continue to evade an open public discussion of the basic question: do we wish to commit the security of nations to a military system which is likely to destroy them?

It is urgent that we face this issue openly, now, before by accident or design we are overtaken by nuclear catastrophe. U Thant has proposed that the United Nations prepare a report on the effects of nuclear war and disseminate it throughout the world. Such a report could become the cornerstone of world peace. For the world would then know that, so long as nuclear war remains possible, we are all counters in a colossal gamble with the survival of civilization.

The costs of correcting past mistakes and preventing the threatened ones are already staggering, for the technologies which have produced them are now deeply embedded in our economic, social, and political structure. From what is now known about the smog problem, I think it unlikely that gasoline-driven automobiles can long continue to serve as the chief vehicle of urban and suburban transportation without imposing a health hazard which most of us would be unwilling to accept. Some improvement will probably result from the use of new devices to reduce emission of waste gasoline. But in view of the increasing demand for urban transportation any really effective effort to reduce the emission of waste fuel, carbon monoxide, and lead will probably require electric-powered vehicles and the replacement of urban highway systems by rapid transit lines. Added to current demands for highway-safe cars, the demand for smog-free transportation is certain to have an important impact on the powerful and deeply entrenched automobile industry.

The rapidly accelerating pollution of our surface waters with excessive phosphate and nitrate from sewage and detergents will, I believe, necessitate a drastic revision of urban waste systems. It may be possible

View on the Monongahela River, Pennsylvania

to remove phosphates effectively by major modifications of sewage and water treatment plants, but there are no methods in sight that might counter the accumulation of nitrate. Hence, control will probably need to be based chiefly on preventing the entry of these pollutants into surface waters.

According to a report by the Committee on Pollution, National Academy of Sciences, we need to plan for a complete transformation of urban waste-removal systems, in particular to end the present practice of using water to get rid of solid wastes. The technological problems involved are so complex that the report recommends, as an initial step, the construction of a small pilot city to try out the new approach.

The high productivity of American agriculture, and therefore its economic structure, is based on the use of large amounts of mineral fertilizer in which phosphate and nitrate are major components. This fertilizer is not entirely absorbed by the crops and the remainder runs off into streams and lakes. As a result, by nourishing our crops and raising agricultural production, we help to kill off our lakes and rivers. Since there is no foreseeable means of removing fertilizer runoff from surface waters, it will become necessary, it seems to me, to impose severe restrictions on the present unlimited use of mineral fertilizers in agriculture. Proposed restraints on the use of synthetic pesticides have already aroused a great deal of opposition from the chemical industry and from agriculture. Judged by this response, an attempt to regulate the use of mineral fertilizers will confront us with an explosive economic and political problem.

And suppose that, as it may, the accumulation of carbon dioxide begins to threaten the entire globe with catastrophic floods. Control of this danger would require the modification, throughout the world, of domestic furnaces and industrial combustion plants—for example, by the addition of devices to absorb carbon dioxide from the flue gases. Combustion-driven power plants could perhaps be replaced with nuclear ones, but this would pose the problem of safely disposing of massive amounts of radioactive wastes and create the hazard of reactor accidents near centers of population. Solar power, and other techniques for the production of electrical power which do not require either combustion or nuclear reactors, may be the best solution. But here too massive technological changes will be needed in all industrial nations.

The problems of industrial and agricultural pollution, while exceedingly large, complex, and costly, are nevertheless capable of correction by the proper technological means. We are still in a period of grace, and if we are willing to pay the price, as large as it is, there is yet time to restore and preserve the biological quality of the environment. But the most immediate threat to survival—nuclear war—would be a blunder from which there would be no return. I know of no technological means, no form of civil defense or counteroffensive warfare, which could reliably protect the biosphere from the catastrophic effects of a major nuclear war. There is, in my opinion, only one way to survive the threats of nuclear war—and that is to insure that it never happens. And because of the appreciable chance of an accidental nuclear war, I believe that the only way to do so is to destroy the world's stock of nuclear weapons and to develop less self-defeating means of protecting national security. Needless to say, the political difficulties involved in international nuclear disarmament are monumental.

Despite the dazzling successes of modern technology and the unprecedented power of modern military systems, they suffer from a common and catastrophic fault. While providing us with a bountiful supply of food, with great industrial plants, with high-speed transportation, and with military weapons of unprecedented power, they threaten our very survival. Technology has not only built the magnificent material base of modern society, but also confronts us with threats to survival which cannot be corrected unless we solve very grave economic, social, and political problems.

How can we explain this paradox? The answer is, I believe, that our technological society has committed a blunder familiar to us from the nineteenth century, when the dominant industries of the day, especially lumbering and mining, were successfully developed—by plundering the earth's natural resources. These industries provided cheap materials for constructing a new industrial society, but they accumulated a huge debt in destroyed and depleted resources, which had to be paid by later generations. The conservation movement was created in the United States to control these greedy assaults on our resources. The same thing is happening today, but now we are stealing from future generations not just their lumber or their coal, but the basic necessities of life: air, water, and soil. A new conservation movement is needed to preserve life itself.

The earlier ravages of our resources made very visible marks, but the new attacks are largely hidden. Thoughtless lumbering practices left vast scars on the land, but thoughtless development of modern industrial, agricultural, and military methods only gradually poison the air and water. Many of the pollutants—carbon dioxide, radioisotopes, pesticides, and excess nitrate—are invisible and go largely unnoticed until a lake dies, a river becomes foul, or children sicken. This time the world is being plundered in secret.

The earlier depredations on our resources were usually made with a fair knowledge of the harmful consequences, for it is difficult to escape the fact that erosion quickly follows the deforestation of a hillside. The difficulty lay not in scientific ignorance, but in willful greed. In the present situation, the hazards of modern pollutants are generally not appreciated until after the technologies which produce them are well established in the economy. While this ignorance absolves us from the immorality of the knowingly destructive acts that characterized the nineteenth century raids on our resources, the present fault is more serious. It signifies that the capability of science to guide us in our interventions into nature has been seriously eroded—that science has, indeed, got out of hand.

In this situation, scientists bear a very grave responsibility, for they are the guardians of the integrity of science. In the last few decades serious weaknesses in this system of principles have begun to appear. Secrecy has hampered free discourse. Major scientific enterprises have been governed by narrow national aims. In some cases, especially in the exploration of space, scientists have become so closely tied to basically political aims as to relinquish their traditional devotion to open discussion of conflicting views on what are often doubtful scientific conclusions.

. . . Unfortunately, under modern conditions there are often close ties between military operations and basic scientific research, and the secrecy which is generated by military demands can work against the progress of science. Particularly illuminating examples can be found in our recent experiences with large-scale space experiments.

One of the main products of post-World War II military work was the development of powerful ballistic rockets. Although these were designed primarily to carry nuclear warheads, they are also able to carry loads of scientific instruments high above the earth. Data reported back from such rockets led to the discovery of a wholly unsuspected feature of our planet—that it carries with it on its passage through space bands of atomic particles held in certain zones around the earth by its magnetic field.

These newly discovered zones—the Van Allen belts—interact strongly with radio waves used in long-range communications, a fact which suggested a particular military application. Government researchers proposed that a nuclear weapon exploded at high altitude might inject additional atomic particles into the Van Allen belts and thereby seriously disrupt radio communication—a capability of some military importance.

This idea, like many military concepts, was "born classified" and was discussed only among those personnel who had access to such secret matters. In August 1958, three nuclear bombs were exploded secretly by the United States over the South Atlantic. When this fact was made public some six months later, the disclosure was met with a vigorous protest from scientists in the United States and abroad. They complained that so little was as yet known about the newly discovered belts that such gross experimental intervention might make long-lived changes in the natural bands and thereby confuse future scientific studies. This is precisely what happened.

In April 1962, the United States government announced that a new test—Project Starfish—was planned, and again scientists protested that the explosion might produce enough atomic particles to cause large and persistent changes in the natural Van Allen belts. It was argued that such effects might damage experimental satellites, increase the radiation hazard to astronauts, interfere with future radioastronomical observations, and hamper further study of the natural Van Allen belts.

A hot scientific controversy developed over these issues, but because of the secrecy restrictions under which the experiment operated, open discussion of differing views was rather difficult. The United States government asked a group of experts for advice. Meeting under secrecy restrictions, the committee reached the conclusion, which was then made public, that "there is no need for concern regarding any lasting effects on the Van Allen belts and associated phenomena." According to the committee, the explosion's effects on the belts would last "a few weeks to a few months."

On July 9, 1962, still governed by military security, the high-altitude explosion was set off over the Pacific. For some weeks no official information about the results was announced. But despite official silence and the project's military classification, the results of the explosion were soon no more secret than the Van Allen belts themselves. Radioastronomers in Boulder, Colorado, detected on their instruments new radio reflections from the Van Allen belts. These showed that, in the vicinity of the explosion, new zones of atomic particles had been created and that, contrary to the prediction of the government's advisory committee, these were persistent. A check with colleagues in Hawaii and Japan quickly confirmed the results. Thus, by pursuing their own quite open studies, the Colorado astronomers found themselves in possession of information which contradicted government statements about a classified military project. When the information was reported to newspapers, the secret was out. Shortly thereafter the presence of persistent bands as an aftermath of the Starfish explosion was acknowledged by an official government statement.

For months afterward there was an intense scientific debate—partly in the open and partly under security restrictions—about the expected longevity of the new belts. After a year of controversy, a scientific review reported a consensus that in certain parts of the Van Allen belt "it may be necessary to wait more than thirty years" before the natural situation is restored. It was also reported that several experimental satellites, including a joint U.S.–British experiment, *Ariel*, were severely damaged by radiation from the Starfish explosion. The report of the government's advisory committee working under the limitations of secrecy had failed to provide an accurate prediction of the consequences of the high-altitude nuclear explosion. . . .

What can scientists do to restore the integrity of science and to provide the kind of careful guidance to technology that is essential if we are to avoid catastrophic mistakes? No new principles are needed; instead, scientists need to find new ways to protect science itself from the encroachment of political pressures. This is not a new problem, for science and scholarship have often been under assault when their freedom to seek and to discuss the truth becomes a threat to existing economic or political power. The internal strength of science and its capability to understand nature have been weakened whenever the principles of scientific discourse were compromised, and restored when these principles were defended. The medieval suppressions of natural science, the perversion of science by Nazi racial theories, Soviet restraints on theories of genetics, and the suppression by United States military secrecy of open discussion of the Starfish project, have all been paid for in the most costly coin—knowledge. The lesson of all these experiences is the same. If science is to perform its duty to society, which is to guide, by objective knowledge, human interactions with the rest of nature, its integrity must be defended. Scientists must find ways to remove the restraints of secrecy, to insist on open discussion of the possible consequences of large-scale experiments *before* they are undertaken, to resist the hasty and unconditional support of conclusions that conform to the demands of current political or economic policy.

Apart from these duties toward science, I believe that scientists have a responsibility in relation to the technological uses which are made of scientific developments. In my opinion, the proper duty of the scientist to the social consequence of his work cannot be fulfilled by aloofness or by an approach which arrogates to scientists alone the social and moral judgments which are the right of every citizen. I propose that scientists are now bound by a new duty which adds to and extends their older responsibility for scholarship and teaching.

We have the duty to inform, and to inform in keeping with the traditional principles of science, taking into account all relevant data and interpretations. This is an involuntary obligation to society; we have no right to withhold information from our fellow citizens, or to color its meaning with our own social judgments. . . .

The moral issues of the modern world are embedded in the complex substance of science and technology. The exercise of morality now requires the determination of right between the farmers whose pesticides poison the water and the fishermen whose livelihood may thereby be destroyed. It calls for a judgment between the advantages of replacing a smoky urban power generator with a smoke-free nuclear one which carries with it some hazard of a catastrophic accident. The ethical principles involved are no different from those invoked in earlier times, but the moral issues cannot be discerned unless the new substance in which they are expressed is understood. And since the substance of science is still often poorly perceived by most citizens, the technical content of the issues of the modern world shields them from moral judgment.

Nowhere is this more evident than in the case of nuclear war. The horrible face of nuclear war can only be described in scientific terms. It can be pictured only in the language of roentgens and megatonnage; it can be understood only by those who have some appreciation of industrial organization, of human biology, of the intricacies of world-wide ecology. The self-destructiveness of nuclear war lies hidden behind a mask of science and technology. It is this shield, I believe, which has protected this most fateful moral issue in the history of man from the judgment of human morality. The greatest moral crime of our time is the concealment of the nature of nuclear war, for it deprives humanity of the solemn right to sit in judgment on its own fate; it condemns us all, unwittingly, to the greatest dereliction of conscience.

The obligation which our technological society forces upon all of us, scientist and citizen alike, is to discover how humanity can survive the new power which science has given it. It is already clear that even our present difficulties demand far-reaching social and political actions. Solution of our pollution problems will drastically affect the economic structure of the automobile industry, the power industry, and agriculture and will require basic changes in urban organization. To remove the threat of nuclear catastrophe we will be forced at last to resolve the pervasive international conflicts that have bloodied nearly every generation with war.

Every major advance in the technological competence of man has enforced revolutionary changes in the economic and political structure of society. The present age of technology is no exception to this rule of history. We already know the enormous benefits it can bestow; we have begun to perceive its frightful threats. The political crisis generated by this knowledge is upon us.

Science can reveal the depth of this crisis, but only social action can resolve it. Science can now serve society by exposing the crisis of modern technology to the judgment of all mankind. Only this judgment can determine whether the knowledge that science has given us shall destroy humanity or advance the welfare of man.

A Fable for Tomorrow

THERE WAS ONCE A town in the heart of America where all life seemed to live in harmony with its surroundings. The town lay in the midst of a checkerboard of prosperous farms, with fields of grain and hillsides of orchards where, in spring, white clouds of bloom drifted about the green fields. In autumn, oak and maple and birch set up a blaze of color that flamed and flickered across the backdrop of pines. Then foxes barked in the hills and deer silently crossed the fields, half hidden in the mists of the fall mornings.

Along the roads, laurel, viburnum and alder, great ferns and wildflowers delighted the traveler's eye through much of the year. Even in winter the roadsides were places of beauty, where countless birds came to feed on the berries and on the seed heads of the dried weeds rising above the snow. The countryside was, in fact, famous for the abundance and variety of its bird life, and when the flood of migrants was pouring through in spring and fall people traveled from great distances to observe them. Others came to fish the streams, which flowed clear and cold out of the hills and contained shady pools where trout lay. So it had been from the days many years ago when the first settlers raised their houses, sank their wells, and built their barns.

Then a strange blight crept over the area and everything began to change. Some evil spell had settled on the community: mysterious maladies swept the flocks of chickens; the cattle and sheep sickened and died. Everywhere was a shadow of death. The farmers spoke of much illness among their families. In the town the doctors had become more and more puzzled by new kinds of sickness appearing among their patients. There had been several sudden and unexplained deaths, not only among adults but even among children, who would be stricken suddenly while at play and die within a few hours.

There was a strange stillness. The birds, for example—where had they gone? Many people spoke of them, puzzled and disturbed. The feeding stations in the backyards were deserted. The few birds seen anywhere were moribund; they trembled violently and could not fly. It was a spring without voices. On the mornings that had once throbbed with the dawn chorus of robins, catbirds, doves, jays, wrens, and scores of other bird voices there was now no sound; only silence lay over the fields and woods and marsh.

On the farms the hens brooded, but no chicks hatched. The farmers complained that they were unable to raise any pigs—the litters were small and the young survived only a few days. The apple trees were coming into bloom but no bees droned among the blossoms, so there was no pollination and there would be no fruit.

The roadsides, once so attractive, were now lined with browned and withered vegetation as though swept by fire. These, too, were silent, deserted by all living things. Even the streams were now lifeless. Anglers no longer visited them, for all the fish had died.

In the gutters under the eaves and between the shingles of the roofs, a white granular powder still showed a few patches; some weeks before it had fallen like snow upon the roofs and the lawns, the field and streams.

No witchcraft, no enemy action had silenced the rebirth of new life in this stricken world. The people had done it themselves.

5

Looking for a Silver Lining

THE HOPE OF LULLING oneself to sleep by reading this book has now disappeared. By now, the reader must have taken sides in one of the most crucial controversies of our times, waxing either mad or sad, or both. Here, made explicit, are the basic errors out of which all of our daily troubles, from Vietnam to increasing crime, have sprung. Thus it was that when I started out, I could not be satisfied simply with collecting antiques, bits of memorabilia, insisting that these pleasant and nostalgic scenes had no meaning in any context but their own, and that I was gathering them together merely to gratify the dilettante. These essays have formidable implications for our future, and I hope that by piecing them together we can understand the things that are taking place all around us. Events that we find disturbing, but which in bewilderment we cannot relate to anything but a malignant fate, arise out of our own preoccupation with the magic of science. We have, so to speak, sown the seeds of our scientific and technical knowledge to the wind, believing that these seeds would grow a material utopia wherein man would have complete mastery of nature. This faith is being broken by our experience. But we have not yet learned the vital arts of cultivation and control.

What hope is there for the future? There may be none, but in the following selections the reader will find wise and perceptive analyses of current trends and hear calm and reasonable voices which I am sure our society cannot afford to ignore.

The Twentieth Century: Dawn
or Twilight?

WHAT PHILOSOPHERS USED to call "the good life" is difficult to define and impossible to measure. In the United States today—increasingly also in all "progressive" countries—we substitute for it "the standard of living," which is easy to measure if defined only in terms of wealth, health, comfort, and convenience. But the standard of living does not truly represent the goodness of a life unless you assume that no other goods are real or at least that the less tangible and less measurable bear a direct functional relation to the tangible.

Even when measuring the standard as such we put greater and greater stress upon its most trivial and, indeed, most dubious aspects. A recent magazine article about Russia by one of the most widely read commentators on the world situation includes these remarkable sentences: "(In Moscow) the day-to-day routine of most citizens is inexpressibly dreary. No local citizen has ever read a gossip column or played canasta. No one has ever seen a supermarket, a drive-in movie, a motel or a golf course. Nobody has ever shopped by mail or paid a bill by check. No one has ever seen an electric toaster, a sidewalk café, a shoeshine parlor or a funeral home. I never saw a girl with dark glasses or encountered a Russian with a cigarette lighter."

Is life necessarily "inexpressibly dreary" without these things? Is our ability to supply them the best proof of the superiority of our civilization to that of Russia? If the answer to both the questions is "no," if these are not major, indispensable items in the good life, then it is obvious that either this writer (who has repeatedly demonstrated his ability to be understood and accepted by a large section of the more serious-minded public) has a wrong notion of what constitutes a high standard of living or the relation between such a high standard and the good life is by no means an identity.

Unless one is prepared to accept as inevitable such confusions as

222

his, or to regard them as a small privilege to pay for prosperity and the other blessings of modern society, then it must appear that not even kindliness and generosity are sufficient to make the good life an inevitable consequence of wealth and power.

Wealth can come to be loved for itself alone, but also and more insidiously for the trivialities and vulgarities it enables one to obtain. Power can be used to oppress and abuse, but it can also become insidiously a threat to those who wield it and the occasion, as in the modern world it is, not of confidence but of an insecurity more acute than any powerful nation ever suffered from before.

Even those who recognize these paradoxes and are troubled by them are reluctant to consider the possibility that they suggest a revision of the fundamental premises which have made our civilization what it is. They may be both offended by the vulgarities of an almost too prosperous economy and frightened by threats which exist only because man has achieved so successfully the power he has for two centuries been seeking. They may even share Albert Einstein's doubt that the modern American is any happier than was the Indian whose continent he took. But they still take it for granted that if there is any right road it is the one we have been following.

If we are no happier than the Indians, that may be because some perversity in the human animal makes more than a certain degree of happiness impossible to him. If that is not the case, and if superabundant bread has so far created a society which only gossip columns and drive-in movies redeem from utter dreariness, then perhaps, so most people seem to believe, this is only because we need still more wealth still more equitably distributed. If power has not brought security, if indeed the most astonishing of new acquisitions has enormously increased the sense of insecurity, then perhaps what we need to know is how to "control nature" even more successfully. At least if none of these perhapses is true then few seem able to imagine any other which could be. Certainly few are prepared to abandon faith in wealth and power as such or able to imagine what else might reasonably be pursued instead.

Ours is not only the richest and most powerful civilization that ever existed, but also one of the most uneasy both without and within —within, perhaps because we feel some undefined lack in wealth and power; without, for a plain and simple reason.

Side by side with the optimism which success in achieving our immediate aims has seemed to justify, there has grown among intellectuals what some see as a perverse cult of despair and a readiness to accept as inevitable "the decline of the West." And though the average man

Across the Monongahela River, Braddock, Pennsylvania.

certainly does not share this pessimism, he is likely to have heard enough about it and about the grounds upon which it is based to be puzzled by certain ambiguities.

On the one hand technology and that ability to "control nature" in which he so profoundly believes is so far from being in a state of decline that it still follows a sharply ascending curve. There are new worlds to conquer and space travel will begin tomorrow. Yet he cannot, on the other hand, fail to be aware that intercontinental missiles are already here and that our enemies may quite possibly have better ones than we have. Do these recent developments mark a new stage in man's triumphant conquest of nature or the beginning of the catastrophe with which a decline will end?

Progress is strangely mixed up with threats, and the release of atomic energy is, among many "firsts," the first technological triumph widely regarded as possibly, all things considered, a misfortune. To be sure, old fogies have always viewed with alarm. They thought twenty-five miles an hour in an automobile too fast; they shook their heads over the airplane; and it is possible that some conservatives among cave men were sure that no good would come of the wheel. But doubts about the atom are not confined to old fogies. They are shared by some of the very men who tinkered with it so successfully. The suspicion that man may at last have become too smart for his own good is nervously entertained in some very respectable quarters. Observing one of those bright new exploding stars called nova in the night sky, a famous American astronomer is said to have remarked with resignation, "Well, there goes another place where they found out how to do it."

The most prevalent opinion among our so confused contemporaries seems to be that tomorrow will be wonderful—that is, unless it is indescribably terrible, or unless indeed there just isn't any. If we are wise enough and lucky enough to escape all the various catastrophes which threaten, then there is no limit to the power and the glory ahead, no limit to the wealth, comfort, and convenience either. But the nagging "if" remains. Have we caught a Tartar or has the Tartar caught us? "He who rides a tiger does not dare to dismount."

There have been ages of hope and ages of despair before now. Historians of ideas inform us that for a thousand years nobody believed in Progress. They inform us also that the general opinion shortly before the year one thousand was that the world was about to end, although, five hundred years later, the notion that the possibilities open to man were limitless was already beginning to be widely assumed. But were the two opinions ever before held simultaneously and progress itself regarded as the possible cause of impending catastrophe?

A recent public relations advertisement by North American Aviation reads: "Supersonic supremacy is the absolute condition of America's future security. It is a day-to-day thing. It must grow with major advances." What we are being told—truthfully enough, it seems—is that we must run as fast as we possibly can if we are to remain where we are. The reward of heroic effort will not be some boon we never enjoyed before, and it will not be the conquest and enrichment which the proponents of military might used to promise. It will be merely the possibility of staying alive. This seems a rather insecure sort of security, though "security" is what it is here called.

If we turn to those of our contemporaries who are professionally occupied, not with the atom, but with the life of our fellow human beings, there is no escaping the fact that man as he appears in the most esteemed contemporary literature, American or European, is an unattractive creature and his life a distressing thing. Our novelists and poets may be wrong. Probably they do exaggerate somewhat and the majority of even their readers does not believe that either man or human existence is quite so unrelievedly dismal as they are made out. But at least this is what the most eloquent and respected among the writers do make out modern man and modern life to be.

It is true that the literary man as spokesman and prophet does not stand very high today even among the more educated classes. Any contemporary Heroes and Hero Worship would have to put the Hero as Man of Letters low in the hierarchy and the Hero as Man of Science at the top. But suppose we turn to these modern heroes. From some of the best of them you will get cold comfort. Here, for instance, is J. Robert Oppenheimer:

"Nuclear weapons and all the machinery of war surrounding us now haunt our imaginations with an apocalyptic vision that could well become a terrible reality: the disappearance of man as a species from the surface of the earth. It is quite possible. But what is more probable, more immediate and in my opinion equally terrifying is the prospect that man will survive while losing his precious heritage, his civilization and his very humanity."

Perhaps the physicists do have the best brains now functioning and it is something to have them used, as here they are, to think about man as well as about the things man makes.

Mr. Oppenheimer has reason to know that doing so has its dangers, and the eight leading scientists (including two Nobel Prize men) who consented some time ago to celebrate the centenary of Seagram's whiskey on TV by taking part in a symposium discussing the prospects for man a hundred years hence, were perhaps only playing safe when they confined themselves largely to predicting such blessings as delicious vegetable steaks, mail delivery from earth satellites, recreational resorts on space platforms, and machines which had abolished all physical labor. Thus they put themselves in the same class as those who write articles for the "service magazines" inviting us to drool over a future full of electronic cookers, family helicopters (at least two in every garage) and two-way household television-telephones in color. The most appropriate comment seems to have been that in the New York *Nation*: "The future of the human race resides in its humanity, not in its ability to construct honeymoon hotels on Venus."

But what is this "humanity" which the *Nation* is interested in and Oppenheimer fears we may lose? It is easier to say what it isn't or to define it negatively. It is that part of man's consciousness, intellect, and emotion which is neither exclusively interested in nor completely satisfied by either mere animal survival on the one hand, or wealth, power, and speed alone. It is that part of him which is least like a machine and therefore least satisfied by machines. It is the part that would like to know itself and that cherishes values to which nothing in the inanimate world seems to correspond and which the nonhuman world of living things only dubiously (though none the less comforting) seems to encourage.

Perhaps we are being a bit provincial to call this "humanness." Man existed for many millennia without, so we guess, exhibiting much of it. Perhaps Mr. Oppenheimer is right in supposing that he might endure indefinitely after he had lost it. Many contemporary men—and especially many contemporary youths—to whom only automobiles, airplanes and television sets seem interesting, have already lost most of it. Perhaps it is primarily a phenomenon of recent man and, in the form we best understand, of Western man. Perhaps what some of us tend to call "the human being" first came into easily recognizable existence about the year 475 B.C. and began to disappear about seventy-five years ago. But though the world may soon belong to other creatures, there are some of us who cannot say simply, "Cultures come and go," without a regret for the passing of what seems to our possibly prejudiced minds more worthy of admiration than anything which ever existed before.

We need not, as some do, insist that the decision whether or not humanness in this limited sense will endure is wholly outside our power to influence. But there can be little doubt that the weight, the pressure, and the demands of the machine we have created make the preservation of "human" life more difficult than ever before—at least since the time when man ceased to be wholly at the mercy of the natural forces he has now mastered almost too well. If we should devote more of our time, energy, and brainpower to the cultivation of "the humanities" in the broad sense that our definition of "human-ness" implies, then we would have to face the fact now so insistently urged upon us that "we need more scientists for survival," and that therefore much more rather than any less of the available brain power must be devoted to the machine and its management, to public educa-tion more and more exclusively devoted to "turning out the scientists necessary to our survival."

It may seem both frivolous and cynical to suggest that if neither we nor any other nation had so many or such successful scientists then we should not be so desperately in need of still more of them now! Yet in sober fact (and as is generally admitted), the greatest proportion of those we do need we need primarily to protect us against their fel-low scientists in other lands. The monster we have called into existence must be looked after, and he is more demanding of time and attention than the creations of any other civilization. Even should we (as does not at the moment seem likely) become bored with it; even should we find ourselves feeling once again that art, philosophy, and what used to be called wisdom, are more interesting than either convenient or destructive machines—we might still not dare spend much time upon them. We are mounted on the tiger and it is hard to imagine how we might dismount.

There are many who give good reasons for believing that overpopula-tion is a threat to humane living second only to the domination of the machine. To them the technicians' assurance that with the desalting of sea water and the cultivation of algae in sewage pools (both of which are already practicable) we shall be able to feed a population many times the present, is not a promise but a threat. They say that what we need is not more men but better men and that there is no immediate prospect of getting them. But the question whether we should risk a stationary or slowly growing population, even if we should all become convinced that from a human standpoint it is desirable, still remains. Population pressures in other countries will make it all the more probable that they will use for aggression the long-range weapons man has supplied himself with, and hence it may well be that any nation not as numerous as it is physically possible for it to become is doomed to conquest by one or another of those bursting at the seams with expendable, more-or-less human beings. A cynical German might speak of the necessity of raising cannon fodder. We will call it only something like "providing for the optimum population from the standpoint of national security."

"Human condition" is a phrase enjoying at the moment a great vogue. In so far as it is more than merely fashionable or means more than simply "the present state of affairs," it must imply a distinction from something else—most legitimately, perhaps, a distinction between what is and what might or what ought to be.

Most current moral and sociological opinion sees little basis for such a distinction. To it the human condition is the only discussable, and, indeed, the only real, aspect, of human nature or society. Society is presumed to be what it is as the result of an inevitable evolution, and human nature merely what a given state of society has made it. Any concept of human nature which implies something permanent, independent, and tending to revert to a norm is dismissed as a myth, since the so-called human nature could not be anything more than what the inevitable human condition at any moment has made it. "Good" and "bad" are assumed to be meaningless terms except in reference to some specific society or condition, and when you have described that condition you are thought to have said all that can be said upon that subject.

Patterns of the Future

I F INDUSTRIAL CIVILIZATION eventually succumbs to the forces that are relentlessly operating to make its position more precarious, the world as a whole will probably revert to an agrarian existence. In such an event history will continue for as long a time as man exists. Empires, republics, and military states will rise and fall. There will be wars, migrations, and revolutions. Art, music, and literature will flourish, wane, then flourish again. As in the histories of the past and of the present, there will be unceasing change. Yet looked upon over a period of thousands of years, history will have a sameness like the repeated performances of a series of elaborate epic plays in which, over the centuries, the actors change, the languages change, the scenery changes, but the basic plots remain invariant.

But if industrial civilization survives—if wars are eliminated, if the population of the world as a whole is stabilized within a framework of low death rates and low birth rates—will there continue to be a human history? The terms "stability" and "security" imply predictability, sameness, lack of change. And these terms further imply a high degree of organization—universal organization to avoid war, local organization to produce goods efficiently, and organization to control the distribution of goods. Organization in turn implies subjugation of the individual to the state, confinement and regimentation of the activities of the individual for the benefit of society as a whole.

Today we see about us on all sides a steady drift toward increased human organization. Governments are becoming more centralized and universal. In practically all areas of endeavor within industrial society —in our systems of production, in the fields of labor, capital, commerce, agriculture, science, education, and art—we see the emergence of new levels of organization designed to coordinate, integrate, bind, and regulate men's actions. The justifications for this increasing degree of organization to which man must accommodate himself are expressed in terms such as "stability," "security," and "efficiency." The end result

Housing along the Dan Ryan Expressway, Chicago, Illinois.

of this rapid transition might well be the emergence of a universal, stable, efficient, industrial society within which, although all persons have complete personal security, their actions are completely controlled. Should that time arrive, society will have become static, devoid of movement, fixed and permanent. History will have stopped.

Here we indeed find ourselves on the horns of the dilemma. To what purpose is industrialization if we end up by replacing rigid confinement of man's actions by nature with rigid confinement of man's actions by man? To what purpose is industrialization if the price we pay for longer life, material possessions, and personal security is regimentation, controlled thoughts, and controlled actions? Would the lives of well-fed, wealthy, but regimented human robots be better than the lives of their malnourished, poverty-stricken ancestors? At least the latter could look forward to the unexpected happening—to events and situations which previously had been outside the realm of their experiences.

In a modern industrial society the road toward totalitarianism is unidirectional. In days gone by men could revolt against despotism. People could arise against their governments in the absence of legal recourse, and with muskets, sticks, knives, and stones as their weapons they could often defeat the military forces of the central authorities. But today our science and our technology have placed in the hands of rulers of nations weapons and tools of control, persuasion, and coercion of unprecedented power. We have reached the point where, once totalitarian power is seized in a highly industrialized society, successful revolt becomes practically impossible. Totalitarian power, once it is gained, can be perpetuated almost indefinitely in the absence of outside forces, and can lead to progressively more rapid robotization of the individual.

Thus we see that, just as industrial society is fundamentally unstable and subject to reversion to agrarian existence, so within it the conditions which offer individual freedom are unstable in their ability to avoid the conditions which impose rigid organization and totalitarian control. Indeed, when we examine all of the foreseeable difficulties which threaten the survival of industrial civilization, it is difficult to see how the achievement of stability and the maintenance of individual liberty can be made compatible.

The view is widely held in our society that the powers of the machine will eventually free man from the burden of eking out an existence and will provide him with leisure time for the development of his creativity and enjoyment of the fruits of his creative efforts. Pleasant though this prospect may be, it is clear that such a state cannot come into existence automatically; the pressures forcing man into devising more highly organized institutions are too great to permit it. If he is to attain such an idlyllic existence for more than a transitory period he must plan for that existence carefully, and in particular he must do everything within his power to reduce the pressures that are forcing him to become more highly organized.

One of the major pressures that give rise to the need for increasing numbers of laws, more elaborate organization, and more centralized government is increase of population. Increase of numbers of people and of population density results in greater complexities in day-to-day living and in decreased opportunities for personal expression concerning the activities of government. But even more important, as populations increase and as they press more heavily upon the available resources there arises the need for increased efficiency, and more elaborate organizations are required to produce sufficient food, to extract the necessary raw materials, and to fabricate and distribute the finished products. In the future we can expect that the greater the population density of an industrial society becomes, the more elaborate will be its organizational structure and the more regimented will be its people.

A second pressure, not unrelated to the first, results from the centralization of industrial and agricultural activity and from regional specialization in various aspects of those activities. One region produces textiles, another produces coal, another automobiles, another corn, and another wheat. Factories require mammoth local organizations. Centralized industries must be connected, and this requires elaborate transportation systems. Regional localization of industries gives rise to gigantic cities, which in turn give rise to elaborate organization for the purpose of providing the inhabitants with the necessary food, water, and services. All of these factors combine to produce vulnerability to disruption from the outside, increased local organization and regimentation, more highly centralized government, and increasing vulnerability to the evolution of totalitarianism.

A third pressure results from increasing individual specialization and the resultant need for "integration," "coordination," and "direction" of activities in practically all spheres of vocational and leisure activity. It results in the placing of unwarranted trust in "integrators," "coordinators," and "directors." Early specialization results in lack of broad interests, lessened ability to engage in creative activity during leisure hours, decreased interest in the creative activities of other individuals, and lessened abilities to interpret events and make sound judgments. All of these factors combine to pave the way for collectivization, the emergence of strong organization, and, with it, the great leader.

Strong arguments can be presented to the effect that collectivization of humanity is inevitable, that the drift toward an ultimate state of automatism cannot be halted, that existing human values such as freedom, love, and conscience must eventually disappear. Certainly if we used the present trends in industrial society as our major premises, the conclusion would appear to be inescapable. Yet is it not possible that human beings, recognizing this threat to the canons of humanism, can devise ways and means of escaping the danger and at the same time manage to preserve those features of industrial civilization which can contribute to a rich, full life? Is it really axiomatic that the present trends must continue and that in the long run industrial civilization and human values are incompatible? Here, in truth, we are confronted with the gravest and most difficult of all human problems, for it is one that cannot be solved by mathematics or by machines, nor can it even be precisely defined. Solutions, if they exist, can arise only in the hearts and minds of individual men.

The machine has divorced man from the world of nature to which he belongs, and in the process he has lost in large measure the powers of contemplation with which he was endowed. A prerequisite for the preservation of the canons of humanism is a re-establishment of organic roots with our natural environment and, related to it, the evolution of ways of life which encourage contemplation and the search for truth and knowledge. The flower and vegetable garden, green grass, the fireplace, the primeval forest with its wondrous assemblage of living things, the uninhabited hilltop where one can silently look at the stars and wonder—all of these things and many others are necessary for the fulfillment of man's psychological and spiritual needs. To be sure, they are of no "practical value" and are seemingly unrelated to man's pressing need for food and living space. But they are as necessary to the preservation of humanism as food is necessary to the preservation of human life.

I can imagine a world within which machines function solely for man's benefit, turning out those goods which are necessary for his well-being, relieving him of the necessity for heavy physical labor and dull, routine, meaningless activity. The world I imagine is one in which people are well fed, well clothed, and well housed. Man in this world, lives in balance with his environment, nourished by nature in harmony with the myriads of other life forms that are beneficial to him. He treats his land wisely, halts erosion and overcropping, and returns all organic waste matter to the soil from which it sprung. He lives efficiently, yet minimizes artificiality. It is not an overcrowded world; people can, if they wish, isolate themselves in the silence of a mountain-top, or they can walk through primeval forests or across wooded plains. In the world of my imagination there is organization, but it is as decentralized as possible, compatible with the requirements for survival. There is a world government, but it exists solely for the purpose of preventing war and stabilizing population, and its powers are irrevocably restricted. The government exists for man rather than man for the government.

In the world of my imagination the various regions are self-sufficient, and the people are free to govern themselves as they choose and to establish their own cultural patterns. All people have a voice in the government, and individuals can move about when and where they please. It is a world where man's creativity is blended with the crea-tivity of nature, and where a moderate degree of organization is blended with a moderate degree of anarchy.

Is such a world impossible of realization? Perhaps it is, but who among us can really say? At least if we try to create such a world there is a chance that we will succeed. But if we let the present trend con-tinue it is all too clear that we will lose forever those qualities of mind and spirit which distinguish the human being from the automaton.

Harlem rooftops, New York City, New York.

The Human Implications

THE STRUCTURAL CHANGE precipitated by mechanization is nowhere more conspicuous than in the sphere of agriculture. The consequences, however, are harder to survey. The figure of the wanderer in his own land, the migrant farm worker, may be abolished. The Second World War proved this. Yet the phenomenon remains. The farmer has been drawn into flux. He has been altered in his relation to the soil. The relationship has become neutralized. Mechanization hastened the process. There can be no doubt of that. . . . Phenomena often regarded solely as the outcome of mechanization had already appeared before mechanization took effect. The relation to the soil began to alter when, early in the nineteenth century, before mechanized agriculture had come into being, the settlers abandoned the old Atlantic States and migrated westward.

Then the tiller of the soil entered into flux. Mechanization did no more than magnify a latent trend into the gigantic. Does the changing farmer reflect, but more conspicuously, a process that is everywhere at work? Can what is taking place in the farmer be a projection of something that is going on throughout? Does the transformation into wandering unemployed of people who for centuries had tilled the soil correspond to what is happening in each of us? In this process, has movement, the basic concept of our world-image, been transposed, in distorted form, into human destiny? . . .

Other periods too have had their mass displacements, whether by free will, violence, or force of circumstance. Yet in due time the people came to rest. Is what we are witnessing today the convulsions of a transition period, different from earlier periods, yet penetrated like them with the need for continuity? Or does it represent a remolding of life into ways for which a form is as yet lacking, and of which the structural alteration of farming, man's basic calling, stands as the first symptom?

Near Spofford Lake, New Hampshire.

Epilogue

Cut is the branch that might have grown full strait,
And burned is Apollo's laurel-bough,
That sometime grew within this learned man.
Faustus is gone: regard his hellish fall,
Whose fiendful fortune may exhort the wise,
Only to wonder at unlawful things,
Whose deepness doth entice such forward wits
To practice more than heavenly power permits.

Christopher Marlowe
Epilogue, to the Tragical
History of Doctor Faustus